When I was about ten years old "I began a book on heraldry of which three completed chapters still exist." Detail of an illustration showing the arms of the city of Norwich.

THE KINDLY FRUITS OF THE EARTH

Clarkson Stanfield, *Vesuvius and the Bay of Naples* (formerly in the possession of Deborah Hutchinson).

The Kindly Fruits of the Earth

RECOLLECTIONS
OF AN EMBRYO ECOLOGIST

G. Evelyn Hutchinson

NEW HAVEN AND LONDON
YALE UNIVERSITY PRESS
1979

Published with assistance from the Louis Effingham deForest Memorial Fund.

Designed by Thos. Whitridge and set in Plantin type by Asco Trade Typesetting, Ltd., Hong Kong. Printed in the United States of America by The Murray Printing Company, Westford, Massachusetts.

Published in Great Britain, Europe, Africa, and Asia (except Japan) by Yale University Press, Ltd., London. Distributed in Australia and New Zealand by Book & Film Services, Artarmon, N.S.W., Australia; and in Japan by Harper & Row, Publishers, Tokyo Office.

Library of Congress Cataloging in Publication Data

Hutchinson, George Evelyn, 1903–
The kindly fruits of the earth.

Includes bibliographical references and index.
1. Hutchinson, George Evelyn, 1903–   2. Ecologists—England—Biography. I. Title.
QH31.H87A34   574.5'092'4 [B]   78-21689
ISBN 0-300-02272-7

In gratitude to all who have helped me
In affection for all those I have tried to help

Contents

ILLUSTRATIONS

ix

PREFACE

THIS LITTLE BOOK WAS WRITTEN because several younger friends interested in the history of science wondered what it was like to learn biology fifty years ago. My answers are doubtless highly atypical, but if interpreted rightly may instruct as well as entertain. The incidents described are chosen not only because they bear on this question, but also because they relate to interesting or beautiful aspects of the world that I have experienced, some of which might easily be forgotten.

In general, no one known to me to be living plays a major role in the part of the story that I tell, though inevitably people who I am delighted are alive come and go, making brief appearances. My debt to the living is, however, even greater than that to the dead. Everyone who has helped me during three-quarters of a century is included in the dedication, even if they do not appear in the narrative. Of them, my wife is the chief.

Among those who have read the manuscript I would particularly thank four friends: Diana Long Hall, for her initial stimulus, Phoebe Ellsworth for her many sensitive, helpful, and appreciative criticisms, Marjorie Garber for illuminating things that I had never before properly seen, and Stan Rachootin for reminding me of much that I had forgotten, and for great help in assembling the illustrations.

In England Sydney Smith and William H. Thorpe have saved me from several errors and have given me the benefit of their longer adult experience of Cambridge. My special thanks are due to my sister, Dorothea, who has not only corrected some erroneous memories but has also added materially to the book, from letters that came into her possession, from her own recollections, and from those of my mother as set down in a brief manuscript. I am also grateful to my cousin, Gilbert Reginald Shipley Stewart, for information about the de Mezzi family. David Boulton, Nancy Davis, Mary de Rachewiltz, Stephen Jay Gould, Donna Haraway, Jaroslav Pelikan, Dillon Ripley, and Keith Thomson have provided helpful comments and useful information.

My thanks again go to Virginia Simon for making my sketches into elegant drawings without loss of character. William K. Sacco has made the photograph for the frontispiece and has helped with other illustrations. Anna Aschenbach assisted in many ways in the preparation of the manuscript, which was typed by Susan Koblitz. My debt to Jane Isay at the Yale University Press will only be understood by those who have had the pleasure of working with her. Maureen Bushkovitch has shown me the importance of humor and grace in copyediting.

I am grateful to the Cambridge University Library, the Fitzwilliam Museum, the master and fellows of Christ's College, the Zoological Museum of Cambridge University, and the Scott Institute for Polar Research for permission to reproduce materials in their collections.

Throughout the book, I have naturally had to rely largely on my memory, which is doubtless far more fallible than I know. I have tried to indicate wherever I suspect an apocryphal element in a story. I have no doubt made mistakes and apologize in advance to anyone who is misled or made uncomfortable by any of my errors.

New Haven, Connecticut
30 January 1978

Belvoir Terrace (Virginia Simon, from a photograph by Stan Rachootin, appearance c. 1903 slightly hypothetical).

CHAPTER ONE

BELVOIR TERRACE

I WAS BORN IN CAMBRIDGE ON 30 January 1903, at home on the top floor of 3 Belvoir Terrace, Trumpington Road. The house was one of a row of five, with a sixth, more elegant, isolated house, built of white brick about 1825.[1] Each of the terrace houses consisted of a basement with kitchen and scullery windows looking out, front and back, into "areas," sunken pits protected by railings and usually inhabited by a toad or two. A small wine cellar, which we populated with ghosts, lay under part of the basement. Above the basement were three floors: the lowest customarily divided into dining room and study, the next drawing room and guest bedroom, and at the top three bedrooms, one perhaps a nursery. A small split-level annex of later date contained a bathroom and maid's room. The house would have been perfectly convenient had it not been so vertical. We lived there until 1912.

After we had left, no. 3 Belvoir Terrace was taken by E. E. Kellett and his tall, very attractive, feminist wife,

1. Belvoir Terrace is no. (284) in *An Inventory of the Historical Monuments in the City of Cambridge*, part 2, Royal Commission on Historical Monuments: England 18, pp. 137–480, 1959. The *l* in the name is mute, as in the genus *Castor*.

whose existence somewhat disturbed my grandmother. Kellett taught English at the Leys School and was the author of numerous historical and literary works. One was called *Ex Libris: Confessions of a Constant Reader*. No subtitle could have been more truthful, for wherever he might be seen in Cambridge, even when crossing the street, he was always deep in a book.

Behind and to the south of Belvoir Terrace lay a large more or less triangular open public meadow known as Coe Fen. This was bounded by the Trumpington Road on the east, by Vicar's Brook, then the haunt of kingfishers, on the southwest, and by the river Cam on the west. Between the terrace and the town lay the Leys School, a large boarding school for boys with an extensive cricket ground and a football field. They were separated from Coe Fen by a fence and a ditch. The latter, usually largely covered with duckweed, supported a good population of the common or smooth newt (*Triturus vulgaris*). A tree that had been struck by lightning stood between the Leys grounds and the terrace. It was clearly visible from the nursery window and made a deep and rather terrifying impression on me.

During the school holidays we had permission to use the Leys grounds, and there I first heard a phonograph, of the old cylinder type, which must have been played by a groundsman, in the deserted cricket pavilion. Edison's invention at this time was regarded as vulgar in Cambridge and I fancy that my hearing it was not reported at home.

Beyond Coe Fen, across the Cam, which was spanned by an iron footbridge, there was another large open space called Sheep's Green. On it there were a number of shallow ponds, partly in former branches of the river. The western side of Sheep's Green was defined by Snobs, a channel that earlier had brought water to run a large watermill of rather forbidding Industrial Revolution brickwork. A *snob* in nineteenth-century Cambridge parlance was anyone not a member of the university. Snobs was a safe place where small boys could bathe; I learned to swim there. Downstream from the bathing place the more engaging inhabitants were moorhens (*Gallinula chloropus*) and water voles (*Arvicola amphibius*).

In front of the house, separated from it by a garden with a lawn, lay Trumpington Road, the main road from Cambridge to London. Across Trumpington Road there was a leisurely brook called Hobson's Conduit, built in 1610 by the town and university acting together and later endowed by Thomas Hobson, the carrier and livery-stable owner, immortalized in Hobson's Choice—the first horse in line—, and by Samuel Potto, who I fear has nothing to do with the attractive prosimian *Perodicticus potto*. The conduit ended a little north of Belvoir Terrace, and from the conduit-head water was piped to a fountain on Market Hill, a flat area in the center of the town. Other channels took the water to other places. Some still runs a short way underground to emerge on either side of Trumpington Street, Trumpington Road having gone urban on its way to becoming King's Parade. The two resulting rivulets flowing past Pembroke and Peterhouse colleges, and originally supplying the water for the neighborhood, are called the Pem and the Pet. Naturally they were a delight to children, who found they provided an easy way to get their feet wet. Another pair of rivulets of like origin existed on either side of Saint Andrew's Street, but they were less elaborately channeled and are now almost dry. I do not remember that they had names. I believe a similar system also survives in Freiburg-im-Breisgau, another beautiful university town.

When I was old enough, I used to go to Hobson's Conduit with a minute hand-net to try to catch sticklebacks (*Gasterosteus aculeatus*) for my aquarium. I remember that once when the water was very low and the channel consisted of a row of muddy pools in which all the fish were concentrated, we found that gudgeon (*Gobio gobio*), a strictly bottom-living fish, also inhabited the brook. Beyond the conduit lay the University Botanic Gardens. It was regarded as ignorant bad form to call the gardens the "Botanics," which we always did, even though we were one of the university families privileged to have a private key so that we could enjoy the gardens on Sunday.

My father was Arthur Hutchinson, at that time university demonstrator in mineralogy and fellow and science tutor of Pembroke College. These positions brought him in close touch with all Cambridge students likely to become economic geologists or teachers of geology in various parts of the British Empire and with all the intending medical students at Pembroke. The college, though very athletic, had a poor intellectual reputation, and I suspect my father was brought in to help raise the tone of the place. It had been founded in 1347 by Marie de Valence (née de Saint Pol), countess of Pembroke and baroness of Wexford in Ireland, and of Montignac, Bellac, and Rançon in France. On the margin of one folio of her psalter and breviary there is a picture (fig. 1) of an aged, bearded knight, clad only in a shirt or tunic, with a belt for his sword, lovingly handling his tilting lance and shield bearing the Pembroke arms.[2] Many country parsonages no doubt contained oars won by Pembroke men, hanging over the fireplace and regarded with the same affectionate nostalgia.

My father had graduated from Christ's College and then taught under Patterson Muir in the chemical laboratory of Gonville and Caius College, at a time when individual colleges sought to give their own instruction in science.

2. Psalter and Breviary of Marie de Valence, Countess of Pembroke, Cambridge University Library, Ms. Dd 55, French, second quarter of the fourteenth century.

FIGURE I Marginal illustration of a knight, in a tunic with sword, lance, and shield blazoned with the arms of the countess and her college. Psalter and Breviary of Marie de Valence, Countess of Pembroke; Cambridge University Library, MS Dd 55; French, second quarter of the fourteenth century.

His training had been mostly chemical; he took a Ph.D. in organic chemistry at Würzburg, where he worked under Emil Fischer and also knew W. C. Röntgen. He was very proud of his association with these two great German scientists. He brought from Würzburg two very early x-ray tubes, and occasionally, as when a fishhook broke off in his forefinger, he would use the more powerful tube, requiring an exposure of five minutes, and take the resulting plate to his doctor. On this occasion, I had the bones in my hand photographed and I think my brother and perhaps my sister did also. When he had returned to Cambridge, my father did some work in the Caius Laboratory with W. Pollard on lead tetracetate, proving clearly that the metal could be quadrivalent, as until recently has been implied on every gasoline pump.[3]

3. A. Hutchinson and W. Pollard, "Note on Lead Tetracetate," *Trans. Chem. Soc.* 1893:1136–37. Lead tetrachloride was known; this short note established the existence of not only the tetracetate, but also the tetrapropionate, so indicating the regular quadrivalent nature of the element.

Rather later he began doing the same sort of thing as Becquerel, only to learn that the latter had discovered what we now call radioactivity. He was also on the point of investigating the alleged nitrogen content of a uranium mineral, when Sir William Ramsay, analyzing the same mineral, announced the terrestrial occurrence of helium. His scientific failures were clearly more spectacular than his successes. He used to say to me, "If you run into anything that looks very important, drop everything to go after it." I think he felt that owing to his responsibility for a rather demanding mother, he had not been energetic enough himself. His version of the parable of the pearl of great price has been only indirectly helpful to me, but it did come in useful when Howard Sanders brought me, in a small petri dish, his first specimen, from Long Island Sound of all places, of the most primitive living crustacean, now the cephalocarid *Hutchinsoniella macracantha* Sanders, diffidently asking me what it was.[4] Remembering my father's injunction, I replied: "I don't know, but I know that it is very important. Drop everything until you have worked it out." He then said, "What about my thesis?" I said, "It can wait until you know what this animal is." A few weeks later another graduate student, in California, found a comparable animal, but I believe he was told by someone, whose father had probably not missed discovering radioactivity and terrestrial helium, to put off studying it until his thesis was finished. He learned of its nature when Sanders' description and figure appeared.

My paternal grandfather, George Hutchinson, formerly of Woodside, Westmorland, had gone to London

---

4. H. L. Sanders, The Cephalocarida, a New Subclass of Crustacea from Long Island Sound, *Proc. Nat. Acad. Sci.* 41:61–66, 1955.

to make his fortune, in which he was succeeding, as an East Indian broker dealing in tea and silks (a West Indian broker dealt in sugar, cf. W. S. Gilbert, "A gentleman of city fame / Now claims your kind attention[5]), when, according to family tradition, he slipped on a piece of orange peel, was largely paralyzed, and died in 1875, when my father was nine years old. I know nothing more of my grandfather, save that when he was courting my grandmother he rode across the river Eden on his horse. I assume my first name was given me at least partly on account of him, though Sir George Stokes of Stokes' Law, whom my father venerated, was dying as I was born. There are still distant Hutchinson relatives around Penrith in Cumbria, successful farmers and rural businessmen.

Deborah Richardson, my grandmother, was the daughter of a farmer in Culgaith in the Eden Valley, about where the old Cumberland-Westmorland boundary crossed the river. Some of the Richardsons had gone to Jamaica and later to New Zealand, but they seem to have been unsuccessful emigrants, and from the numerous letters that my brother found and studied, very dull correspondents. There were, however, various family connections with Powleys, Fothergills, and Nelsons who were perhaps more interesting. One even compiled a book of Lake District folk poetry.[6] Though the Richardsons seem to have had rather modest intellectual aspirations, Deborah was sent from the Culgaith farm to a Parisian finishing school.

The imaginative genealogist has, however, some further scope for speculation. From the account given by

5. W. S. Gilbert, "A Discontented Sugar Broker," in *The "Bab" Ballads, Much Sound and Little Sense* (London: J. C. Holton, 1869).

6. Mary Powley, *Echoes of Old Cumberland, Poems and Translations* (London: Bemrose & Sons, 1875).

Aeneas Sylvius Piccolomini, who claimed descent from Romulus and later became Pope Pius II, of the very odd behavior of the village women in the lower Eden Valley, when he and two of his servants, leaving the court of Edinburgh where he was engaged in a diplomatic mission, traveled incognito into England, it is conceivable that a few Italian Renaissance genes might be still around in the local population.[7] Moreover, the builders of Long Meg,

7. Aeneas Sylvius Piccolomini may have spent a curious night, apparently having crossed the Solway, at some village in the lower Eden Valley. After supper, in the second hour of the night, all the men left, with their children, to flee to a tower where they would be safe from the Scots, leaving Aeneas, his two servants, and his guide with about a hundred women, "quamvis adolescentulae et matronae formosae complures essent: nihil enim his mali facturos hostes credunt, qui stuprum inter mala non ducunt." He goes on to say that the women sat round a fire carding hemp and gossiping with his interpreter. An alarm was given by dogs barking and geese gabbling; Aeneas remained in the stable given him as a chamber, though the women all disappeared; later they returned saying that friends rather than enemies had come. As a young man, Aeneas was of a notoriously amorous disposition, some of the women were pretty and saw no harm in casual lovemaking; he does not say, however, that he had a companion in his stable, but he might have preferred not to mention her. The whole strange event is regarded by the Rev. Canon James Wilson in The Passage of the Border by Aeneas Sylvius in the Winter of 1435–6, *Trans. Cumberland Westmorland Antiq. Archaeol. Soc.*, n.s. 23:17–28, 1923, as an elaborate ruse to get rid of a troublesome foreigner, sending him on his way to Newcastle early next morning. This explanation I find quite unconvincing. Though Canon Wilson gives some reasons for thinking that Aeneas had come into Cumberland by a western passage, rather than into Northumberland by an eastern route, the geographical evidence is, to me, not fully adequate. Whatever did happen, the scene is most beautifully described: "Mansit ergo illic solus Aeneas cum duobus famulis et uno itineris duce inter centum feminas, quae corona facta medium claudentes ignem, cannabumque mundantes, noctem insomnem ducebant, plurimaque cum interprete fabulabantur (*Commentarii Pii Pape II*, bk. 1, ff. 6–8, Rome, 1584).

five miles north of Culgaith, the third largest stone circle in Britain and one laid out on an elaborate geometrical plan, may well have left female descendants, even if, as is not too likely, all the men were killed off by every later Celtic or Nordic invasion.

By the death of her husband, my grandmother was left a widow with a good income, strong low church convictions, and a belief in respectability. She must somehow have discovered that my father had a bent for science, of which she was totally ignorant. Someone more knowledgeable than herself must have suggested that she settle in Clifton, near Bristol, so that he could go to school at Clifton College, which had recently been established to give a more scientific education than was available in the older public schools. When he was ready for a university, she moved with him to Cambridge, and apart from a short time in Germany, lived there for the rest of her life. There was much that was attractive about her, but she never understood my father's intellectual aspirations nor his intellectual friends. She put her foot down on a friendship with Roger Fry, who read science at Cambridge, but having an unexpectedly good eye for pictures she treasured, not only a lovely study of Vesuvius and the Bay of Naples by Clarkson Stanfield (frontispiece), but also a very pretty early Fry watercolor on her drawing-room wall.

My grandmother lived next door to us, in 2 Belvoir Terrace. My father arranged to have a door cut through the wall of the top floor so he could always reach my grandmother easily. The room into which the door opened was incorporated into our house and was used as a dressing room and as a laboratory. Since it housed a goniometer, it was called the goniometer room. Occasionally my father did some optical work on crystals in the evening and it was a great joy to be allowed to watch quietly as a thallium, sodium, or a lithium flame was produced so that refractive

indices in the green, yellow, and red could be determined.[8]
My mother was Evaline Demezy Shipley.[9] Though

8. A. Hutchinson, The Chemical Composition and Optical
Characters of Dolomite Crystals from Algeria, *Rep. Brit. Assoc. Adv.
Sci.* (Dublin Meeting) 78 : 701, 1908. This note probably reports the
results obtained that evening.

9. My mother's father, Alexander Shipley, was the eighth child
of John Shipley, himself the son of William and Catherine. John Shipley
kept a saddler's shop at 181 Regent Street, over which the large family
lived. His eldest son, John, inherited his father's business but not his
sweet temperament; he numbered Napoleon III among his customers.
My mother remembered staying in the house above the shop, but her
most vivid recollection was that the drinking water, having always to be
boiled, was relieved of its "flatness" by the addition of toasted crusts
of bread.

William Shipley's father-in-law was presumably the son either of
Guiseppe de Mezzi, mayor of Cocconato, who seems to have died in
1763, or of his brother Pietro Antonio. A third brother was killed at the
battle of Madonna dell'Olmo in 1744; he had a son Guiseppe who like
his uncle became mayor and left a number of descendants in Italy.
Neither Guiseppe the elder nor Pietro Antonio are credited with issue
in V. Spreti, *Enciclopedia Storico-nobiliare Italiana* (Milan, 1931, vol. 4,
pp. 577–78). Quite likely children who became Protestants and left
Italy were regarded as more or less nonexistent. Since in what is recorded
of the de Mezzi genealogy by Spreti, sons do not have fathers' Christian
names, I suspect Guiseppe was the father of the three emigrants,
Antonio, Angelo, and Niccolo. It is, however, possible that the latter
belonged to an unrecorded branch of the family that became extinct
and so was not treated in the *Enciclopedia Storico-nobiliare*. Spreti gives
some biographical details about the more interesting de Mezzi, including Basilio. He is described as *priore mitrato* of Saint Thomas's in Brno,
which probably indicates that he was the head of the monastery, though
unlike Mendel not an abbot.

Little is known about the Burge family, save that my mother's
grandfather had a tobacconist's shop in Windsor before starting his
brewery. The Burges seem to have come from near Sherborne in Dorset.
It was said that some of them made so much money in the wool trade
that one Miss Burge had, as her dowry, her weight in gold coins; her
husband soon squandered it.

she once told me that the Shipley family was supposed to have produced a publisher early in the eighteenth century, I can find no trace of him. As my mother did not allude to him in a short manuscript on her family that she left with my sister, I have little doubt that he is apocryphal. The first undoubted record of a Shipley ancestor is the entry in the marriage register at Hartley Wintney church, in the northwest corner of Hampshire, of the marriage of William Shipley of Saint Martin's in the Fields to Catherine Demezy of Hartley Wintney, on 24 January 1782. William was doubtless in business in London, but his family had probably been living in this part of Hampshire, where he must have met his bride. Catherine, my great great grandmother, was the daughter of Count Antonio de Mezzi (1730–1812), naturalized as Anthony Demezy, who had left Italy, according to family tradition, on becoming a Protestant. He settled in Hartley Wintney, but I have learned nothing of his mode of livelihood.

The de Mezzi were an ancient Piedmontese family, probably ultimately from Venice, who owned property at a place called Cocconato, a little east of Turin. In the sixteenth and seventeenth centuries, several members of the family were learned ecclesiastics holding positions, not only in Italian universities, but also in Bohemia and Bavaria. One of them, Basilio de Mezzi, became prior of the Augustinian house in Brno, where, rather over two hundred and fifty years later, Gregor Mendel was abbot.

My mother was a strong but strictly nonmilitant feminist, though she always maintained that she got her ideas on the subject from my father, who saw no reason to believe that the two sexes differed in ability. In view of the rate at which women are now developing, as social restraints are abolished, he may ultimately prove to have been wrong. My mother's great interest in middle life was in seeing that women were properly treated in the

Cambridge police court, where she did much good, though, by a rather dominating and at times intolerant personality, possibly also some harm. Three of her brothers survived into adult life. One, Sir Arthur Shipley F.R.S., was a zoologist, responsible for part of the text and much of the administrative work of the *Cambridge Natural History*, which, after three-quarters of a century, is still much used, and for part of the organization of the *Fauna of British India*. He was a rotund man who liked his port and became the subject of many stories, mostly no doubt apocryphal. He is said to have been found supporting himself on the knob of the chapel door late at night on degree day and, on being asked what he was doing, he replied, "I came to give thanks to Almighty God, but Almighty God has sported his oak," the usual expression for shutting one's outer door for the night. Once it was alleged that the Mistress of Girton (one of the two women's colleges) wanted to complain to Professor Sedgwick about the treatment her students were receiving and went to the zoological laboratory, asked the very dignified head lab man, called Brockett, if he would tell the professor she had called, and was asked to sit down. Nothing happened for an hour, so she approached Brockett again. He disappeared and went up to announce to the professor that Miss Jones was still waiting. "Tell Miss Jones to go to the devil." Brockett descended and tactfully remarked, "Professor Sedgwick suggests that you see Mr. Shipley."[10]

10. I give this story as it used to be told when I was an undergraduate. In a more authentic version given by Shipley himself (in *"J" A Memoir of John Willis Clark* [London, Smith, Elder & Co., 1913], see p. 280), the importunate lady is not the Mistress of Girton but a student. The incident seems to have taken place entirely within Shipley's hearing. "After a third or fourth interruption Adam, whose temper was in those days always within easy call, said 'Oh tell Miss "Chose" to go to the Devil.' I was not best pleased a moment later to

Shipley wrote a number of papers early in his life on invertebrate morphology, development, and systematics. He also played an important part in an investigation of a serious epidemic affecting red grouse (*Lagopus lagopus scoticus*). When he failed to get the professorship of zoology on Sedgwick's leaving Cambridge in 1909, he seemed to have given up research and devoted himself to writing, becoming a very successful exponent of the art of *haute vulgarisation*. His *Minor Horrors of War* and *More Minor Horrors* are masterpieces in this genre. They discussed all the parasites and pests that might have been significant to fighting men or food supplies in the First World War. There is a beautiful comparison of the eggs of cockroaches ranged on either side of the egg capsule to the choirboys on the Gospel and Epistle sides of the chancel of a church. He became master of Christ's College and appropriately discovered, when the master's lodge was being restored after years of neglect, the mummified bodies of four black rats (*Rattus rattus*) that had died in the space between the dining-room ceiling and the floor of the room above, in a nest made of the chewed-up leaves of a number of books and documents dating from c. 1500 to 1820. There were fragments of a page of Virgil (fig. 2) and rather more of

---

hear Brockett, who is always a diplomatist, saying to the lady, 'Mr. Sedgwick, Miss, thinks you'd better see Mr. Shipley'."

Professor Adam Sedgwick was the grandnephew of his namesake "Old Adam" Sedgwick, the professor of geology at Cambridge that Darwin knew and after whom the Sedgwick Museum was named.

It is interesting, in view of what I remember about the use of names (see pp. 26–29), that the younger Sedgwick seems to have been Adam to his contemporaries. Here the Christian name and the nickname are perhaps identical. He had a daughter Daphne, much older (i.e., about ten years) than I was, who was believed by Christina Innes and others of my friends to have seen a fairy, a little old woman spinning, sitting at the mouth of a rabbit hole on the Yorkshire moors.

Horace, as well as scraps of didactic works printed by Caxton and Wynkyn de Worde. Since the latter styled himself "printer unto the most excellent princess my lady the King's Grandame" (i.e., Lady Margaret Beaufort, the foundress of the college), the rats may well have been chewing a publisher's presentation copy.[11]

From this discovery I learned of the invasion of Britain by *Rattus rattus* and its subsequent displacement by the brown rat, *Rattus norvegicus*. I think my interest in interspecific competition was first aroused at this time.

My mother's other two brothers ran the Burge Brewery, which came into the family through their mother,

11. A. E. Shipley, *Minor Horrors of War* (London: Smith, Elder & Co., 1915); A. E. Shipley, *More Minor Horrors* (London: Smith, Elder & Co., 1916). For the rats see A. E. Shipley, *Cambridge Cameos* (London: Jonathan Cape, 1924). A more accurate and detailed account of the manuscript and printed fragments is given by Charles Sayle, Cambridge Fragments, *The Library*, 3d ser. 2:339–55, 1911.

Since the litter of which the nest was made varied much in date, I suspect that much of the paper was recycled by the rats. No perfect copies of the books from which the Caxton and Wynkyn de Worde fragments are derived were recorded by Sayle. The Caxton fragment was from his *Donatus Melior* of Mancillinus, of which another fragment, from a binding, exists in New College, Oxford. The Wynkyn de Worde *Primer* is known in several editions, at least two of which are different from the Christ's fragment.

In addition to these works of Britain's earliest printers, the rats were using fragments of Virgil and Horace and of documents relating to Thomas Thompson, master of the college from 1510 to 1517. There were also some pages from children's books from about 1820, but their relation to the rats' nest is not clear.

At the same time as this discovery, when plaster had been removed from the ceilings of the rooms of the ground floor, it was found that the joists had been covered with paper bearing a printed design, and that the paper used was in fact the back of copies of Henry VIII's first proclamation and of a poem on the death of Henry VII. My uncle used copies of the reconstructed printed design, made up in fabric, for upholstery in the restored lodge.

FIGURE 2   Mummified black rats (*Rattus rattus*) found between the ceiling of the ground floor and the floor above, which was intended as an apartment for the foundress, Margaret Countess of Beaufort, with two fragments of the *Aeneid* (2. 331–35, 385–400) from their nest. Note the diagnostically long tail of the uppermost individual (by courtesy of the master, librarian, and fellows of Christ's College, Cambridge).

Amelia Burge, who had married one of her father's appren-
tice brewers, Alexander Shipley, the grandson of William
and Catherine. Amelia, my maternal grandmother, was an
intrepid horsewoman and a very sweet, good, and intelligent person whom my mother loved dearly. She and her
sister, Sarah, who married another brewing pupil, were
skilled musicians, Amelia playing the piano and harp and
possessing a fine mezzo-soprano voice. In those days living
in Windsor led to occasional encounters with the royal
family; Queen Adelaide once stopped her carriage to talk
with little Millie and Tallie, out for a walk with their nurse,
Miss Fussell, just as if they were inhabiting an early poem
of Edith Sitwell.

One brother, Sir William, became mayor of Windsor.
The other, Colonel Reginald Shipley, was militarily gifted
and had a distinguished short career in 1914–18 in the
Ypres sector of the western front. He was much too old
for this and broke down completely after the war. He was
a brave and very generous man. I think he probably showed
me my first protist, namely yeast, under the microscope
of the tiny control laboratory of the brewery.

I was the oldest of three children. My brother, Leslie,
just under two years younger than I, ultimately became
Director of Education in the Isle of Wight. My sister,
Dorothea, was a psychiatric social worker and still lives
in Cambridge. I can remember my brother when I was four
and he two years old, crawling about on the sands of a
place called Buckland on the Devonshire coast. For my
sister's birth we were sent away to Corton on the Suffolk
coast, but I just remember her christening party, where
I was found with my friend Christina Innes under the
table picking up the bits of icing from the christening cake
dropped by the guests.

Much later, in the First World War, a girl who was
working as a technician in pathology in connection with

a military hospital came to live with us. She was called Gwendoline Ethel Rendle, immediately contracted to Gwendle, and soon became an elder sister. Later, as Sah Oved, she became a most distinguished jeweler and silversmith, and a very learned historian of her art. During the Second World War we had her small daughter to live with us.

I remember keeping little aquaria with red watermites and I think a water spider (*Argyroneta aquatica*), about the time my mother was teaching me to read and write, when I was aged five or so. I certainly realized then or a little later that different kinds of animals lived in different kinds of water, so that one would not look for the red watermites of the ponds on Sheep's Green in Hobson's Conduit across Trumpington Road, where, however, sticklebacks might be caught.

About this time I was taken to the London Zoo; I have no memory of the visit, but later my mother told me that I was entranced, almost literally, by the array of animals.

I had started collecting butterflies and moths before I was eight; the killing-bottle was made by my father in his lab, but the art of setting (or *spreading* in American English) I learned from a nurse, a very good woman called Jane Bumstead. Incidentally, she provided most curious links with two of the important traditions of British natural history. She had friends who lived in a cottage on a small estate for which the man was the gardener. He was an enthusiastic if quite unlearned moth collector, one of the workmen naturalists of whom there were numbers in the nineteenth century and whose role needs to be explored.[12]

12. Alfred Russel Wallace, in his biographical introduction to Richard Spruce, *Notes of a Botanist on the Amazon and Andes* (London: Macmillan, 1908), vol. 1., writes (p. xxiii) of Spruce, who made immense contributions to our knowledge of the bryophytes of South America:

The other link, in the opposite, aristocratic, direction, was that she had previously held a position in the small Hertfordshire town of Tring. From her I learned of the animal wonders of Lord Rothschild's estate. Though her recollections were muddled and secondhand, they prepared me for cassowaries and giant tortoises, the last named having become great favorites.

From this period I have a distinct recollection of the magnificent Morehouse comet of 1908, seen from a west window on the stairs at 3 Belvoir Terrace. Unfortunately the comet in my memory is upside-down.

I remember very clearly my earliest reading lessons. P-O-T *pot*, H-O-T *hot*, but what, I asked my mother, was the meaning of *ot*? The idea that there were potential

---

"Sam Gibson was his first adviser in the study of mosses. This Gibson was a whitesmith or 'tinman' at Hebden Bridge, about six miles west of Halifax, and was one of a considerable number of North-country working-men botanists of the early nineteenth century."

My friend Donna Haraway of Johns Hopkins University has called my attention to a discussion of the intense study of natural history by Yorkshire weavers early in the nineteenth century, in E. P. Thompson, *The Making of the English Working Classes* (New York: Vintage Books, 1963), p. 291.

I have used data collected by two unnamed Yorkshire working-men, one tentatively identified by Professor Geoffrey Fryer, F. R. S., as Ben Morley, in calculating the frequency of the *varleyata* gene in the population of the currant moth, *Abraxas grossulariata*, near Huddersfield in Yorkshire in the first few years of this century (Some Continental European Aberrations of *Abraxas grossulariata* Linn. (Lepidoptera) with a Note on the Significance of the Variation Observed in the Species, *Trans. Conn. Acad. Arts Sci.* 43:1–24, 1969). I understand that one of the policemen in the city of York is an authority on staphylinid beetles, so this admirable tradition is still alive. The influence of such people on the history of biology in Britain greatly needs study. As Thompson hints, the records of local natural history museums and societies should provide rich material. There is unfortunately little on the workmen naturalists in D. E. Allen, *The Naturalist in Britain* (London: Allen Lane, 1976).

words that somehow had not yet acquired meanings, puzzled me at the time, and always comes back into my mind when I am thinking about any kind of formal system. I know my sister was taught by my mother and imagine that my brother was also. I am pretty sure I early learnt some arithmetic from my father. Such teaching implanted the idea that letters and numbers are a natural part of life in the home, for which I am most grateful to both my parents.

After starting my education with my mother, I went daily to Miss Innes, who also taught her niece Christina, in a two-child school, for several years. I am said to have pushed Christina, of whom I was really very fond, into a pond in the University Botanic Gardens to see if she would float, an early interest in the hydromechanics of organisms of which I am not proud, but I know that the victim has forgiven me.

We were taught in a large schoolroom in Christina's parents' house on Saint Eligius Street. This street got its improbable name from a medieval hospital for lepers that had once existed in this part of Cambridge (then outside the Trumpington Gate) and been dedicated to Saint Anthony and to the Merovingian goldsmith saint, also called Saint Eloy.

My main recollection of this phase of my education was learning "John Gilpin was a highway-man [sic] of credit and renown," and "Sir Ralph the Rover tore his hair and cursed himself in his despair," and more fortunately considerable doses of Greek and Latin mythology, so that, as with Renaissance youth, the ancient gods and heroes were as much a part of my life as the characters of the Bible. My grandmother I think was still a fundamentalist as to the creation story of Genesis, but my parents of course took it as an allegory. In 1909, when I was six, I was taken to see the academic procession of delegates to the centennial of Charles Darwin's birth and the jubilee of the *Origin of Species*. I remember a white academic robe from Portugal and a general impression of brilliant diversity representing all corners of the earth.

Saint Eligius Street, accidentally though appropriately, since the saint was the patron of farriers, also contained a stable from which one could hire a cab to go to the station, or for any purpose for which a taxi is now used. There being no telephone, one of us would go round with a note to the proprietor asking for a cab at the appropriate hour next day. The carriages were of three kinds: a brougham, which was closed and was regarded by my mother as masculine and unhealthy; a landau, the divided top of which could be opened; and a victoria, seating two adults, with a collapsible top, ordinarily thrown back.

When the cowslips (*Primula veris*) were in flower on the Granchester Meadows along the river Cam a couple of miles south of the town, my grandmother took a victoria in which she sat with her sunshade, feeling very elegant, while one or two of us wriggled about on the other seat. Being a widow, she always wore black, but sunshades could be green, purple, or white with a pair of narrow black submarginal stripes. She also had pierced ears, supposed in her girlhood to improve vision, and nice Victorian earrings of which my parents greatly disapproved. We picked large bouquets of cowslips that filled her house and ours. Later I realized that primroses (*P. vulgaris*) were not commonly found wild in our part of England while cowslips were, and I vaguely wondered why. I knew of, but never got to, the woods in western Cambridgeshire where the true oxslip (*P. elatior*) grows, to some extent replacing the primrose ecologically.

Later, when we could bicycle, the blooming of the Pasque flower (*Anemone pulsatilla*) justified in April another floral expedition, this time to the Fleam Dyke, one of three large earthworks with ditches on the southwest and ramps on the northeast, built either in late Roman or early Saxon times to block invasions from the southwest. The ramp, being of chalky soil and uncultivated, provided a refuge for this very attractive plant.

Horses provided not only transportation for the living, but also for the dead. The horse-drawn hearse was a vehicle of great elegance, with glass sides, a railing of silvery posts and chains to surround the flower-covered coffin, and a low pyramidal roof of shiny black painted ornamental woodwork.

When a funeral passed, one was expected to stand with uncovered head. I was, unfortunately, terrified of hearses and went to considerable pains to avoid them. Other children took a different view. I was told by my brother that Jim Pearce, who later became a great friend, had ascertained in a comprehensive study of the burial customs of Cambridge that Roman Catholics habitually covered the coffin with strawberry jam before inhumation. I am sure that he took a respectful attitude to his alleged discoveries. There was, however, still some absurd religious prejudice around.

My mother, to her great credit, took a strong line about such matters. I remember that when a family of Jews came to live near us we were told that they followed the practices of the Old Testament and were to be respected as a living demonstration of what the Bible was about. They immediately acquired a quite legendary aura. I recently learned from my sister, who knew one of the Salzman daughters, that the father of the family, though professionally a physician, was by avocation the great medievalist who has placed all users of the Victoria County History in his debt.

Of my friends before I was plunged into tough

masculine society at the age of eight or nine I can remember little. My cousin Gilbert Reginald Shipley Stewart, whom we called Bill or Rex, the second son of my mother's younger sister, was a little older than I was, but very important in my life. My memories of him when we visited Dulwich, or when he came to stay in Cambridge, are nearly all concerned with discussions of conjuring tricks. His father, professionally in medicine, was an enthusiatic moth collector and therefore a venerated figure. He had a number of scientific friends and I remember when staying with the Stewarts being taken to tea with Sir Jethro and Lady Teall; he was a very distinguished geologist who became head of the British Geological Survey. I was also taken rather later to see Dr. H. H. Dale, later Sir Henry Dale, president of the Royal Society, to which visit I shall refer later.

In Cambridge, apart from Christina, I have early memories of Anna Bidder, now well known for her beautiful work on the biology of *Nautilus*;[13] her father was to have a decisive influence on my intellectual development. I also think that I knew the small daughter of the master of Caius, who later, as M. D. Anderson, wrote admirably on English medieval art, including a small book on animal carvings which I treasure.[14] Apart from my brother and my cousin, my close acquaintance was evidently largely feminine.

13. A. M. Bidder, Use of the Tentacles, Swimming and Buoyancy Control in the Pearly Nautilus, *Nature* (London) 196:451–54, 1962.

14. M. D. Anderson, *Animal Carvings in British Churches* (Cambridge: Cambridge University Press, 1938).

CHAPTER TWO

AYSTHORPE

WHEN I WAS NINE I was enrolled in one of the three private schools for boys, in local parlance, preparatory schools, in Cambridge, this one being Saint Faith's. We had moved from Belvoir Terrace to a larger house set in a garden of just under an acre, and the school was about three minutes walk from this house that we called Aysthorpe. The house was built on land leased from Trinity College. The road on which it stood, Newton Road, was the first of several in a small development and was called after Trinity's greatest alumnus. Next came Bentley Road, and after my time Barrow Road followed.

The house looked out on meadows, over which kestrels (*Falco tinnunculus*) hawked and skylarks (*Alauda arvensis*) sang. The yellow and black warningly colored caterpillars of the cinnabar moth (*Hypocrita jacobaeae*) fed on numerous plants of ragwort (*Senecio jacobaea*) among the grasses, while in the swampier places ghost moths (*Hepialus humuli*) could be seen appearing and disappearing as they fluttered in the summer dusk. A flowering almond stood by the front gate, and I remember one Sunday evening in May, when the tree was in full bloom, a nightingale (*Luscinia megarhynchos*) chose it as a singing place.

Aysthorpe was a name synthesized by my parents from Ayscough, Sir Isaac's mother's maiden name, and Woolsthorpe, where he was born. The house was built for my parents by an architect called Alan Munby, an old friend of my father, who had spent most of his professional career designing laboratories, on which subject he wrote a book. His son was later librarian of King's and a very respected bibliographic scholar. Munby secured from somewhere a set of plaster zodiacal signs that he set, to our great delight, in a circle in the ceiling of the dining room. My parents must have become rather sick of hearing us chant at mealtimes:

The Ram, the Bull, the Heavenly Twins
And next the Crab, the Lion shines
The Virgin and the Scales
The Scorpion, Archer and He-goat
The Man who holds the watering pot
And the Fish with glittering tails.

This room was the scene of the disgraceful incident I described in "Cambridge Remembered," where my brother and I locked in all the guests, including Sir George and Lady Darwin, at a dinner party with my parents, and then turned out the lights at the main.[1] Being presumably now the only living person to have incarcerated one of Charles Darwin's sons, has often provided a useful link with the past when giving a class on evolution.

Saint Faith's, at the corner of Newton Road and Trumpington Road, taught everything that a young gentleman was supposed to know: English poetry, at first Macaulay's *Horatius* and *The Battle of Lake Regillus*, which

1. G. E. Hutchinson, *The Enchanted Voyage* (New Haven and London: Yale University Press, 1962), (reprinted., Greenwood Press, 1978) see pp. 149–56.

didn't have enough about the lake for me, but later, to my
lasting delight, we did Chaucer's *Prologue to the Canterbury
Tales*, Gray's *Elegy*, Milton's *L'Allegro*, *Il Penseroso*, and
Lycidas, and Coleridge's *Ancient Mariner*. English history,
geography—in retrospect largely lists of the products of
the British possessions in Africa, each list ending in pignuts
—arithmetic, algebra, and geometry, French and Latin
constituted the rest of the curriculum, with, for all but me,
Greek. My father insisted that I do more mathematics
instead, which was his only educational mistake. His
similar insistence that I was also to do algebra instead of the
ridiculous exercise of writing unspeakably bad Latin verses
was obviously wise. It did, however, keep me from the
unconscious English riches of some of the textbooks on
that infertile subject, which, among the examples to be
done into Latin, rise to the heights, so I understand, of:

> Grinder, jocund-hearted grinder
> By whom Barbary's agile son,
> Deftly poised upon his hinder
> Paw, accepts the pro-offered bun.

Organ grinders went round the streets of English towns,
pushing barrel organs which they played at intervals. The
better ones each had a monkey in a red jacket with a mug
in which to collect the "penny to play in the next street."
As children we loved them. They all came from Cassino in
central Italy, but, alas for the veracity of the poet, the
monkeys I believe were mainly *Cebus* from South America.

The place of Greek in education had for long played
a large role in university politics. The language was
required for entrance to the older universities, but at least
at Cambridge a growing number of dons were opposed to
its retention in what was officially the Previous Examination, and colloquially the Little-Go, which gave entrance
to all higher studies. A few Hellenists were violently

opposed to this change, and among them none more so than T. R. Glover.

My sister relates in a letter of 12 October 1977 that "Mother had sat next to Glover at a dinner party on a Saturday night and had had a heated discussion on the value of compulsory Greek in schools, he defending and she attacking it. Next morning he was to give one of a series of Ecumenical sermons at St. Edward's Church, so we abandoned St. Botolph's and trooped down to St. Edward's. Arriving (as usual) rather late, we were shown into the front pew. When the time came for the sermon Glover leaned forward from the pulpit and announced his text 'And the centurion said unto Paul, canst thou speak Greek?' Collapse of Hutchinson family, as mother had regaled us with an account of the discussion all through breakfast." I have no recollection of this, but if it occurred in term time with more than one child at home it must have been during my time at Saint Faith's. Greek was finally made optional in the Little-Go shortly after the First World War.

A very important aspect of going to a boys' school involved changing one's name. In the largely feminine world of childhood I was Evelyn; now I had become, at school, Hutchinson. Of course, I already understood about Christian names and surnames, but the latter were empirically unimportant. My cousin who was very close to me was a Stewart, my uncle who was important to me, a Shipley. Becoming "Hutchinson" was in a sense a process of initiation. It meant belonging in a large world in which a few other people whom I learned to feel were relatives had the name, but, more importantly, belonging in a small world, the school, where it happened that initially no one else bore the name. It was, moreover, a process that only happened to boys. In some cases it would emphasize primogeniture. My brother had had rheumatic fever when he was about eight years old; in Cambridge it was commonly, if unconsciously, believed that Hippocrates would have disapproved of the local air, much preferring that of Surrey. Accordingly, it was felt wiser for Leslie to go to a boarding school at Hindhead, so he escaped being Hutchinson 2 at Saint Faith's after a year. Later he was Hutchinson minor at Gresham's School, Holt, which must inevitably have been somewhat galling. Moreover, it could happen quite accidentally. Robinson tertius was no relative of Robinson major and minor. Not being well liked, he soon became Robinson dirt and was still less liked.

Though most adult men called each other by their surnames ("My dear Darwin" and "My dear Huxley" would be typical Victorian salutations), there was some use of nicknames, often derived from the surname in a way parallel to derivation within a family from a Christian name. Thus E. A. Wilson of the Terranova Expedition seems to have been Dr. Bill on the Antarctic continent. There was another usage denoting intimacy, namely the use of Christian-name initials. This was very common in some circles in late Victorian and Edwardian times. My father never called my uncle anything but A. E. Moreover, he used to call me G., which I think was an elision of G. E. and denoted a desire to think of me as a close contemporary friend. Among people of my age the practice must have been virtually extinct, though one American who became a fellow of Saint John's in the 1930s always addressed me as G. E. when we met. By the time that I was an undergraduate, men were beginning to use Christian names for their close friends. This involved, I think, some rejection of the arrogant masculinity of the schoolboy and an acceptance of more mature values in which tenderness was not out of place. While adolescent, the boys I knew, when we went to young people's dances, would always call the girls by their Christian names, Diana, Barbara, and so on. When one got to college, every new acquaintance was, in ordinary mixed contexts, Mr. and Miss, until one was ready for kissing, of which there was far less than today. The Christian name was not merely adult, but it had a definite sexual connotation; thinking of its use to someone attractive thus became a mild but very charming erotic fantasy.

The full sequence of names used for one's close associates in late Victorian times would then have been,

childhood	Christian name
boyhood	surname, often with nickname
early manhood	surname, initial name, or nickname
courtship, love, and marriage	Christian name.

By my time the Christian name was beginning to play both the last two roles.

About women's names I know little, but I suspect an almost universal use of Christian names in private, with Miss becoming more used publicly as the girl matured. There was, of course, a movement by "advanced" young women in the 1920s to imitate men, of which movement poor Carrington is perhaps the only significant memorial. Insofar as the practice was not a meaningless imitation of a rather tiresome male world, it obviously denoted faith in one's powers to do something as well as a man could. Unfortunately, in Carrington's case, everyone knows that she wanted to be called Carrington and that she died for the love of someone who was no doubt personally much inferior to her, however eminent a Georgian he may have been. Between name and death practically nobody till recently considered the fate of her pictures and whether she had been a good painter.

The mandatory change in all this was the adoption of the surname as the main appellation of a boy going to school. Whether later a nickname or an initial name were used, and when a young woman was no longer Miss, depended on personal judgments. One could always be wrong and so any situation involving names initially might be embarrassing. It generally was not, but the fear that it might be was real.

The headmaster of Saint Faith's School was Henry Lower; he was assisted by his sister and a small staff. Mr. Lower taught the two upper classes side by side and in retrospect he gives the impression of having been able to teach Greek, Latin, and algebra simultaneously. I can remember nothing much about the other teachers, save that I was first taught arithmetic by a Miss Chrystal, who I think recently had been, or was about to become, a student at the university. I hope, and indeed suspect, that she was the daughter of Professor George Chrystal of Edinburgh, the great investigator of the seiches or periodic water movements of lakes.

The curriculum was completed by cricket, in which I excelled negatively, in spite of the beauty of the game, and by soccer, which on one occasion I played very well. My subjective experience of adrenalin is ultimately based, so I imagine, on that one match. Almost everything I learned at Saint Faith's has proved of great value, but while I was there I was also conducting my own education in other ways.

The country around Cambridge lies on Cretaceous rocks and in my boyhood there were exposures of the whole sequence from the Lower Greensand to the Upper Chalk in cuttings, clay pits, and more or less abandoned chalk pits, from some of which, with tenacity, very nice fossils could be obtained. Further north at Upware on the edge of the fen country a lime pit exposed late Jurassic coral rock with fragments of tropical-looking sea-urchin spines, an unbelievably romantic circumstance to a small boy. In geological studies I had of course help from my father, who always traveled on our holidays with a geological atlas of the British Isles, so that we could appreciate from the window of the train the ultimate nature of the countryside through which we passed. The geological structure of Britain, with the usually great dip of the beds, permitting one to pass one formation after another in a distance of a few tens of miles, was just what one needed to learn about rocks or, in my case, where to look for fossils. I was also greatly helped by two other older friends. One was Dr. Cowper Reed, a very eminent professional paleontologist and curator of the Sedgwick Museum of the Department of Geology in the university. The other was the Reverend J. W. E. Conybeare, a local antiquarian and fossil collector who had been vicar of Barrington, famous for a gravel pit that had yielded many *Hippopotamus* bones. He had, however, become converted to Roman Catholicism and now lived privately in Cambridge. He had a large collection of specimens from the Cambridge Greensand, a very narrow bed full of phosphatic nodules which had been extensively worked in the nineteenth century and had produced an extraordinary fauna, including a few bird bones. Only one exposure still existed, at the top of a very deep clay pit; I managed to make friends with the workmen and visited the locality, but I cannot remember what I found. Fortunately I presented the one or two really good fossils I had collected near Cambridge to the Sedgwick Museum, for the rest were given away, without my knowledge, when I went to South Africa.

The churches in the country around Cambridge contain a number of medieval brasses, and brass rubbing, now so popular that its devotees flock from Bengal and Oklahoma to Oxford and Westley Waterless, was a favorite avocation of a few of us. I had learned the art, rather imperfectly, from an older boy called George Anderson who

was technically a superb brass-rubber and who had traveled in Belgium and Germany rubbing some of the extraordinary brasses in the Continental or "Flemish" style.
I hope his collection survives, as some of the originals, after
two wars, well may not, and his rubbings could hardly
have been excelled. I am told that I passed on the art to
Michael Ramsey, later one-hundredth archbishop of Canterbury, though I greatly regret not having any memories
of this; the Ramseys were valued friends. I have written
elsewhere of Frank Ramsey mystifying a children's party
by choosing the "left horn of a dilemma" as the object to
be guessed in a game of Animal, Vegetable, or Mineral,
which we called "clumps."

Three miles south of Cambridge lay Sir Roger de
Trumpington, a magnificent knight and the second oldest
survivor in Britain.[2] A short bicycle ride to Fulbourn
brought one to William de Fulburne in a splendid cope,
under a canopy, and on the way home one could speculate
on the meaning of lunacy when passing the county asylum.
At Hildersham a skeleton in a shroud yielded a rubbing
useful for scaring the housemaid. Brasses, moreover, led
to heraldry, which when once recognized greeted one from
every building. "Barry argent and azure, an orle of martlets

2. Sir Roger de Trumpington, whose effigy must adorn walls
all over the world, died in 1289; his armor fits this date, but the figure
was originally surrounded by a fillet, of which only the indent remains,
bearing an inscription. No other brass or indent before 1300 has such
a fillet, the earliest inscriptions always consisting of letters set separately
in the stone matrix. If the figure and fillet are coeval, the brass probably
dates from c. 1300. However, it is set on an altar tomb under an ogival
arch, which looks even later. There is some indication that the heraldry
of the figure has been altered. Sir Roger's brass may well have been
reused on the tomb of his son and successor Sir Giles, who died in 1327.
If this happened the inscription on the fillet would be later than the
effigy (see *Inventory of the Historical Monuments in the City of Cambridge*, part 1, pp. cvii–cviii).

gules," which describes the blue and white bars and ring
of little red birds of one half of the Pembroke arms, is
surely one of the most beautiful abstract lines in any
language. I began a book on heraldry, of which three
completed chapters still exist. It was to have been very
learned and exhaustive, so it had to mention all the very
rare tinctures or heraldic colors used occasionally by Continental heralds but regarded in England as foreign bar-
barisms. I remember trying to make *cendré* paint out of
ashes from a fireplace to illustrate a coat of arms with this
ash-gray field.

The loss of brasses at the Reformation and after was
appalling, initially because they asked in Norman French,
Latin, or English, "Dieu de sa alme eyt mercie," and later
because, broken and outmoded, they reached a good price
as scrap metal. Other remarkable things, however, might
be found in Cambridgeshire churches. Ickleton, which
takes its name from the pre-Roman Icknield Way, has a
set of Roman monolithic pillars capped by Norman arches
and is said by Pevsner to be "far too little known."[3] I won
a prize for a highly unoriginal essay on its architectual
history when I was at Saint Faith's, thirty-five or forty
years before Pevsner wrote.

Another favorite was Hauxton, a small church with a
beautiful Norman south door by which, in the wall, is a
scratch dial, a very primitive sundial with a hole for the
gnomon, for which the user of the dial supplied his own
piece of stick. Inside, at the end of the south aisle of the
church, is one of the very few surviving medieval paintings
of Saint Thomas of Canterbury, a bête noire of Henry VIII,
who attempted as far as possible to blot out the archbishop's
memory. Sundials were a great part of my childhood, as

3. Nikolaus Pevsner, *The Buildings of England*, B. E. 10 Cambridgeshire (London: Penguin Books, 1954), see p. 331.

my father had a passion for them. He not only possessed some very good sixteenth- and seventeenth-century pocket dials, now in the Whipple collection of the Department of the History and Philosophy of Science in Freeschool Lane in Cambridge, but also loved regraduating, for the contemporary epoch, any painted wall-dial in Cambridge that had become illegible.

Fortunately, for some inexplicable reason I did not visit Whittlesford Church, very close to Hauxton, until I was an adult; it would either have been lost on me or would have worried me greatly. On the tower is a sheela-na-gig,[4] a squat, intensely erotic female figure, being approached by a zoomorphic man (figure 3, above). Such female figures, of which there are over thirty conspicuously set on British churches, more than twice that number in Ireland, and some in Normandy, raise unsolved questions of medieval belief. As a great contrast, in a glass case in the same church, among a number of broken fifteenth-century alabaster figures found bricked up in a wall, a lovely fragment of a *virgo lactans* seems, by her very low gown, a late medieval symbol of the unmarried state, exposing her breasts, to convey with great elegance both the virginity and maternity of Mary (figure 3, below).[5]

4. For the most recent account of sheela-na-gigs, see J. Andersen, *The Witch on the Wall* (London: Allen & Unwin, 1977). See also G. E. and A. L. Hutchinson, The "Idol" or Sheela-na-gig at Binstead with Remarks on the Distribution of Such Figures, *Proc. Isle of Wight Nat. Hist. Archaeol. Soc.* 6:237–81, 1970.

5. The Whittlesford alabaster fragments are described in J. H. Middleton, On Fragments of Alabaster Retables from Milton and Whittlesford, Cambridge, *Proc. Cambridge Antiquar. Soc.* 7:106–11, 1893. H. J. E. Burrell and G. M. Benton, The English Alabaster Carvings of Cambridgeshire, with Special Reference to Fragmentary Examples at Wood Ditton Church, *Proc. Cambridge Antiquar. Soc.* 34:77–83, 1924.

The Whittlesford *virgo lactans* is clearly very close to a large (c. 90

In the winter of 1917–18, the weather was abnormally cold and many birds died. I remember just after Christmas finding six redwings (*Turdus iliacus*) dead in a ditch over a stretch of about fifty feet along the Trumpington Road. One would have thought that so boreal a bird would have known how to look after itself. I tried to skin one; my father mentioned this to Dr. F. H. H. Guillemard,[6] possibly at a meeting of the vestry of Saint Botolph's Church,[7] where they were both sidesmen. Guillemard had been a remarkable traveler and collector in early life, was the author of a book on the birds of Cyprus, and had for a short time been lecturer in geography at Cambridge, though he never lectured. He was eccentrically conservative and eschewed gas or electricity in the Old Mill House in Trumpington where he lived. He immediately asked my father if I was aware of the importance of paper in skinning

---

cm.) and perfect figure of Saint Catherine illustrated in an advertisement in *Burlington Magazine*, Dec. 1968, p. xxxix; the two pieces may well be by the same hand. The occurrence of broken images embedded in walls may suggest that such images were, in spite of Puritan desecrators, believed to have some numinous significance that they could continue to exercise even though fragmented and unseen.

6. For F. H. H. Guillemard see S. C. Roberts, *Adventures with Authors* (Cambridge: Cambridge Univ. Press, 1966), pp. 26–29; D. R. Stoddart, The RGS and the Foundations of Geography in Cambridge, *Geogr. J.* 141:216–39, 1975, where two fantastic photographs of Guillemard are published.

As I indicated in *The Enchanted Voyage*, Guillemard, till he was in his seventies, made it a practice to attend every auction of a great auk (*Alca impennis*) skin or egg held in Britain.

7. The rector of Saint Botolph's, the Reverend Canon A. W. Goodman, was, I believe, the last examiner in Paley's *Evidences of Christianity*, which could be taken instead of chemistry or logic as a subject in the university entrance or previous examination, usually called the Little-Go. Very few students can have elected Paley in my day, but the existence of the subject is of some interest in view of the influence of the book on Darwin.

FIGURE 3   Whittlesford Church. *Above*, sheela-na-gig on the tower, early twelfth century; *below*, fragment of *virgo lactans*, now on north wall of nave, c. 1480.

a bird. My father must have answered no, because next morning I rode out on my bicycle to Trumpington with a dead redwing, scissors, and scalpel. The secret of preparing a good study skin was to have a supply of small pieces of toilet paper about one inch square, with which every piece of flesh exposed was immediately covered. No blood or exudates ever soiled the feathers. Many years later, my wife pointed out to me that Mary Kingsley, the great African explorer, had had lessons from Guillemard, about a quarter of a century before I did, in the preparation of natural history specimens. I am delighted to have this link with her.

Before my last year at Saint Faith's I had come to regard the Lepidoptera, quite wrongly and indeed snobbishly, as too commonplace a subject for study. Later I realized that they carry all the major problems of evolutionary biology set out in colored two-dimensional diagrams on their wings. At thirteen I had decided that they were too much collected, by too uninteresting people, to be worthy of my attention.

The most remarkable butterfly in the area was the swallowtail, *Papilio machaon britannicus*, which occurred only at Wicken Fen and in the Norfolk Broads. The British race has heavier black markings than the Continental, is usually univoltine, or with one brood each year, and feeds as a larva on milk parsnip, *Peucedanum palustre*, while the paler form in France is bivoltine and feeds on cultivated carrot and some other plants. French individuals often blow over and many have been taken in southeastern England, but the insect cannot now establish itself.[8]

8. Most of the information available on the distribution of the British and Continental swallowtails in England is summarized in E. B. Ford, *Butterflies* (London: Collins, 1945), pp. 302–03; T. G. Howarth, *South's British Butterflies* (London and New York: Frederick Warne, 1973), p. 38; and R. L. H. Dennis, *The British Butterflies* (Faringdon,

About the time I was born, the swallowtail occurred on Burwell Fen near Cambridge as well as on Wicken Fen. During my boyhood it was common at the latter locality, a large stretch of undrained fenland covered with sedge and in places with buckthorn. In the 1940s it died out at Wicken but has now, after considerable efforts, been introduced from Norfolk. It was hard to catch. On my first trip to the fen I was riding on my bicycle along the lode or ditch that separated the fen from the lower drained pasture to the north. Along came a swallowtail. I swept at it with my net, more or less falling off my bicycle. On getting up I picked up the net, and out flew the butterfly. At least I have both caught a *P. machaon britannicus* riding a bicycle and in retrospect need not feel I have contributed to the decline of an endangered species. I think this incident may have contributed to a temporary disillusionment with the Lepidoptera.

Rather later in my school days my interest in the Lepidoptera revived, partly as the result of seeing, at tea-time on one or two Sundays, the splendid collection of European butterflies made by Dr. J. Neville Keynes, Registrary of the university and father of Lord Keynes, the economist, and Sir Geoffrey Keynes, the surgeon and incomparable bibliographer. My interest in variation early led me to the magpie or currant moth, *Abraxas grossulariata*, and I have published papers on this protean organism in recent years.

The two elder sons of William Bateson, John and Martin, both to die tragically, to the world's great loss, overlapped me at Saint Faith's and turned me momentarily to beetles. I was also failing to learn to play the piano, and

---

Oxon.: E. W. Classey, 1977), pp. 120–21, 140. It is quite possible that the Continental *P.m. bigeneratus* was a regular inhabitant of southern England until the early nineteenth century.

after my lessons Francis Jenkinson, the University Librarian and husband of my teacher, often showed me, through his binocular microscope, the flies that he had been collecting. If I had been told about counterpoint I might have combined music and entomology successfully. As it was, the flies proved more fascinating but hopelessly difficult. There were too many species and no handy guide to their identification. I felt, moreover, that I should look into something not otherwise studied at Cambridge. The true bugs or Hemiptera seemed appealing. Good books existed on them and my father could borrow them from the university library. Moreover, my friend Jim Pearce, who had become very interested in pond life, was a devotee of beetles, so that on our expeditions we could divide the spoils without contention. We formed a Cambridge Junior Natural History Society. I think the members were Jim Pearce, David Pollock, who I suspect went into law, Audrey Lloyd Jones, whose medical father was an amateur paleontologist, but of whom I know nothing more, and probably my brother Leslie, who was drawn in by Jim and myself. For a time he collected caddis flies, though largely through my prodding. As the group was so little known and as he had superb manual dexterity in mounting such things, his specimens were ultimately added to the national collection, along with many of my bugs. My sister, whom I persuaded to collect shells, tells me she also occasionally attended our meetings, which were held in the dining room of the lodge of Corpus Christi College, where Jim's father was the master. Later I was to discover that there had been a similar society more than a century before in Bottisham, east of Cambridge, brought into existence by Leonard Jenyns, whose greatest contribution to science was arranging for Darwin to sail on the *Beagle*.

Jim Pearce, now an Anglican monk at Mirfield, became an authority on the Haliplidae, and later Pselaphidae and Scydmaeidae. The coleopterist will realize that he

had a passion for the minute, allied I think to the Blessed
Dame Julian of Norwich seeing the universe as a hazelnut
placed in her hand and to other medieval attitudes that
appear in miniature painting. Alas, he is now too blind to
see his beloved little beetles.

Through David Pollock, I met a woman, I imagine
of about thirty, called Dorothy Elizabeth Thursby-
Pelham. She had been a postgraduate student of or assistant to Richard Assheton, a mammalian embryologist of
great distinction who died relatively young. Assheton had
started some work on the placentation of the coney or
dassie, that curious little relative of the elephant, scientifically then known as *Hyrax*. After Assheton's death, Miss
Pelham completed the work. She used to take me to her
laboratory to show me what she was doing, with an extremely discreet flirtatiousness, which was just right for
my age and insured that for the appropriate time I should
be in love with her. Later she got involved with defenses
against gas warfare under Barcroft and then went into
fisheries biology at Lowestoft. I owe her a great deal.

At about this time, through Jim Pearce, I also got
to know E. J. Bles, whose name is to be found in the
bibliographies of all the early biological work on *Xenopus*,
which he was the first to breed in captivity. He was a man
of private means who had built a beautiful laboratory
behind his house. Initially his interests were in the life
histories of Amphibia, but later he turned to cell physiology
and did a remarkable study on the production of gas
vacuoles in *Arcella*, a work continually interrupted by
illness and most tenaciously completed.[9] Bles remained
my friend through the rest of his life and was a continual
source of exciting biological conversation.

In the winter months, when little was stirring in the

9. E. J. Bles, Arcella. A Study in Cell Physiology, *Quart. J.
Microsc. Sci.* 72:527–48, 1929.

field, the various university museums in Cambridge were a constant source of delight. I probably knew the specimens shown in the old University Museum of Zoology by heart by the time I was fourteen. Most of them were displayed in a large hall on a site that had been the University Botanic Gardens until the middle of the nineteenth century. The ground floor of this hall was occupied by stuffed mammals and even more numerous skeletons. A gallery ran round the hall and was devoted to lower vertebrates.

Hanging from the roof and easily studied from the gallery was a magnificent skeleton of a rorqual or finwhale, *Balaenoptera musculus*. I remember hearing a most romantic story of this whale being stranded on the east coast sometime in the last century. Its body was said to have been brought to Cambridge by train, on a line of flatcars, by the Great Eastern Railway. When it arrived, during the Long Vacation, everyone connected with the museum was away. The decomposing whale, lying near the station, caused more and more distress, until the vicar of Little Saint Mary's, who held a position once occupied by George Herbert, valiantly assembled a group of osteological volunteers to prepare the skeleton. Unhappily this elaborate and beautiful story is completely untrue. The animal was beached dead, at Pevensey Bay, Sussex, on 13 November 1865. Claimed by the Crown, it was sold at auction and ultimately was exhibited by a speculator who had roughly prepared a skeleton. Later the skeleton was auctioned again, purchased by the university, and properly mounted. The romantic tale is an interesting example of a myth generated from the flimsiest factual foundations.[10]

In two galleries at the side of the main hall invertebrates and specimens to illustrate the principles of zoology were installed. In the museum I was able to learn

10. The true story is given in A. E. Shipley, "*J.*" *A Memoir of John Willis Clark* (see chap. I, n. 10), pp. 265–66.

of Mendelism and of sex-linked inheritance in the magpie moth, *Abraxas grossulariata*, of cryptic coloration and mimicry, of the sequestering of carotinoids from chilis in the plumage of orange "color-fed" canaries, of Abbott Thayer's discovery of countershading, giving meaning to the dark upper and paler lower surfaces of most vertebrates, as well as of a host of strange beasts such as the Surinam toad and its compatriot with an enormous tadpole and small frog, which fooled Maria Sibylla Merian, or one of her daughters, into thinking she had found a frog that grew up into a tadpole. Upstairs in a building which mostly housed the department of zoology and the study collection of insects, the bird room contained skeletons of the dodo and of both male and female solitaires, among the best testimonies of these extinct beings in existence. All these things and doubtless many more were essential ingredients of my life.

I was first taken to the Sedgwick Museum across the street from the Museum of Zoology, by my father, on my birthday, probably my eighth. We went specifically to see the skull of an aurochs, the old wild ox of Europe, in the forehead of which a Neolithic ax was embedded. It was supposed, I imagine, that the beast had been killed by a Neolithic hunter but had fallen into a water-filled pit in the fen country and been covered with peat. In later times the skull was certainly discovered in a peat cutting, but I believe that there is some doubt about the authenticity of its association with the ax. In the museum, however, the specimen fitted in perfectly with the bones of *Hippopotamus* from Barrington nearby and with all the marine fossils from the Chalk. Not only in space was an extraordinary variety of creatures to be found but the geological collections showed that my home itself had once been on the seafloor and that later it was inhabited by large exotic animals and wild men.

The Museum of Ethnology and Archaeology close by

contained a number of superb casts of Maya stelae and great collections of artifacts from Malaya and the Pacific Islands. On another birthday, either my tenth or eleventh, we were shown some of its special treasures by the curator, Baron Anatole von Hügel, the brother of the well-known theologian. I had for a minute or so a magnificent Hawaiian feather cloak draped over my shoulders, the sartorial high point of my existence. I remember also on the same occasion Baron von Hügel telling my mother of the extraordinary personal cleanliness of the Fijians. She received this information with great relief and obvious skepticism.

The last and greatest museum in Cambridge was the Fitzwilliam; with its beautiful vases of flowers, it is, perhaps, the most welcoming art gallery in the world. The style that has characterized the Fitzwilliam throughout most of this century is fundamentally due to its former director Sir Sidney Cockerell. He had a reputation in Cambridge for being impossible; in Oxford *to cockerell* an object meant to acquire it by any means, fair or foul. I distinctly remember him, when I was eleven or twelve, going out of his way to show and explain to me a number of Dürer prints.

When I first knew the Fitzwilliam it retained the crowded appearance of a nineteenth-century gallery, picture ranged above picture, closely covering the whole wall. I was very small, probably about five years old, when I was taken there to see an ivory model of the Taj Mahal. This object, no doubt an embarrassing gift, was later removed, but it was a source of real delight to children. Throughout my early life it gave me a haunting hope that one day I should see the building itself. When I did see it, it did not let me down. Of another, more adult work in the collection, I shall have a little to say on a later page. Revisiting the Fitzwilliam has always been one of the great pleasures of returning to Cambridge. Over the years my favorite painting there, or indeed perhaps anywhere, has come to be a small annunciation by Domenico Veneziano, a predella panel originally associated with an altarpiece now in the Uffizi. In this painting the two figures are in a cortile opening into a garden with a path leading to a wooden double door, which must be that *ex qua mundo lux est orta.*

Opposite the Fitzwilliam was a confectioner's shop called Mason's which produced a special large sponge cake; officially called a Fitzwilliam Cake, everyone called it a Fitzbilly. A legend grew up that the recipe had been invented by Sir Ellis Minns, a great authority on the Scythians and my father's dearest friend in Cambridge. He was also supposed to have blended a tea, before he was knighted, known as "Mr. Minns' Mixture," which could be obtained many years after his death at a grocer's shop called G. P. Jones. It was, I think, the best tea that I have drunk. Alas, G. P. Jones has closed and all efforts to learn the nature of the blend have failed.

Shortly before his death I asked Sir Ellis why Michael Rostovtzeff, who became the most significant member of the department of classics in my early days at Yale, had left Oxford, where he had come from Berlin in the early 1930s. Sir Ellis replied: "In Oxford if you disagree radically with someone, you say to him, 'My dear fellow, don't you think it is *just* possible that there is an alternative explanation, somewhat along the following lines?' But Rostovtzeff said, 'You are wrong, and I will tell you why you are wrong.'" Henry Andrews suspected that the words had been said to Sir Maurice Bowra. At Yale, however, Rostovtzeff, in spite of a rather leonine appearance, had a reputation for his very mild treatment of examination and term papers; attending the course rated a C, handing in some sort of an exercise a B, knowing anything at all an A.

During the time when I was at Saint Faith's, real

tragedy first touched my life. E. A. Wilson, the medical officer of the Terranova Expedition led by Captain Robert F. Scott to explore Antarctica, was a friend of my uncle. I can well remember the horror that struck us when we learned that Scott and four of his companions, including Wilson, had perished on their return from the South Pole. Wilson was an admirable ornithologist, a good landscape painter, and a most saintly man.

Later I discovered a curious link with the expedition. I had, as a boy, known that a Cambridge undergraduate called D. G. Lillie, at the end of the first decade of the present century, had been an extraordinary caricaturist.[11] He had painted William Bateson holding up two dark chickens labeled F_1 while a white F_2 emerged from his pocket. He had also done Sir Sidney Harmer, later the meticulous director of the Natural History Museum in South Kensington, with a red-tape worm in a museum jar.

About 1933 my father, who had found four of Lillie's works among my uncle's papers, gave them to me. They hung on my study wall until 1972, when I gave them to the National Portrait Gallery in London. Mr. Kingsley Adams, late director of the gallery, and I engaged in considerable research on the artist. It turned out that Lillie had been marine biologist on the Terranova, had done a

11. All the documentary evidence relating to Lillie that Mr. Adams, Lillie's goddaughter Miss Muriel Arber, or I have been able to discover is now in the National Portrait Gallery in London, with the four caricatures that I gave to that institution. There are four more Lillie originals in the Scott Institute for Polar Research at Cambridge, including the one of Wilson here reproduced. Besides those of William Bateson (see *The Enchanted Voyage*, frontispiece), and of Harmer, my four included one of Sir William Ridgeway (see A Cambridge Caricaturist, *Country Life* 144:644–45, 1968) and one of Tansley and Blackman (see G. E. Hutchinson, *An Introduction to Population Ecology* [New Haven and London: Yale University Press, 1978], figure 83).

oun Bill

FIGURE 4   D. G. Lillie, Caricature of E. A. Wilson. Scott Institute for Polar Research, Cambridge University.

wonderful caricature of Wilson as a penguin with a human head (figure 4), and had spent some time after the other survivors returned to England studying whales off New Zealand. He became involved in medical research in the First World War, but he had a mental breakdown in 1919 from which he never recovered, dying in 1963.

The loss of Scott's party seems in retrospect to have been the beginning of the carnage of 1914. Any day one might learn that someone close had been killed. Christina lost both her brothers. John Bateson was killed. Every boy of my age must have felt that if the stalemate in the trenches went on indefinitely, his turn one day would come.

Early in the war a camp was established in the University Polo Ground south of Aysthorpe, and my father decided that the soldiers there lacked all facilities for recreation. He got permission to set up two marquees, one as a writing and reading room and one as a sort of café. The camp was very temporary, but I remember serving ginger ale in the café and selling Woodbine cigarettes throughout one summer vacation.

Later, when gas warfare began, my father was much worried by the insensitivity of the navy to the dangers of a gas attack by sea. With a high naval medical officer, Fleet-Surgeon Hewitt by name, he managed to get invited to Scapa Flow to convince the high command. He did this by letting out a little brombenzene downwind, which immediately sent Admiral of the Fleet Lord Jellicoe below, weeping. This earned my father an O.B.E.

Apart from selling gingerpop and Woodbines, my wartime career consisted of being a boy scout orderly at the First Eastern General Hospital, erected on the King's College cricket ground, now the site of the Cambridge University Library.

The matron did not like me; she was a good authoritarian and much preferred subservient working-class boy scouts. My duties at the hospital were mainly sorting out good fruit from very mixed barrels of apples. I think, however, that at this point I began to realize that the world in which I really lived consisted of people who were passionately devoted to the fascinating and beautiful wonders provided naturally or artificially by the world, though the troubles of the times might force them to defer their passion. Insofar as we shared interests there was love between us, even though I was a small boy and they might be grown and eminent men and women. The Cambridge philosopher J. M. Ellis McTaggart believed that reality consisted of selves loving each other. People complained that he modeled the universe on an ideal conception of the fellowship of Trinity College. Certainly not all fellows at Trinity loved one another, but looking back on my own boyhood I see a little of what he meant, even though he insisted that he derived his ideas from first principles and not merely from the best that Cambridge could then offer empirically.

What I have written will I hope indicate the extraordinary richness of the environment in which I grew up. My first thought as a teacher has been to try to pass on as much of that richness as possible. Quite recently, in studying the career of Maria Sibylla Merian, the remarkable entomological artist who worked in Surinam about 1700, I have been impressed with the artistic and intellectual quality of her family environment, ranging from her father's connections with the De Bry publishing firm to her granddaughter marrying Leonhard Euler.[12] Through her stepfather and his student Abraham Mignon, who

12. G. E. Hutchinson, The Influence of the New World on Natural History, in *The Changing Scenes in Natural Science, 1776–1976*, ed. Clyde E. Goulden. Academy of Natural Sciences, Philadelphia Special Publ. 12, 1977, pp. 14–22.

taught Maria Sibylla as a girl, she inherited the tradition of Dutch flower and insect painting that goes back to the late Middle Ages. Wherever she went she seems to have been helped by other naturalists, as I was. The role of social structure in providing a really rich mental and artistic environment might well be a most significant subject of study for an intellectual historian. I suspect that quite unexpected parts of society may be involved.

CHAPTER THREE

WOODLANDS

I WENT TO BOARDING SCHOOL, or public school in the English sense, at Gresham's School, Holt, Norfolk, in September 1917, staying there until 1921, when I went up to Cambridge.

The school had been founded in the sixteenth century by Sir John Gresham. His family had lived in Holt but became immersed in affairs in the City of London. Sir John's father had been Lord Mayor, and he himself was elected to that office in 1547. He must have made a considerable fortune trading with the Levant, and he was also an original member of the Russia Company, established in 1555. His better known brother, Sir William Gresham, founder of the Royal Exchange and promulgator of Gresham's Law that bad money drives out good, inherited the family estate at Holt but sold it to his brother in 1546. Sir John proceeded to convert it into a free grammar school which he endowed with property in Norfolk and in London, putting it under the governorship of the Fishmongers' Company. The London properties were leased and increased greatly in value. Late in the nineteenth century, when the leases had expired, the Fishmongers' Company found that their small local school had become immensely rich. They forthwith decided to develop it as a very modern educational establishment.

Holt is a small market town about four miles inland from the north coast of Norfolk. The country around is mainly agricultural, but at the time of my school days there were a number of large and partly wooded estates in the neighborhood, though I do not think any belonged to people of great importance.

When the school was reconstituted, the old building in the town was converted into a preparatory or junior school, known officially as the Old School House and colloquially as the Osh. A complete set of new buildings for classrooms, library, and the like were set up east of the town and residential quarters for the boys were constructed by adding dormitories and studies to preexisting houses, in each of which a house master lived. Three of these retained the old names that they had had as private residences; the fourth, the School House, may have been entirely new.

The School House was under the headmaster, G. W. S. Howson; Woodlands under the second master, J. R. Eccles, always called J. R. E.; Farfield under Major Miller, usually called the Major; and Kenwyn under the school chaplain, whom we knew as Beaky Field.

Howson was a most peculiar man. He had been a master at Uppingham before being asked to undertake the rejuvenation and development of Gresham's in 1900. He imported the Uppingham custom of insisting that only school prefects, the half dozen or so senior and most important boys, be allowed to wear trousers with pockets. His sister kept house for him, as he, like J. R. E., was unmarried. They both gave me the impression of being, though in very different ways, extremely repressed homosexuals, which may well be in line with their obvious commitment to what they thought to be the welfare of the boys in their charge. On the one occasion of a public caning, of boys caught outside at night and smoking, both very serious offenses, Howson gave an impression of immense authority. Apart from a very rare event of this kind, there was, as far as I can remember, practically no punishment except moral obloquy.

Howson could entertain very unconventional ideas. He once got greatly interested in an article foreshadowing Marshall McLuhan's views about the decline of the written word and one evening sent for me and one or two other boys to discuss the matter with him. We found him in evening clothes, both he and J. R. E. always dressed for dinner, lying on a hearth rug in front of the fire in his study. He also got excited about a book claiming that men, rather than written words, were becoming obsolete and that the future belonged to women.[1] Though this very reasonable idea was not likely to appeal in so essentially masculine a society as an English boys' school, he adopted the book as required reading in a course that he gave on political theory.

I imagine that Howson was ultimately responsible for the very high intellectual level of the education we received. To him, presumably, must also be attributed the most peculiar requirement, on which the moral life of the school was supposed to depend, of each boy on entrance being put on his honor not to do certain things that were so awful that they could not be mentioned, let alone defined. In this aspect of school discipline he was ably assisted and I think surpassed by J. R. E., who was apocryphally related to have announced at house prayers, in his brusque and

1. Benjamin Kidd, *The Science of Power* (London: Methuen, 1918). Renewed acquaintance with this exasperating and at times prophetic work mainly emphasizes the value of humility as an intellectual virtue. Kidd's phrase "the iron law of renunciation" to me suggests a concealed forcible masculinity.

icy voice: "A certain boy, in a certain place, at a certain time, did a certain thing. I do not wish this to happen again." Many of us realized that the system might contain the germs of its own destruction. We all expected that a significant proportion of the boys leaving school would "go to the dogs" as a reaction. However wise we may have been about this and however much we may have learned from the Encyclopaedia Britannica, such ambiguities imposed a considerable strain on many of us, though this strain was probably less in Farfield than in Woodlands or the School House. David Lack, the best biologist that the school has produced, who was at Gresham's rather after my time and who later became a close friend, told me that he had felt about the system much as I had done. To my brother, who overlapped us both in Woodlands, the problem seemed to have been of no importance at all.

The fact that a house concert at the end of term might give an opportunity to fall in love with a small boy in a crinoline dress and blond wig singing Thomas Campion's "There is a garden in her face" merely shows that the form of the line separating good from evil can provide fascinating problems for the moral topologist.

On the whole we were more humanely treated than were the boys in practically every other public school in Britain. The fag system, by which new boys were assigned as messenger boys and the like to the prefects, or senior boys who had certain responsibilities, existed at Gresham's but was not abused.

The food was atrocious, but this was partly because we were nearing the end of a world war. I achieved a certain notoriety by secreting from the breakfast table a sample of scrambled "Cook's Farm Eggs" and demonstrating in the chemistry laboratory that since it gave no reaction for sulfhydryl it could not be derived from eggs. Microscopic examination suggested the debris from a cracker factory.

J. R. E. had been a student of my father's and I was placed in his house. I never liked him nor I think did he like me, but we achieved a modus vivendi, ultimately based on mutual respect. He taught me always to be careful about units in stating a quantitative result. I doubt he envisioned calories per square centimeter per centimeter per second, which may occur in limnology. Much later in his life, when I had published my first book and he had retired from teaching, he wrote a most generous letter about me to my father. He succeeded to the headmastership in 1919, after Howson's death; the change made very little difference to the school while I was there, though he was intellectually less adventurous than Howson. He had a peculiar habit of marking the important passages in any book that he was reading by drawing a straight line with a meter rule parallel to the margin of the page. If he liked the book every paragraph was so marked. We used to see him do this every evening while he was supervising the preparation or study period from seven to eight-twenty, but I have no idea what he read. The only person I remember standing up to him was John D. Hayward, later T. S. Eliot's friend, who was asked to remove his most cherished possession, a signed photograph of Karsavina, from his study wall, on the grounds that the great dancer's costume was inadequate. Hayward snapped back, "Madame Karsavina, Sir, is a very beautiful woman," but the photograph was no longer displayed.

Of the other houses and their house masters I knew very little. I think I once went to W. H. Auden's study in Farfield to read some of his very early poems, but this may have been after I had left the school, during a short visit to Holt in the early summer of 1922. Kenwyn I visited only to be coached in Plautus' *Captivi* for the entrance examination to Cambridge or to attend confirmation classes with Beaky Field. He was a sweet person and a good Latinist, but I think a rather inadequate house master.

I chiefly remember his attachment to J. E. Flecker's *The Golden Journey to Samarkand*. We were not allowed in the town so I never examined the Osh and do not know if any traces of the Greshams' Norfolk seat were still incorporated in its structure. There was obviously very little contact between the houses and all close friendships developed within the house.

Apart from the house masters and those who taught in the Osh, there was a population of a dozen or two assistant masters, some married and living in houses scattered round the outskirts of Holt, near the school, some unmarried and sharing a large house called "The Crossways," with inevitable Meredithian overtones. During the war their ranks were depleted and many were rather halt if not blind. The staff also underwent mysterious transformations, sometimes accompanied by vague whispers of adultery. Though nearer to their homes than if they had been at some small station in India, there was of course no club in Holt, and the social life of the wives of the married masters must have been restricted and often dismal. Some of the younger ones were very nice to us on the occasions when we met at their houses to read plays by Wilde, Shaw, or Galsworthy. I hope we were nice to them, though at the time this would not have entered the minds of most of us.

Among them I remember particularly an elegant young woman with reddish-gold hair, the left side of her face extremely beautiful, the right wholly disfigured by a birthmark which, with great courage and skill, she made to add to her charm. In my time I think she was the only master's wife with whom boys fell in love. I hope life rewarded her with the happiness she deserved.

Of the autochthonous inhabitants of the region we saw but little. J. R. E.'s gardener rather fancied himself as an ornithologist and claimed to have seen an American robin near Holt, which is just possible but very unlikely. The less sophisticated inhabitants could be observed only with difficulty. Once as I sat in a gallery at the back of the Big School or main assembly hall, which gallery contained part of the library, I heard two cleaning women conversing below me. Their speech was totally incomprehensible, though I was used to Cimbridgeshire as talked in the east end of my own home town or to the rich dark accent of Cumbria. Later I learned from W. W. Skeat's book on English dialects that the one spoken in Norfolk was among the more impenetrable variants of English speech.[2]

This linguistic peculiarity must have increased the isolation of the small colony of masters and their families, again just as if they had been shoring up the British Empire in Cawnpore or the Caprivi Strip. Like the colonial administrators, the schoolmasters could make fearful mistakes, but on the whole they were devoted men with a vocation; because of this they taught us well.

The school was intended to break away from the exclusively classical tradition of most boys' boarding schools at the beginning of the twentieth century. Greek was not taught and great emphasis was placed on modern languages, mathematics, science, and history.

The physics was a bit old-fashioned and one entirely missed mechanics if placed fairly high on entrance. This was partly made up for in my case by a mathematics master, I think called Sparling, taking a fancy to me and asking me over one evening a week to talk about relativity, as he was deep in one of Einstein's more general books. For

2. W. W. Skeat, *English Dialects from the Eighth Century to the Present Time*, Cambridge Manuals of Science and Literature (Cambridge: Cambridge University Press, 1911); see pp. 125–26. Though much older than my father, Skeat was a great friend. I believe my father acted as a trustee for the Skeat children. I remember Skeat as an ideal sweet-tempered scholar.

some obscure reason, I hope unconnected with relativity or with me, he was not reappointed the next year.

When I began physics with J. R. E. we started with optics, using his own "Lecture Notes on Light" as a textbook. The whole treatment was deductive and, to the English countryside empiricist that I had become, completely revolting. I realize now that I was studying something basically grounded in Euclid's Geometrical Optics and that what was good enough for Dante might, for a twelve-week term, have been good enough for me.[3] It would have helped greatly to have been told how a deductive theory was supposed to be related to physical reality. I probably did not realize until well into adult life that what looked to me to be a rickety scaffolding of unknown derivation represented one of the most daring flights of imagination yet taken by the human mind.

The chemistry was superb, owing largely to the senior chemistry master D. Ll. Hammick, who had a private research laboratory under the seats of the lecture theater in which the science was taught. Unfortunately, he left early in my career to teach at Winchester and I have no memories of his successor, "Gummy" Evans. Hammick later returned to Oxford and became an F. R. S. He did some work on dyes while at Gresham's but more importantly was concerned with van der Waals's forces and

3. Come quando dall'acqua o dallo specchio
    Salta lo raggio all' opposita parte,
    Salendo su per lo modo parecchio
  A quel che scende, e tanto si diparte
    Dal cader della pietra in igual tratta
    Si come mostra esperienza ed arte
                    [*Purgatorio* 15. 16–21]
Though Dante must have derived his knowledge of the law of reflection ultimately from Euclid, it is interesting that unlike J. R. E. he puts *esperienza* before *arte*, observation before theory.

surface phenomena. Being able so to excite a group of schoolboys about this subject in a single lecture that the feeling has lasted sixty years in one of them is quite an achievement.

Biology was not taught until my last year, so for my entrance scholarship examination for Cambridge I took mathematics, physics, and chemistry. My only recollection of the examination was having to illustrate the principles of mechanics by an analysis of the act of riding a bicycle. I like to think that in spite of having missed mechanics, I handed in a reasonably elegant answer. The question anyhow could hardly have been better. Had I studied biology formally I should have got a bigger scholarship instead of the minimal forty pounds per annum, which would have saved my parents some money, but in every other way I was much better off getting an unimpeded grounding in the physical sciences.

Mathematics included the simpler differential equations and some linear algebra. No one, of course, had ever heard of set theory.

Latin to me was mainly the sixth book of the Aeneid. I have worked extensively on crater lakes in Italy, knew Avernus well in its present state, and once when visiting Nemi found, near the site of the Sanctuary of Diana, a branch of holm oak with chlorotic golden leaves, obviously the Golden Bough. I have particularly studied the Lago di Monterosi, north of Rome, a crater lake whose medieval name *Ianula* suggests a little gateway to the infernal regions. However, the only quite specific Virgilian memory I have from school is of a boy, I think called Wilson minor, who, when told that he could do his translation into English verse, produced as an opening couplet:

Under the columns Tisiphone sits
Clipping the tickets and reading Tit-bits,

which my friend Professor Edmund Silk almost immediately identified as a concise if somewhat free translation of:

Porta adversa ingens, solidoque adamante columnae,
Vis ut nulla virum, non ipsi exscindere bello
Caelicolae valeant; stat ferrea turris ad auras,
Tisiphoneque sedens, palla succincta cruenta,
Vestibulum exsomnis servat noctesque diesque,

[*Aeneid*, 6.552–56]

where the Fury is indeed sitting at the gate of Tartarus. *Tit-bits* was a very low grade journal, but it might well have been read by a ticket inspector on the London Underground.[4]

The capacity to produce unforgettable nonsense seems to have been well developed in the school. Two examples by G. R. Hayward, the elder brother of J. D., come to mind:

I consign
A porcupine
To Proserpine

Goddess divine
If you wish to dine
You'll find its flesh is superfine.

Or this, entitled "A Libel Action."

The offense was intense.
The expense was immense.

We got adequate French. My teacher was called

---

4. Somewhat less concisely and less freely:

A huge door opposite and columns with solid adamant; strength that no man, nor the dwellers in heaven, can lay low in battle; an iron tower reaches up into space, and Tisiphone sitting, her blood-stained mantle girt about her, guards the entrance unsleeping night and day.

Trèves. He had a lively mind and perhaps a too sardonic sense of humor. He insisted that there were six spatial dimensions, three objective outside our minds and three subjective to which they could be compared. This seemed a remarkably Continental idea to me, as it doubtless was.

For those of us in science there was some special but not very good teaching in German, a language which otherwise was considered a low-grade commercial substitute for Latin. We did a great deal of history and had an excellent course in political theory under the odd title of "General English." I suppose that there were some quite conservative members of the Fishmongers' Company among the governors; if they knew that we studied Marx it did not worry them.

Nearly all the teachers were excellent, but I think, apart from Hammick, I got most from C. H. Tyler, whom we called Toc. He loved and taught English, was a fearsome but helpful critic, and once startled us greatly, since the school had a strong teetotal tradition, when he announced, "Drinking wine is a very delightful thing, but we must not do it too much." We did lots of Shakespeare, supplemented by a performance each summer of one of the comedies—*Twelfth Night*, *A Midsummer Night's Dream*, *The Taming of the Shrew*—in the beautiful outside theater, located in the school woods behind the playing fields. The female parts were of course played by boys and the stage was defined merely by bushes and screens of verdure, which we believed gave a very authentic atmosphere to the performance. Some of the more senior boys who were uninterested in cricket, which was otherwise compulsory, worked as the "Labour Party," which each summer put the theater into shape for the performance. This was as near to the productions as I got, but I loved the results.

These plays were I think my first real experience of

the theater, though early in my time at Holt, I imagine just after the war, I also saw a performance of *Cyrano de Bergerac* in London. The ladies in the play were all wearing lovely off-shoulder gowns, and for the first time I experienced a little of the delight that the uncovering of a woman's body may give to a man. I am grateful to Edmund Dulac who designed the dresses and to the ladies who wore them for showing me this in so beautiful a way. I do not think, however, that it was the reason for my mother giving my cousin and me the tickets for the performance.

One tiny point arose when we were studying *King Lear*; though I did not mention it at the time, it still intrigues me. When I first read the passage:

> The wren goes to't and the small gilded fly
> Does lecher in my sight.
> Let copulation thrive; for Gloucester's bastard son
> Was kinder to his father than my daughters
> Got 'tween the lawful sheets.

[4.6.114–18]

it put me anachronistically in mind of the thousands of *Drosophila* being bred in genetic experiments in Columbia University. Now, in later life, I have been taught to see more deeply. The larger things, sin and the serpent, that are gilded in the play, are clearly evil, and this is true of some other gilded beings in other plays. The gilded butterflies are foolish, but the little fly probably stands for gilded sin, flies having such a meaning in medieval symbolism. I therefore take it that the fly is Gloucester. The wren has a most elaborate and curious folklore, involving a ceremonial hunt; it is the king of the birds, but a king destined to die. I suspect therefore that the wren is Lear, and that with the fearful irony of Edmund's kindness, we have the whole play condensed into these few lines.[5] Both the wren and the fly are small, so that ultimately their tragedy may be overlooked as they bring new life into the world. Yet the new life may bring tragedy again.

Of the more recent poets, Tennyson seemed just right then, but much less so later. I am told his turn is coming round again and wonder at these cyclical changes in literary fashion and what elegant mathematical structure lies beneath them. Wordsworth, at least in the best sonnets, still is what he was in those days.

In prose we seem to have missed my great love, Sir Thomas Browne. Jane Austen we had had at home, but I do not think I sensed her extraordinary greatness until my wife showed it to me much later. Ruskin I read with avidity, always in the large paper edition, one or another volume of which I carried around for a time wherever I went in school.

One further aspect of language was of great importance

5. E. A. Armstrong, *The Folk Lore of Birds: an Enquiry into the Origin and Distribution of some Magico-Religious Traditions* (London: Collins, 1958). In this most important book, Armstrong gives a full account of the ceremonial hunting of the wren, which S. Dillon Ripley has shown to be the origin of the Audubon Christmas bird census (The World of Birds and Books, *Yale Library Gazette* 52, 1977, p. 5).

In one way the whole tragedy of King Lear can appear as a rationalist inversion of the Golden Bough, fertility leading to the death of the king rather than the magical reverse.

Marjorie Garber, who started me thinking along these lines and may perhaps now wonder what she has done, points out to me that "Edmund Crispin" (R. B. Montgomery), in *Obsequies at Oxford* (Philadelphia and New York: Lippincott, 1945), identified the little gilded fly as *Chrysotoxum bicinctum*, a hover-fly of the family Syrphidae. This is based on an analogy with an ancient Egyptian ring supposedly in the British Museum. Though a careful study of small iridescent British Diptera might throw light on the subject, this particular identification, though interesting, to me lacks visible means of support.

in my education. This was the use of Gregorian chant in singing the psalms in the school chapel. From this I got an experience of prose rhythm that is invaluable in writing. It also helped in a real discovery of music, in an almost chronological manner, going from the psalms to Tudor pieces played on the organ and from there to Bach and Mozart after I had left school.

I was, from my first term to my last, always third in whatever form I happened to be in, the list at the end of each term running Glanville, Gooch, Hutchinson. . . . Of the destinies of Glanville and Gooch and how they were accomplished I have been unable to learn anything.

When biology was introduced, along with quite sophisticated physical geography or geomorphology, in my last year, the laboratories were opened (figure 5) by my uncle, Sir Arthur Shipley, a rotund figure with one essential button not fully adjusted, who gave a lecture on practical work in education, beginning with a late medieval statute about the provision of naughty boys to be thrashed by intending schoolmasters as part of their instruction in the University of Cambridge.

Biology was taught by H. W. Partridge ("P"). He had studied with Crew in Edinburgh and first introduced me to the work of Darbishire, who played an important, though initially unappreciated, part in closing the rift between the biometricians and the Mendelians in the early part of the century.[6] "P" got Crew to come to give a school lecture on "Sex-reversal in Frogs." It was beautifully delivered and for about a week was the only subject of conversation at meals. It undoubtedly provided a symbolic but much needed release.

At school I had plenty of opportunity to continue the

6. A. D. Darbishire, *An Introduction to a Biology and Other Papers* (London: Cassella, 1917).

FIGURE 5   Sir Arthur Shipley, the short figure in the center, opening new laboratories at Gresham's School, with my father to his left, wearing a hat, and J. R. E. to his right, in academic dress but bareheaded, a little in front of the others.

study of insects, and in 1918 I published my first scientific note, in the *Entomologist's Record*, on the swimming ability of a tettigid grasshopper which I had observed in the pond in the school woods.[7] As the Gresham crest is a grasshopper, the observation was most appropriate. Several records of rare Hemiptera followed in the *Entomologist's Monthly Magazine*. One of these was based on an incident that represents, in a childish way, the sort of thing that so often must have happened in the old days of the British Empire.[8] We were expected to belong to an OTC unit which went for a week's training at a camp during the first week of the summer holidays. Lying on the ground, pretending to be military, on an open grassy hillside at Tidworth Pennings on Salisbury Plain, I saw an unfamiliar insect which I coaxed into the cavity in the butt of my rifle, supposed to contain the piece of cloth called a two-by-four, used for cleaning the barrel. When I got the specimen back to Cambridge I discovered it was the first British example of the fully winged form of a rather uncommon carnivorous hemipteran, *Stalia boops*; it is now in the insect collection at Cambridge.

The military expedition just mentioned was responsible for another interesting event. To reach Salisbury Plain we left Holt early in the morning and had several hours to wait in London before boarding our troop train. Some of us decided to visit the National Gallery, partly to see El Greco's *Agony in the Garden*, which had caught our attention in the *Times* and no doubt also in the *Illustrated London News*. The acquisition of this painting by the nation had set off a controversy, the conservatives damning

7. G. E. Hutchinson, A Swimming Grasshopper, *Entom. Rec. J. Var.* 30:138, 1918.

8. G. E. Hutchinson, *Nabis boops* Schioedte in Wiltshire etc., *Entom. Month. Mag.* 57:18, 1921.

and the avant-garde praising it, as if it were a work of Picasso, Matisse, or Cézanne. There was another picture by El Greco in the national collection, *The Expulsion of the Money Changers from the Temple*, but this, though depicting violent action, is an early, less extreme, more Venetian work and attracts little attention. The newly cleaned and, to many, strident *Agony* naturally came to represent El Greco to most of the educated British public.

Many years later Henry Andrews told me of a Parisian dealer who classified the works attributed to Domenicos Theotocopoulos as "Greco," "très Greco," and "trop Greco." It now seems that the National Gallery, seeking a work of the second category, had acquired one of the third, which is at best a studio piece. It has been banished to the study collection in the basement of the gallery. Yet it gave us boys, in small-sized khaki uniforms, on our way to Boer War–style and totally unrealistic military training at Tidworth Pennings, an extraordinary feeling of excitement. Later in life the problem raised by that excitement in the face of something that is not what it is supposed to be has worried me considerably. Though I have not seen *The Agony in the Garden* for many years, I think that again standing before it I would inevitably recapture the original thrill.

My adult concern with such matters arose from seeing and thinking about a painting that had been found in Delacroix's estate on his death and which entered the collection of the Fitzwilliam Museum in Cambridge in 1954, as a work by that painter. It had been exhibited in London and had received great praise in reviews of the exhibition in which it was included. It admittedly looked to be quite alien to the style of several small early paintings of Delacroix already in the museum's collection; to me it was far more satisfying than these genuine works. Later it was removed from the gallery where it had been shown

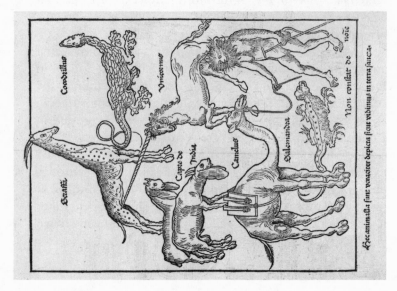

FIGURE 6 *Left*, animals supposedly observed on Bernard von Breydenbach's journey to the Holy Land. The anthropoid in the bottom right-hand corner is copied by Tyson, without the camel, for comparison with his specimen; *right*, Edward Tyson's juvenile chimpanzee, misnamed orang-outang.

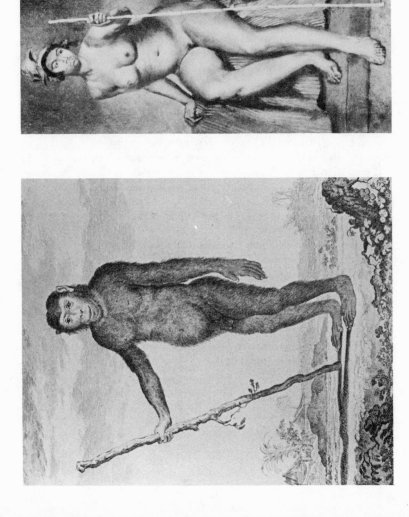

FIGURE 7 *Left*, Buffon's jokko; *right*, study of a mulatto woman possibly by J. R. Auguste (Fitzwilliam Museum, Cambridge). The animals in figure 6 and figure 7 left are shown with sticks to emphasize erect posture and bipedality; in figure 7 right the stick seems to have become a theatrical property conferring a degree of primitiveness on a fully human figure.

and placed in the study collection, as certainly not by the painter himself, though possibly a work of Jules-Robert Auguste, a rather second-rate artist whom Delacroix knew. These changes in attribution and critical esteem have of course no effect on the splendid erotic geometry of the figure.

Very recently, as this book was being written, I had occasion, in helping to prepare an exhibition of animals in art, to consult Tyson's famous work on the anatomy of the chimpanzee, which he called an orang-outang. In the figure of the young animal before it died, it is supporting itself on a walking stick and so achieving a fully upright stance (figure 6, right). The same convention is used a number of times[9] in the eighteenth and nineteenth centuries (figure 7, left). It now seems to me likely that the

9. G. E. Hutchinson, The Naturalist as an Art Critic, *Proc. Acad. Nat. Sci. Philadelphia* 115:99–111, 1963.

Examples of sticks being used to emphasize bipedality and the erect stance in anthropoid apes may be found in: E. Tyson, *Orang-Outang, sive Homo Sylvestris or the Anatomie of a Pygmie Compared with that of a Monkey, an Ape, and a Man* (London: T. Bennett and D. Brown, 1699) fig. 1; C. E. Hoppius, *Anthropomorpha* (Erlanger, 1760); G. L. Leclerc, Comte de Buffon, and L. J. M. Daubenton, *Histoire Naturelle, générale et particulière, avec la description du Cabinet du Roi* (Paris: Imprimerie Royale, 1766) vol. 14, pl. I opp. p. 82 (pp 72–83 are by Daubenton); A. Vosmaer, *Beschryving van de zo zeldzaame als zonderlinge Aap-Soort, genaamd Orang-Outang, van het Eiland Borneo* (Amsterdam: Pieter Meijer, 1778), unnumbered second plate; P. Gervais, *Histoire Naturelle des Mammifères: Première Partie* (Paris: L. Curmer, 1854), figure of *Simia satyrus* opposite p. 30.

All the earlier naturalists seem to have overemphasized the bipedality of the great apes (see Vernon Reynolds, *The Apes* [New York: Dutton, 1967], p. 53).

Tyson reproduces a figure from Gesner showing a long-tailed primate with a ruff of hair round the face and well-developed breasts, holding a walking stick, with a short cross bar at the top, in her left hand. This is said to be "from a *German* book, wrote about the *Holy Land*"

painter of the little picture in the Fitzwilliam Museum wanted to do a romantic savage, a primitive being who was certainly a woman of his own species, but one set, as far as a French studio allowed, in an exotic context. This is done by introducing the long cane, evoking a memory of earlier anthropoid iconography, possibly Buffon's Jokko, in a very widely known book. The model herself seems to show in her face that she is bored and unhappy about the whole proceeding. Perhaps we can recompense her by seeing in her our own evolutionary condition. The long thin bamboo cane still points upward (figure 7, right).

The school natural history society was very active and I belonged to all the sections. Slightly senior to me were G. H. Lockett, who became one of the main authorities on spiders in Britain, and Ian Hepburn, later a distinguished plant ecologist. Natural history was more than tolerated, though it did not have the prestige of cricket.

On certain Saturday afternoons in the summer term we went on quite long expeditions on bicycles to places of biological interest. I have particularly vivid memories of first seeing the glow on the underside of a roseate tern as it flew over me at Blakeney Point, a wonderful breeding ground for seabirds just northwest of Holt, and of hearing

---

and obviously Bernard von Breydenbach's *Peregrinatio in Terram Sanctam* (Mainz, 1486), in which a like organism with a similar stick is depicted, leading a camel with her right hand, on a plate also showing a unicorn and some more probable animals observed during the journey. H. W. Janson (*Apes and Ape Lore in the Middle Ages and Renaissance*, London, Warburg Institute, 1952), concludes that von Breydenbach's primate was a humanized *Papio hamadryas*. Having been adopted by Gesner it clearly underlay several later drawings including two of those of Hoppius. Though Tyson's chimpanzee was certainly from life, its stick is evidently a traditional late medieval attribute.

the booming of one of the very few bitterns then living in Britain, at Sutton Broad.

Most of my insect collecting, however, was done in the neighborhood of the school and it raised a social and ethical problem of considerable general interest and importance.

The only time when we were free to roam around by ourselves was on Sunday afternoons between lunch and evensong in chapel. Throughout Sunday we had to be dressed in our best clothes: striped trousers, black waistcoat and jacket, stiff turn-down collar with black tie, and a straw hat with the school arms on its ribbon. It was believed that this was the regular daily costume of both boys and masters until one day when J. R. E. had bent down to get some apparatus from a cupboard in the physics laboratory; a boy passing with a meter ruler in his hand thought he was another member of the class. Thereafter all boys wore grey flannel trousers, blue blazers, and ties of distinctive colors indicating their houses. This story has various parallels in literature and folklore and is probably not true. The everyday dress was much more convenient in the physics laboratory, though a Sunday suit was tiresome and uneconomical to wear when studying the biology of ponds and streams.

Thus attired, with pond-net, killing-bottle, and jars for live specimens, I set out each week for some favorite locality, which ordinarily was on the private estate of a more or less absentee landlord. There I sometimes encountered a gamekeeper intent on turning me out peremptorily; he might threaten the law. I had learned from my parents that simple trespass cannot lead to an arrest in England provided that the trespasser had tendered a shilling to pay for any supposed damage. We were in general careful about closing gates and the like, but we also always had the shilling handy, though I do not remember actually using it. The ethical question, however, remained unresolved. The landowner certainly believed that he had the right to the privacy of his woods and to the welfare of his pheasants until the time came, on October 1, to shoot them. Most of our instruction in social theory at school had a liberal or socialist cast, which implied that it was in the public interest to break up large estates by means of heavy inheritance taxes. The landowner with his pheasants and gamekeepers was, at least to a mild degree, an enemy of the people. Yet had he not inherited his property and set guards over it, the habitats for my insects would certainly have been endangered, as they may well be now. To me it was amply worthwhile to run the risk of being caught by a gamekeeper for the sake of finding the rare pond-skater *Gerris lateralis asper*, hitherto supposed, in the British Isles, to be almost confined to Scotland, adding a few specimens to my collection and publishing a note on the occurrence in the *Entomologist's Monthly Magazine*.[10] I was always careful in my collecting and the population of the insect did not suffer during the years that I had it under observation. The system, for all its theoretical unjustness, thus provided exactly what I wanted. The political and moral dilemma here exposed to view lies at the base of much contemporary debate on conservation and liberty in a welfare state. My conclusion has been that quite unexpected and seemingly irrational systems sometimes can provide the only satisfactory compromise solutions of such problems, a conclusion that goes far beyond the occurrence of *G. lateralis asper* in Norfolk. The role of the selfish country gentleman and his gamekeepers in providing, at an acceptable risk, the environment in which field biology has developed in

10. G. E. Hutchinson, Gerris asper Fab. in Norfolk, *Entom. Month. Mag.* 55:33, 1919.

Britain deserves some attention from the historians of science.

In my last year at Gresham's School I had become aware of the American work on *Drosophila* genetics: my copy of T. H. Morgan's *The Physical Basis of Heredity* is dated September 1920 and I am pretty sure that I understood the significance of what the book contained as well as any other of its original readers.[11] This interest was part of a general concern with variation. I made a study of the incidence of the various color morphs of *Philaenus spumarius*, the common spittlebug, and submitted it for the Holland Martin Natural History Prize, awarded annually at the school. Revisiting one of the localities forty years later I was able to show that there had been no statistically significant change in the proportions of the various morphs, though from place to place there are significant differences.[12]

My interests were also unconsciously becoming more ecological. I had begun to realise that organisms had chemical environments. I remember one Good Friday, probably 1919, when the day was free after chapel, using much willpower to practice titrations in the chemistry laboratory over and over until the results were quite concordant, before I allowed myself a visit to my favorite ponds and woods, feeling that I should have to be an adequate chemist if I were to become a good field zoologist.

While I was at Gresham's, my father had inherited the house in Culgaith next to the Richardson farm, long since sold, in which my Great Aunt Jane had lived a

11. T. H. Morgan, *The Physical Basis of Heredity* (Philadelphia and London: J. B. Lippincott, 1919).

12. G. E. Hutchinson, A Note on the Polymorphism of *Philaenus spumarius* (L.) (Homopt. Cercopidae) in Britain, *Entom. Month. Mag.* 99:175–78, 1963. I would take this opportunity to point out that the male and female signs are transposed in table 1 of this paper.

placid, bedridden existence. This meant at least one holiday in the north of England each year, and a whole new region to explore. The occurrence of a more northern fauna, with a special pond-skater, *Gerris costae*, on the pools of the mountains, fascinated me, and all the zoogeographic aspects of glaciation and the postglacial recolonization of Britain kept dancing around in my head. I was particularly excited about a group of small, very shallow lakes, Great Rundale, Little Rundale, and Seymour Tarns, lying on limestone but surrounded by thick peat, on Dufton Fell, a stretch of the Pennine Range about seven miles southeast of our house, but a thousand feet or so higher. These lakes proved to be teeming with a waterbug quite unknown to me, though quickly identified as *Arctocorisa carinata*, with sparse long hairs on its wing cases and a keel down the center of the exposed part of its thorax. The genus is generally northern and montane in both the New and Old Worlds and some years later I was delighted to find a new species in a flat mountain lake in Indian Tibet which I called *A. kesar* after the Tibetan hero.[13]

My mind full of problems of distribution and variation, in a great state of excitement, I left school to start a real scientific career at Cambridge.

13. G. E. Hutchinson, A Revision of the Corixidae of India and Adjacent Regions, *Trans. Conn. Acad. Arts Sci.* 33:339–476, 1940.

CHAPTER FOUR

EMMANUEL : BEING TAUGHT

ONE ALWAYS WENT UP TO CAMBRIDGE and, when there, went down to London. From all other parts of the world, unless one was an Oxford man, one went up to both places.

The university was an association of eighteen colleges, the oldest being Peterhouse, founded in 1286, the youngest Selwyn, founded in 1882. A group of noncollegiate students were, however, assigned to Fitzwilliam Hall, which has now turned into a college. Two major new colleges, Churchill for both sexes, primarily in science, and New Hall for women have now been added, along with several colleges for postgraduate students, notably Darwin. Many of the older colleges are becoming coeducational. The colleges in many ways are separate legal entities but contribute funds and people to make the university. This fundamental structure differs radically from that of Yale, Harvard, and a few other American universities which have adopted a college system, for in them the colleges are produced by internal differentiation, while in Oxford and Cambridge the university has been developed by a symbiosis between colleges. The two major theories as to how multicellular animals evolved differ in much the same way.

There were in 1921 two colleges for women, Girton,

some way out of town, and Newnham, occupying the site of a hamlet of that name very close to the rest of the university. Women did not get real degrees and technically they were not part of the university. Senior undergraduates, at least in the biological sciences, regarded the women students as equally as much a part of the place as themselves. There were, however, real disadvantages for the men as well as the women, for the fellows of Girton and Newnham, however learned, took very little part in teaching outside college supervision, though they were not completely excluded from university classrooms. The sexes were slightly segregated in class, the women sitting in the front rows. A very decorative girl whom I think was called Dibs made a point of being a minute or so late for lectures so that she could make an entrance. Such behavior, however, was unusual.

One very peculiar and almost unnoticed kind of sexual discrimination existed at the time in Cambridge, and perhaps still does so. All women who owned bicycles had bicycle baskets on their handlebars. This seemed a most practical way to transport gear for zoological field-work, so I attached a basket to my own machine. My father was very upset; since he professed feminist beliefs I am inclined to attribute his attitude to a horror of homosexuality, unconsciously expressed in this way. After more than half a century, modern speculation on the enormous importance of containers to our female ancestors when they started to become gatherers brought this memory back to me; it may well express a quite fundamental sexual dichotomy of deep interest.

In my time a large minority of students lived in lodgings in town, though they were members of colleges. They were still under strict disciplinary supervision, and their landladies were required to report if they were out after midnight. They ate dinner in hall. Breakfast and lunch were always eaten in one's own rooms. The wealthy could get a meal sent up from the college kitchen, but most of us cooked eggs and made toast and tea on a gas stove or on the fire in our living room. There were elderly women, discreet matrons from the working-class, eastern part of the town, called bedmakers, or "bedders," who cleaned our rooms. Mine was called Mrs. Misen, which I suspect was the Cimbridgeshire, Austrilian, or Shikespearean version, as you will, of Mason. They always wore black with elaborately decorated black hats which had some stylistic affinities with a horse-drawn hearse. At least in Pembroke they were only engaged after being interviewed by the master. Each bedmaker might have an help or 'elp.

Some colleges put their freshmen in lodgings, and second- and third-year students in college; a few adopted the contrary practice. It was usual, however, for scholars, or students who had won a scholarship by taking an open examination, to live in college for their entire career. Since, as a Swedish woman put it to my father, when shown the rooms where her son was to live, such lodgings might "not satisfy the pretensions hygienic," this was a considerable privilege. In return one took turns to read the Latin grace before dinner and the lessons at morning prayer and evensong daily in chapel. Saint Paul's Epistles are hard to read well on a cold dark morning before breakfast.

Whether in lodgings or in college, it was necessary to have lived in Cambridge for three terms, in each of three years, to qualify for a degree. If a night was missed, by an urgent need to leave Cambridge, it could be made up by residence in a short period at the end of the *full term* in which classes were given. Beyond residence nothing was expected of the individual so completing his term. Two of the three terms, the Michaelmas from October to De-

cember and the Lent from January to March, were of
eight weeks and two days, while the third, the May, from
April to the beginning of June, was of seven weeks and
two days.

During the Long Vacation a sort of semiofficial Long
Vacation term was instituted, largely for science students.
In the humanities one was supposed to read during the
summer, but this could be done anywhere.

My college was Emmanuel. This was primarily
because I had a cousin who was more anxious to follow
the family tradition of going to Christ's and my family did
not want me to compete against him in the entrance
scholarship examination. Emmanuel is architecturally
charming and has a distinguished intellectual tradition
going back to the greatest alumnus of the college, Thomas
Young, and before him to the Cambridge Platonists. It
was very Puritan at its foundation, in 1584, but I am told
that the long Latin grace beginning *Oculi omnium in te
sperant Domine*, which the scholars had to read in turn
before dinner, has a distinct Dominican flavor, in line
with the original use of the college site as a black friary.
This is probably accidental, for at the foundation of the
college the friary church was turned into the dining hall
and the college chapel oriented north and south to avoid
all hint of superstition. Later Wren built a lovely new
chapel pointing east. I like to think that during the Middle
Ages at least some of the brothers living on the site knew
of the existence of Albertus Magnus and his writings on
natural history.

As a Puritan foundation Emmanuel developed a
strong American connection, though John Harvard's
career there, as far as it is documented, was not particularly
distinguished. The founder of the college, Sir Walter
Mildmay, was a strong proponent of free speech, but

unlike some of his followers he believed that freedom should be tempered by politeness.[1]

When I entered the college it had been more successful in training than in retaining the really eminent among its former students. J. D. Bernal and Canon C. E. Raven, the historian of British natural history, bear witness to the truth of this. The science tutor, Alex Wood, was a physicist, but he was mainly interested in college affairs, in Thomas Young, on whom he wrote well, and in a strictly Christian non-Marxian socialism. He was an important figure in local politics and a most endearing person. He read both the ultraconservative *Morning Post*, until that daily disappeared, in order to keep his socialist faith intact and untarnished, and the *Daily Herald*, the Labour Party paper, to avoid holding his convictions uncritically. At one time I was closely associated with him in arranging a set of meetings at which religious people, scientists, and

1. S. E. Lehmberg, *Sir Walter Mildmay and Tudor Government* (Austin: University of Texas Press, 1964).

A decade before I came up, Emmanuel had been disrupted by serious intellectual and spiritual troubles. The college had retained, into the beginning of the twentieth century, through some historic continuity and by periodic religious revivals, much of the low church piety of its founder. In 1911 the master, William Chawner, delivered two lectures to the Religious Discussion Society of the College, which were published as: *Prove All Things* (Cambridge: Bowes, 1911) and *Truthfulness in Religion* (Cambridge: Bowes, 1911). The more conservative fellows of the college and many others throughout the university regarded these pamphlets as attacks on Christianity. Serious questions of the effect of the master's rash action on undergraduate enrollment were raised. The fellowship and the university at large were badly divided on the issue, some sympathizing with the master, others, both inside and outside the college, signing a document protesting his position. I think this episode probably did more damage to the college than would now seem credible. The wound was evidently still somewhat open when I came up, though I doubt more than one or two undergraduates knew of it.

philosophers were to debate the eternal issues of being human. Unfortunately at that time the Holy Ghost, with a characteristic sense of humor, was speaking mainly through the mouth of atheists and agnostics, and the professed Christians were greatly discomfitted.

My own views on these matters were then much as they are today, though held far less defensibly. I have of course oscillated somewhat in the intervening half century. The subjective intuition of the presence of God seems obvious to me, though of course saints and mystics have it to an incomparably greater degree than do most of us. Some people do not recognize it, others unhappily are taught to ignore it. I have no idea what the solution to the questions that the intuition raises, such as the problem of the existence of evil, may be. This ignorance, however, is not an exceptional defect. I am aware of the explanations in objective terms that can be given for the intuition. None of them explain why that which is supposed to underlie the experience translates subjectively into what is experienced. As far as I can see the problem raised by any such translation is, in principle, insoluble. We do, however, possess a capacity for metaphor which seems to absolve us from total silence in the face of that of which we cannot speak. Such metaphors may hint at formal relations without being available as bases for logical deduction. All theology to me consists of metaphors, some less totally inadequate than others.

I was brought up as a Christian in the Church of England. I realize that as a historical document the New Testament is not the sort of work that would confer Ph.D. degrees on Saint Paul and the Evangelists. Its value is in the fact that, in an ultimate and general way, it works. It is interesting that in the time of Christ it was the second fundamental Commandment, to love one's neighbor, that needed explication on the road to Jericho. Today it is more likely to be the first, to love God. To me this certainly includes Simone Weil's definition of science as the study of the beauty of the world. It can, however, only become fully realized if someone else is shown the beauty. Loving one's neighbor not only involves charity but also all the intelligence and foresight that can be brought to bear on our behavior. If our action has an evil, unloving consequence, it must be wrong, even if it appears to be recommended by a code of ethics. The whole history of the moral control of reproductive behavior is replete with examples. Religious institutions have done wonderful things in preserving the sacramental way of loving God, though there are of course also other ways, and many have promoted heroic charity. They are all, however, literally apt to lose their heads when confronted by sex, a part of living behavior which at least in man, and no doubt in some other vertebrates, is largely on the side of love. The result has been appalling human misery. Love, in its deepest sense, and intelligence seem to me the twin heights of our evolutionary progress, but they must be linked together to be effective. I know from my own life how difficult this can be.

The master of Emmanuel, Peter Giles, was an eminent philologist. He was short, wide, and genial, and as a boy I had once taken one of his daughters to a dance. He made little direct impression on the undergraduates that I knew.

A quite eminent mathematician with a beard, whom we called Beaver Bennett, was, I suspect, the only Fellow of the Royal Society in the college. He is said to have bicycled every afternoon to Saint Ives near Huntington, to the west of Cambridge, to have a glass of beer at a favorite pub. The college organist, E. W. Naylor, had made a critical study of the Fitzwilliam Virginal Book, one of the great collections of manuscript sixteenth-century music, placing all lovers of the period in his debt.

The other fellows, insofar as I remember them, appear as adequate scholars and devoted mentors of youth, no doubt each in his idiosyncratic way.

The student body was fantastically varied. There were athletic hearties who were apt to break into one's rooms at night if one had forgotten to sport the oak. I was also once woken up in rather different circumstances, by a man banging on my door who assured me that a lady who had mysteriously and, I could only suppose, illegally appeared in the college urgently needed to see me. When I collected my wits, dressed, and went into my living room, I saw an auburn-haired woman of about thirty-five in a black evening dress. Greatly puzzled I started to make conversation rather lamely, while she seemed upset that I did not remember her. It gradually dawned on me that the low voice was familiar. It belonged, in fact, to a friend who had great transvestite skill and had been playing a woman's part in an amateur theatrical production.

There was an exquisite with immense floppy silk bow ties and fringed gloves who had the enormous courage of his convictions in the face of the hearties who grossly mistreated him. I believe he is now rewarded by having become a most imaginative student of the protohistoric archaeology of the eastern Mediterranean and Black Sea region. There were some Puritan Protestants, in keeping with the tradition of the founder, but they did not, I think, include the contemporary representative of the Mildmay family, who had his way eased through college as Founder's Kin. There were ordinary run-of-the-mill students. There was one man with a pond-net or a handful of stoat skulls. There were quite a few musicians.

One other member of Gresham's School had come up in my year, W. A. H. Rushton, later to become a very eminent student of the physiology of vision. Since he had been in Farfield I had only known him slightly at Holt.

He spent a good deal of his time playing Bach on the viola or violin and trying to solve Fermat's last theorem. We became great friends. From him I learned unconsciously much of what I needed to know to enjoy music deeply. Cambridge offered extraordinary opportunities for this. I remember particularly what was supposed to be the first modern performance of Byrd's Great Service, the alleged first English performance of Handel's *Semele* as an opera, and performances of Bach's B Minor Mass and Mozart's Requiem in Ely Cathedral. The soprano passage *Te decet hymnus Deus in Sion* in the latter struck me as the most beautiful thing I had ever heard.

In the days when I was up, serious students "read for honours;" there were also students who took an ordinary or pass degree, which was said to involve working on alternate Wednesday afternoons in full term. "Reading for honours" involved taking one or more triposes or final examinations in a group of subjects. The word *tripos* originally referred to a bachelor of arts appointed, until late in the nineteenth century, to argue humorously or satirically with the candidates at an honors examination. This he did sitting on a three-legged stool. The humorous verses which he recited were published on one side of a sheet of paper, with a list of successful candidates on the other. The list thus became a tripos list. The mathematics examination thus became known as the Mathematical Tripos, and examinations in other subjects were so named later. The custom of providing some sort of comic relief at final examinations is very widespread in Europe and presumably has affinities with other customs, such as the Lord of Misrule, the Boy Bishop, and the Ass officiating at Mass on the Feast of Holy Innocents.

In most subjects there were two triposes, part I and part II. In the natural sciences, which in my day included physics, chemistry, mineralogy, geology, botany, zoology, physiology, and anatomy, passing in three subjects in part I at the end of three years was the minimum requirement for an honors degree. There were also examinations called Mays, taken at the end of the first and second years, which were preliminary and, if passed, merely gave one entry to the next stage without affecting one's final position. No other examinations or tests were required, so most of the year was mercifully free from such interruptions. Any combination of subjects was possible except mineralogy and anatomy, which were supposed to be so far apart that no one would ever want to combine them and so had their tripos examinations at the same time. I write this having met at lunch today (23 May 1977) a mineralogist and an anatomist who had been working together on the development of the human femur. The results of the triposes were given out as lists, now no longer backed with comic verse, of candidates receiving first-class, second-class, and third-class honors. A few people doing too badly to get a third might be given a pass degree for a very bad but not *completely* hopeless paper. This happened to one friend of mine who had hardly ever been involved in any zoological studies at Cambridge except a little systematic mammalogy. If one was a really serious science student one took part I after two years, with second-year Mays at the end of the first year, and then went on to part II in one science, or occasionally to some other subject such as anthropology. It was commonly believed to be impossible to get a first in part II without staying up for a fourth year. The examinations were always conducted by both internal and external examiners and the results were regarded as unquestionable.

The way of ordering the results of the triposes curbed excessive competitiveness. If a year should have produced a batch of geniuses and nothing else in some group taking part II, then everyone would get a first; if only nonentities were available everyone a third. This system was a deliberate innovation, introduced by degrees early in the present century; earlier, candidates who passed were listed in order of merit. In part II of the Mathematical Tripos, those achieving a first class are called wranglers. The top man was the senior wrangler, the next the second wrangler, and so on. The candidates placed in the second and third classes were senior and junior optimes. The senior wrangler in any year achieved national distinction; though he was obviously the best man at passing examinations in mathematics, it was widely recognized that he was by no means always the best mathematician. William Thomson, later Lord Kelvin, was second wrangler and the man who beat him is said generously to have remarked that he was about worthy to mend Thomson's pens.

The abolition of the system of ranking the successful candidates individually, though certainly wise, inevitably involved the disappearance of the picturesque custom of the wooden spoon. On degree day, candidates were led up to receive their degrees, each holding a finger of a college official called the praelector, who presented each candidate by name as he knelt, his hands raised in an attitude of prayer, before the vice-chancellor. The latter placed his hands outside those of the kneeling candidate and conferred the degree in Latin. When my uncle, Sir Arthur Shipley, was vice-chancellor, a candidate of the same surname was presented. Instead of "auctoritate mihi commissa admitto te ad gradum baccaulaurei in artibus in nomine Patris et Filii et Spiritus Sancti," he was left wondering if he had really received a degree on hearing the rhythmical intonation of "I didn't know there was another man in the university called Shipley, come to lunch with me tomorrow at Christ's Lodge at one-fifteen." In the days of the well-ordered Mathematical Tripos list, when the lowest junior optime had stood up, bowing to the Vice-chancellor after receiving his degree, his friends on either side of the gallery of the Senate House let down an enormous wooden spoon, playing it so that at first he had some difficulty in seizing the symbol of his lowly rank. I never saw this happen, but everyone talked about it when it was done for the last time, and I distinctly remember seeing the spoon, when I suppose I was six years old, with the recipient's college arms painted in the bowl, on display in a shop window on King's Parade. Since the last "Wooden Spoon" was much better at rowing than at mathematics, he had won his oar, and the oar blade was incorporated into the handle of the spoon. I hope it is still treasured somewhere. There was, I believe, considerable ingenuity exercised by candidates, who could not aspire to become wranglers, in doing just well enough to pass, but hopefully no better.

The only extra distinctions inside the first class in botany and zoology were the two Frank Smart prizes then given to the top male candidates in part II in these subjects. Women, not being fully legal students at the time and only receiving titular degrees, could not be considered for the prizes. I am pretty sure that Sydnie Manton should have got the Frank Smart prize that I received, though I have no certain way of knowing. When I got it, I immediately went off to Heffer's book shop and bought the recently published *Times Atlas*, which I still have, and constantly use in spite of its decrepit state, in my laboratory.

Such competitiveness as existed between individuals mainly arose after graduation, but in those days positions were freely available for the really gifted. Personal competition, with its envy, hatred, and malice, was very little in evidence. After one had achieved a first or even a second in part II one regarded oneself as a finished product, much like a Ph.D. today, but with the additional advantage that one usually immediately got something to do. The Ph.D. program was largely reserved for visiting Americans and in my day in zoology was hardly a success. The M.A. degree followed automatically three years after the B.A. on payment of a fee. Anyone who wanted anything better could publish enough significant work to get an Sc.D. By the time I had done this there was no point in spending fifty pounds for the degree fee, though the scarlet gown would have been fun.

When I came up to Cambridge the biological eminence of the university was very unevenly distributed among the various departments of what are now often called life sciences. This was indeed true of any group of subjects, as is inevitable in a university. To my certainly prejudiced mind it seems that in the thirty years from about 1890 to 1920, Cambridge was the intellectual capital of the world, much as Berkeley was for a few years during the past decades. Within the period of which I am thinking Russell and Whitehead were writing the *Principia Mathematica*, G. E. Moore the *Principia Ethica*, J. G. Frazer *The Golden Bough*, and Jane Harrison *Themis;* Marshall and later Keynes were establishing modern Western economics and W. W. Skeat providing the basis for modern studies of Middle English; J. J. Thomson and Ernest Rutherford were beginning to dissect the atom and F. Gowland Hopkins doing more than his share of founding biochemistry. Vague indications of all this were apparent throughout my boyhood. By the time I was an undergraduate some of the glory had departed, partly because of the First World War and partly because the rise of the other universities was spreading the most exceptional talent, which might be recognized wherever it appeared, more thinly than before. Nevertheless the tradition was still strong. The greatness, however, was not uniform through the university, being concentrated in Henry VIII's huge foundation of Trinity, in King's, and to some extent in Saint John's.

The role played by the college in undergraduate

education was undefined and very varied. In the natural sciences it was possible never to have any college instruction at all, and in fact, I never did. Most science students had a supervisor, who was either a college fellow or had been appointed from outside the college fellowship to do this work. My father once noticed a student leaving his laboratory before he had finished the exercise and asked him why. He replied he had to go to see his supervisor. My father then discovered that the supervisor was a postgraduate student in mineralogy, and he pointed out to the young man that it might be better to stay and learn from the university lecturer rather than from his student. I was, therefore, warned against all supervision. In contrast, in some arts subjects, one could get all the teaching needed in college, particularly in a large college. There was, I think, always an advantage in having really eminent men around, but I had plenty of ways of meeting them, so that their comparative rarity in Emmanuel did not worry me.

In zoology the great days at Cambridge had been the late nineteenth and very early twentieth centuries, with F. M. Balfour and later Adam Sedgwick, both very distinguished embryologists. By the time I came up no one of first-class distinction was apparent to the beginning undergraduate; and the group of students to which I belonged was rather impatient with their teachers. The professor, J. Stanley Gardiner, had been a leader in the exploration of the coral reefs of the Indian Ocean. His expeditions had done a great deal to make known not only the marine biology but also the terrestrial life of the Maldives, Laccadives, Seychelles, and Aldabra. In 1931, he published a very good book on coral reefs, still read with profit by modern workers.[2] He was, however, odd

2. J. Stanley Gardiner, *Coral Reefs and Atolls; Being a Course of Lectures Delivered at the Lowell Institute at Boston, February 1930* (London: Macmillan, 1931).

and uncertain and an adept at putting one at dis-ease. He could not inspire students, at least in my time, and I have heard him called a "very bad man." Yet when he came to recommend me to Yale he wrote a superb and most understanding letter. The three more senior lecturers were L. A. Borradaile, F. A. Potts, and J. T. Saunders. They cooperated in that excellent textbook *The Invertebrata.*[3] Borradaile was a classical morphologist, interested primarily in the body plan of arthropods. He was immensely learned and very generous to anyone who really wanted to learn from him, but by the time that I knew him he seemed somewhat disillusioned intellectually and was said to spend more time on his stamp collection than on zoology. What I learned from him and the files of notes that he lent me was invaluable on the two occasions when I was called in as intellectual midwife at the birth, or at least recognition, of the two major new groups of living Crustacea to become known in this century, the Mystacocarida of Pennak and Zinn and the Cephalocarida of Sanders.

Potts had done very nice work on parasitic Crustacea but again had lost interest to some extent. Saunders taught in the main invertebrate laboratory and gave a hydrobiology course to part II students. He did some of the best, indeed, for a time the only critical work on the ecological role of pH, but he drifted into academic administration and ended as the principal of Ibadan University.

Vertebrate zoology was taught by Hans Gadow, a marvelous relic of the nineteenth century who walked in from Shelford, four or five miles, to give his lectures. He began the course by writing in transliterated Greek the first verse of the first chapter of Saint John's Gospel. He

3. L. A. Borradaile, F. A. Potts, L. E. S. Eastham, and J. T. Saunders, *The Invertebrata* (Cambridge: Cambridge University Press, 1932).

had pronounced orthogenetic views of evolution, in which he clearly felt the Logos operating. As a good Lutheran he once nailed to the door of the zoology laboratory a set of theses on the homologies of ear ossicles, but I never heard that anyone took up the challenge.

F. Balfour Brown taught entomology. A committed Scot with a passion for water beetles, he gave a good straightforward course; not a powerful intellect, he is dear to me for having introduced me to the Hebrides.

Friends, particularly Bill Thorpe, with more inside experience of the department than I could have had, tell me that much of the tension that we felt was a psychological aftermath of the First World War. This fits in with my general impression that the university had lost some of the early-twentieth-century glory before I came up. British intellectual society, however excellent it was in other ways, clearly had no completely effective mechanism for absorbing the shock, as well as the loss of life, resulting from the war.

More exciting people appeared when one got to part II. H. Munro Fox, with a reputation as the best-dressed man in British zoology, had done beautiful work on the lunar periodicity of breeding in sea urchins and later on chlorocruorin and other animal pigments. He was also much interested in the passage of animals through the Suez Canal. He soon left Cambridge for a chair in Birmingham and later in London.

James Gray was certainly the most generally distinguished man in the department at the time. He was tall, long-legged, and was believed, I think falsely, to have served in 1914–18 in a camel corps. He was working on ciliary movement and gave a very good, skeptical course on experimental cytology. He tended to disbelieve in any structure not visible in intact living cells, all the rest of cytology being a study of artifacts. At this time such a

restriction greatly reduced the range of the subject. Fortunately, S. T. P. Strangeways in the pathology department
was demonstrating mitotic figures in living fibroblast cells;
his films, in fact, may still be used in teaching. This demonstration was very helpful if one took Gray a little bit more
seriously than he intended. It is also interesting to recall
his worry that the histones of the sperm head were among
the simplest of proteins, quite unfit to be the stuff Mendelian factors are made of. Gray succeeded Gardiner as
professor in 1937 and at once began turning the department
into one of the outstanding centers of experimental
zoology in the world.

The last teacher in zoology that I would mention was
to me the most important, G. P. Bidder. He was an eccentric of considerable wealth, largely nocturnal, with beard,
moustaches, and cloak in truly operatic fashion. He gave
a course on sponges, or rather on some aspects of the
calcareous sponges and any related ideas that came into
his head. This disorganized piece of teaching was the most
important that I ever had. The ideas that he implanted
kept on working and growing and still do so when trans-
planted. His great theme was the ecological significance
of size as such and the complete difference of living in
aquatic worlds in which Brownian movement, viscosity, or
inertia was the dominant force. This concept is not only
extremely interesting in itself but provides a model of ways
of classifying the spaces in which organisms live, by using
properties that are not intuitively obvious.

As well as the teaching faculty, and Bidder was, I
fancy, only an honorary member, there was an important
zoological museum. The curator, C. Forster Cooper, the
discoverer of *Baluchitherium*, the largest known terrestrial
mammal, fossil or living, was a charming and able man who
had fallen out with Gardiner and was obviously glad to be
called to the directorship of the Natural History Museum

in South Kensington. The other full-time member of the museum staff was Hugh Scott, a meticulous taxonomist working mainly with beetles, who had been involved with the *Fauna Hawaiensis* and with the terrestrial insects of the Seychelles. He was obviously, but very quietly, in love with the diversity of the insect world and was a good, sweet-tempered man. His entomological learning was extraordinary and he was also an amateur archaeologist and collector of old English ironwork. We became great friends though he must have been thirty years older than I was. I spent many happy hours helping arrange Hemiptera in the museum. Quite recently his successor, Dr. John Smart, showed me a couple of death's-head hawkmoths, *Acherontia atropos*, preserved in a cabinet drawer, with a long and characteristic label by Hugh Scott that identified them as having appeared in George III's bedroom late in his career.

The physiology department was housed in a building much newer than the rather ramshackle zoological laboratory. The professor, J. N. Langley, who had done important work on the autonomic nervous system, seemed, like Gardiner, to have mislayed his earlier eminence. I was in fact advised not to take his elementary lectures, so I signed up only for the lab, which was half histology and half nerve and muscle frog physiology. Instead of Langley's course I therefore took Adrian's Nervous System in my first term, followed by Hartridge on special senses, Marshall on the physiology of reproduction, and a few other unimportant offerings of which I have almost no recollection.

Langley had one engaging quality. If there was good ice on a large field, flooded for the purpose, south of Coe Fen, he put up a notice indicating that the laboratory was closed on account of the inclemency of the weather. This was a treat that only happened in some years.

Adrian's course was a tremendously exciting experience. The audience was immense, including every intended medical student in the university, and had to be held in the examination schools after the first meeting, no other available room being big enough. Adrian always strode in rapidly, a few minutes late, removing an immense pair of fur gloves. He never wore an overcoat even at the height of winter. He gave a lively summary of all the contemporary research on neurons and on the mammalian spinal cord and brain, beautifully arranged and clearly delivered. He always used yellow chalk, the dust from which supplied admirably macabre makeup for an impersonation of a Jacksonian epileptic going into a fit. At the beginning of the course he recommended Bertrand Russell's *Analysis of Mind* as the best treatment of the mind-body problem, adding that it had nothing to do with psychoanalysis. His death, while this book was being written, removes the last person whose formal lectures I attended at Cambridge.

The other exciting member of the department at the time was Barcroft, but I do not think he took any part in the part I teaching, and though I had met him on and off during my school days, I did not really get to know him until much later.

Marshall, who taught what I imagine was the first course in the physiology of reproduction given in Britain, was a member of the agriculture faculty and not of the department of physiology. He spoke with a pronounced lisp, "In the pretheding leththure we dithcuthed the phenomenon of ptheudopregnanthy in the bitth." To those of us in zoology the excitement of Marshall's course lay in its comparative aspects. The bitch might become pseudopregnant but some other female mammals could not. Women ovulated spontaneously, but rabbits at least needed to be stroked. In Adrian's treatment of the nervous system the hominid or medical emphasis was not only practical but intellectually reasonable, since we after all did have the best one available. Marshall, coming from a non-medical area, provided something comparative that was specially informative, though of course the subject itself had an immense inherent fascination. Of the other teachers of physiology I will only mention, as an antiquarian footnote, Dr. Shore, who had worked with Maray in Paris, and whom we all believed had kept the horse happy with continual wisps of hay as the gauge was being slid into its heart in the first *in vivo* measurement of intracardial pressure. An Englishman should, of course, have understood horses.

Though when I took part I, biochemistry was still part of physiology, the development of a separate department was fast going ahead. This department *in statu nascendi* was the great intellectual center of Cambridge biology in the 1920s. As was the tradition in most science departments, the lectures of the introductory course were given by the professor, in this case F. Gowland Hopkins. He was able to impart an aura of authority even when, as once happened, he tried twice to put the structural formula of tryptophan on the board and then gave up with the remark, "I knew what this was when I elucidated it in 1911."

Hopkins, in 1906 and 1907, had done experiments that indicated the essential nature of some minor constituents of an unknown kind in the diet of growing rats. The results had been mentioned in lectures at Guy's Hospital, but illness had prevented their publication. Funk's classic paper on the substance, now vitamin B_1 or thiamin, which was derived from the outer coat of rice seeds and prevented the polyneuritis produced in pigeons by a diet of polished rice, appeared in 1911. Immediately after, in 1912, Hopkins published the results of a new set of experiments confirming those done five or six years earlier. In Cambridge we always regarded Hopkins, I think justifiably, as a codiscoverer of vitamins with Funk, as indeed did the Nobel committee.[4] Some time between 1912 and 1914 I had been taken with my cousin Bill Stewart to see Dr. H. H. Dale (later Sir Henry Dale, president of the Royal Society), at the Wellcome Physiological Research Laboratory and was there shown

4. F. Gowland Hopkins, Feeding Experiments Illustrating the Importance of Accessory Factors in Normal Dieteries, *J. Physiol.* 44:425–60, 1912. Hopkins writes (p. 425) that the "particular experiments ... were undertaken to put upon a more quantitative basis results which I obtained as far back as 1906–1907." He adds a note that publication was delayed on account of illness but that the "results of experiments made at this time were summarized in lectures delivered at Guy's Hospital in June 1909." It would be interesting to know if any notes exist, taken by someone in his audience. Hopkins also writes in the same paper (p. 449): "Convinced of the importance of accurate diet factors by my own earlier observations, I ventured, in an address delivered in November 1906, to make the following remarks. 'But further, no animal can live upon a mixture of pure protein, fat, and carbohydrate and even when the necessary inorganic material is carefully supplied the animal still cannot flourish.'" This remark is quoted from F. G. Hopkins, The Analyst and the Medical Man, *The Analyst* 31:385–97, 1906, which was based on an otherwise dull lecture given to the Society of Public Analysts on 7 November 1906.

Funk's results were published, from the Lister Institute, as: C. Funk, On the Chemical Nature of the Substance which Cures Polyneuritis in Birds Induced by a Diet of Polished Rice, *J. Physiol.* 43:395–400, 1911.

Funk and Hopkins were certainly on friendly terms, as is clear in S. L. Becker, Butter Makes them Grow, *Conn. Agri. Exp. Stat. Bull.* 767, 1977, which gives an excellent account of the early work on nutrition by T. B. Osborn and L. B. Mendel.

It had, of course, been obvious for a couple of centuries that the lack of something in diets could cause scurvy, and comparable knowledge had existed in Japan with regard to beri-beri. Perhaps one should not try to say vitamins were discovered at a specific time and by certain workers, but rather that a knowledge of such substances started growing rather rapidly in the second decade of the twentieth century.

FIGURE 8   Sir Frederick Gowland Hopkins O. M., F.R.S. (Barnet Woolf, originally published in *Brighter Biochemistry* 1925; by permission of the Department of Biochemistry, Cambridge University).

experiments on the cure of polyneuritis in pigeons by extracts of the material removed in polishing rice. These were presumably an early confirmation of Funk's work. When I was a student Hopkins was best known for his recent discovery of glutathione (figure 8).

The elementary laboratory in biochemistry was run by Sydney Cole, who was I think really more interested in golf than in science. He and his wife would in fact have fitted, as minor characters, into a silent film of a Wodehouse novel. During the First World War he was worried by what seemed to him the calamitous scarcity of blood charcoal, then widely used as a sorbent in certain analytical and preparative processes. He wrote a letter to *Nature* about it.[5] This gave rise, I suspect in the fertile mind of M. A. Rushton, to:

> Sydney Cole
> Would sell his soul
> For half a bowl
> Of blood charcoal,

which in the perfection of its sound rhyme, set against varying eye rhymes, has a certain fascination for the student of minor verse. Cole liked to improve on the work of his predecessors, so that most of the standard procedures appeared, in the laboratory manual that he wrote for the course, as Cole's modification of——'s method. All the apparatus was set up ahead of time by the lab boy, as such attendants were usually called, so that even the most thick-headed aspirant to an MB degree could complete his experiment. As a result the course was entirely useless as an exercise in biochemical technique. It had for me, however, an extraordinary fringe benefit, namely that one of

5. S. W. Cole, The Preparation of "Blood Charcoal," *Nature* 99:226, 1917.

the demonstrators was Joseph Needham; so having let the apparatus complete Cole's modification of this, that, or the other, I heard about the work being done in chemical embryology and many other things.

J. B. S. Haldane, then reader in biochemistry, was active in his experiments on salt metabolism, which on occasion involved running round and round Market Hill, a crowded flat area in the middle of the town, with a bottle to be filled for analysis in the subterranean men's room, which on another occasion had been used as Tutankhamun's tomb in a mock excavation. Haldane was also beginning his classical work on the mathematical theory of natural selection, which is a major foundation stone of modern population genetics and evolutionary theory.

Though I do not think he ever worked on enzyme kinetics himself, he gave an excellent course on enzymes which later turned into a book. Once when I was the only student to appear on time for a lecture in this course, he began in a deadpan manner, "When John Hunter found himself having to address an audience of this size, he was accustomed to bring a skeleton into the room so that he could address them as gentlemen."

I soon got to know another biochemist, Robin Hill, as he was an Emmanuel man who sought me out as soon as I had settled in. Although officially working on photosynthesis, which of course ultimately led to the Hill effect,[6] he was devoting a great deal of time to calculations for a fish-eye lens that would photograph the entire sky and so, by the use of two cameras synchronized electrically, permit the triangulation of lightning flashes. Hill was also much

6. R. Hill, Oxygen Evolved by Isolated Chloroplasts, *Nature* 139:881–82, 1937. Hill found that chloroplasts suspended in a medium containing ferric oxalate produced oxygen when illuminated, the ferric iron becoming reduced to ferrous. This was the beginning of modern work on the nature of the reactions occurring in photosynthesis.

interested in the preparation of permanent mineral pigments for artists painting in oils. Mention of Needham, Haldane, and Hill indicates the extraordinary range of intellectual interests that centered around biochemistry, but it does not exhaust the list of significant people. R. A. Peters soon left for Oxford and I did not really meet him until much later in life. Marjorie Stevenson was founding the comparative biochemistry of bacterial metabolism.

In spite of the great strength of the nascent department of biochemistry, it is possible that the most important biochemical work done in Cambridge about the time that I was up was the discovery of cytochrome by David Keilin, an entomologist interested in parasitic fly larvae, working in the Molteno Institute of Parasitology. He was a friend of E. J. Bles, and I came to know him quite well. I think he put me on to Delcourt's work on what we should now call introgression, to which I shall return on a later page. He took such evolutionary studies rather lightly and evidently felt that Delcourt, in attempting to raise *Drosophila* axenically on a medium of known composition, had gone on to do something really serious and worthwhile.

One further name, that of the Honorable Huia Onslow, must be added to the list of Cambridge biochemists who influenced me. He perforce worked as an amateur at home, but though I never met him personally, he has haunted my life in a most curious and beneficial way. The son of Lord Onslow, governor general of New Zealand, and named for an extraordinary extinct bird, the Huia or *Heteralocha acutirostris* (Gould), Onslow had had a serious diving accident as a student and did all his scientific work in a more or less recumbent position. This included a very important analysis of apparent blending inheritance of yellow ground color in the currant moth, *Abraxas grossulariata*. By applying a quantitative colorimetric method, he showed the inheritance to be Mendelian. He did very early biochemical work on the genetics of melanin production in rabbits and also an extraordinary study of irridescent physical colors in insects.[7] When I was admitted as a fellow of the Royal Entomological Society in 1923 Onslow's death had just been announced at the meeting, as his name was coming up for election. Many years later, Sir James Gray (in a letter of 7 February 1966), wrote "D[oncaster] introduced me to Onslow who was the first biochemist I ever met— a terribly nice and modest man with superb courage." Onslow's work on *A. grossulariata* has been most useful to me when in recent years I have tried to give an interpretation of the fantastic range of variation in this moth. Onslow's wife, Muriel Wheldale, was also a distinguished and very early biochemical geneticist, working on anthocyanins. The Cambridge interest in such matters, insofar as it was not an obvious next step, probably derived something from Bateson.

Genetics was taught twice a week, at five o'clock in the Michaelmas term, by R. C. Punnett, who had been Bateson's close collaborator and aid. He was a mild man with an overdominant wife who had been a major tennis player. Her opponents must have been terrified. Punnett had fine collections of Chinese porcelain and Japanese

7. H. Onslow, A Contribution to Our Knowledge of the Chemistry of Coat-Colour in Animals and Dominant and Recessive Whiteness, *Proc. Roy. Soc. Lond.* 89 (B): 36–58, 1915. In this paper Sydney Cole is thanked for "his invaluable suggestions and help." Helping Onslow in this work may have been Cole's greatest contribution to science. H. Onslow, The Inheritance of Wing Colour in Lepidoptera. I. *Abraxas grossulariata* var. *lutea* (Cockerell), *J. Genetics* 8:209–58, 1919; H. Onslow, On a Periodic Structure in Many Insect Scales and the Cause of their Iridescent Colours, *Phil. Trans. Roy. Soc.* 211 (B): 1–74, 1923.

prints in a delightful house backed by an experimental garden, and he devoted himself largely to the genetics of sweet peas. The Punnetts gave Sunday lunches with superb wine to an incongruous set of students, half biological intellectuals, half athletes, all I think men. Only about half a dozen students took Punnett's course. It was given in the large zoology lecture theater. All but one of us sat in the front row. My friend Ivor Montagu, on the very rare occasions that he attended, sat in the back row. Punnett was a strong believer in the presence and absence theory of dominant and recessive factors (genes were not yet respectable in Cambridge); I used to argue, in retrospect interminably, that his defense was circular. He seemed to enjoy these arguments. The chromosome theory was still widely debated. Bateson was usually skeptical, though I know he accepted it for about a fortnight shortly before his death. Punnett tended to be more receptive to the idea. One evening the high point of the course arrived unexpectedly; Punnett came in demurely and then announced that he had just finished all the calculations of linkage of the various characters he had studied in the sweet pea and that indeed there were as many linkage groups as haploid chromosomes. The chromosome theory had worked for a plant as well as an animal and therefore might be reasonably expected to be of general validity.

I have said nothing about chemistry, which I also took for part I. I remember little of the teaching except Fenton writing with both hands at once on the board, and an organic lab run by the dourest Scot I have ever had the misfortune to encounter. His scientific interests were supposed to be the synthesis of more and more poisonous gases for military purposes. He may have been misjudged; as a fellow of King's perhaps he was an interesting and humane man. Anyhow,

It's certain that some of the ultimate things
Are hidden from even the fellows of King's.[8]

I have little to say of botany either except to express, as so many others have done, gratitude, admiration, and affection for H. Gilbert Carter. He was a great knower of plants; his labels in the Botanic Gardens told one what the Latin, Greek, Hebrew, and Persian poets had called them. On field trips, he insisted that the leaf of each species studied, unless he knew it was poisonous, had to be tasted to supply a new set of taxonomic characters. He ran a private seminar on Virgil and was the only person whom I knew who really understood my passion for the folklore of *Mandragora*, which he grew.

In general, the relations between botany and zoology were much less satisfactory than between zoology and biochemistry. Tansley was mainly concerned with psychoanalysis when I was taking botany for part I of the tripos and without H. Gilbert Carter I should have learned nothing from the course.

8. I suspect this appeared in *Punch* during the First World War when some fellows of King's were much criticized for their pacifism.

CHAPTER FIVE

EMMANUEL: LEARNING

A VERY IMPORTANT PART OF CAMBRIDGE LIFE consisted of the various college and university societies. Many of these were of fundamental importance in our education. The Cambridge University Science Club elected only senior students of outstanding ability, mostly in their third year. The meetings began with the junior member being called on to "eat the whale," which was a sardine on toast. The club then turned to the more serious business of a paper and discussion, usually at a very high level. It was commonly believed that one in three of the members of the club would ultimately become fellows of the Royal Society. I never addressed the club, being ill the day of my paper in my last year. Fortunately, it had been written out and was read for me. It dealt with the problem of local variation and subspecies.

Every college had at least one science society of some sort. In Emmanuel, in those days, there were two, the Science Club, which elected only scholars, and the Science Society for the rest. Robin Hill called on me to introduce me to the Science Club. He was incredibly shy and unaudible, but I did gather we were going to a meeting at which he was speaking. When the room was hushed he presented a brilliant but unresolved discussion of the problem of why art appears to involve an element of illusion. At a later meeting he gave, under the title "Cumulonimbus," a beautiful account of his work with the fish-eye lens on thunderstorms. Though I must have attended some dozen meetings, these are the only ones that I can remember.

The Cambridge Natural History Society was an old-established body consisting of both professionals and amateurs, some associated with the university and others with the town. It was a very healthy organization in my day. The most enthusiastic and prominent amateur member from the town was William Farren. D. G. Lillie had in fact drawn a caricature (figure 9) of the society showing three members, my uncle Arthur Shipley, as president, C. G. Lamb, an academic engineer who was deeply interested in flies, particularly from the islands of the Southern Hemisphere, and Farren, then secretary, sitting round a table looking at a small stuffed bird, the first smoking a cigar and the second a self-rolled cigarette. Farren had a taxidermist's shop on Regent's Street in Cambridge, later converted into Farren the Furrier, that I had known from childhood, flattening my nose against the window whenever I could persuade nurse or mother to pass that way. Farren had been an industrious collector of moths and later a very successful bird photographer, and during my undergraduate days he became a great friend. I had got interested in the geographical variation of the ermine or stoat, and he pointed out to me that in East Anglia, where these animals rarely became even partially white in the winter, if extensively whitened individuals were found, they were always females. Later Hamilton reported the same phenomenon in the North American *Mustela*

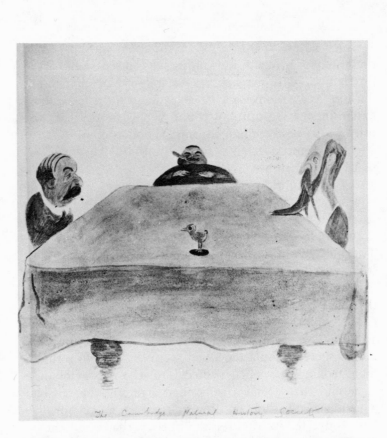

The Cambridge Natural History Society

FIGURE 9   D. G. Lillie, *The Cambridge Natural History Society*. The broad figure presiding is A. E. Shipley; on his right is C. G. Lamb, and on his left William Farren (by courtesy of the director of the Zoological Museum of Cambridge University and of Dr. John Smart).

frenata, in parts of New York State where whitening is inconstant.[1] Quite recently Pamela Parker and I reviewed the matter, concluding that this may be an example of a rather obscure and little-known phenomenon that also occurs in a few insects. In any region of sufficient environmental instability, if there is a gene adapting the species to one set of environmental conditions and its allele adapting the species to the opposite condition, it would be advantageous for the gene to be dominant in one sex and recessive in the other, so that as long as both alleles are present, even if one is quite rare, both will be phenotypically visible in the population. When the environment changes selection can get to work immediately without waiting for rare homozygous recessives to turn up. When Farren showed me the stoat skins in his shop over half a century ago, I had no idea that I was looking at the result of a recondite and minor but quite interesting evolutionary principle.

Farren was president of the society during part of the time I was up and Michael Perkins senior secretary, a post to which I later was elected.

The most celebrated, or perhaps notorious, meeting of the society was one at which Paul Kammerer gave an account of experiments that he believed demonstrated the inheritance of acquired characters. This meeting is a central episode of Arthur Koestler's *The Case of the Midwife Toad*; all my recollections of it were communicated to him.[2]

Kammerer's case was generally supposed to rest most

1. W. J. Hamilton, The Weasels of New York, *Amer. Midl. Natural.* 14:289–344, 1933; G. E. Hutchinson and P. J. Parker, Sexual Dimorphism in the Winter Whitening of the Stoat *Mustela erminea*. To appear in Mammal Notes in *J. Zool.*

2. A. Koestler, *The Case of the Midwife Toad* (New York: Random House, 1971).

critically on his claim that if the midwife toad, *Alytes obstetricans*, is reared under very hot humid conditions, it can be converted into an animal breeding in water like other amphibians rather than one breeding on land. This change involves the development of a ridged horny nuptial pad on the front leg of the male, which though present in most other frogs and toads, is lacking in ordinary fully terrestrial *A. obstetricans*. Kammerer found minute indications of the pad in the second aquatic generation and a clear small pad in the third, which became more pronounced in the fourth and fifth generations reared in water. Much of Kammerer's material disappeared in the First World War, but a fifth generation specimen, showing the pad, survived and was photographed in Vienna for J. H. Quastel in 1922. The pad is clearly ridged. The same specimen was shown in Cambridge at a conversazione of the Natural History Society. I had some organizational duties and did not see it when it was taken out of its jar and placed under a binocular microscope. J. B. S. Haldane did examine it and remarked on the ridges, though just before his death he could not remember the incident. Later what was supposed to be the same specimen was found by Dr. G. K. Noble, a very distinguished student of the Amphibia, to have no true nuptial pad but rather a dark mark apparently produced by the injection of India ink.[3] Six weeks after this discovery Kammerer committed suicide.

I believe with Koestler and so far as I know with everyone who met Kammerer in Cambridge, including his hosts Mr. and Mrs. E. J. Bles, that Kammerer was indeed honest. I do not, however, think that the experiments indicate what he thought they did. Three reviewers

3. G. K. Noble, Kammerer's Alytes, *Nature* (London) 118:209–10, 1926.

of Koestler's book, an anonymous writer in the *Times Literary Supplement*, Stephen Gould in *Science*, and Lorraine Larison in the *American Scientist* all point out, after studying Kammerer's original accounts, that the investigation began with a very large number of specimens, among which there was considerable mortality.[4] There is also evidence of rudimentary pads occurring very rarely in nature. The original stocks may well have been genetically heterogenous, and very intense natural selection could have taken place in Kammerer's vivaria, leading to conventional Darwinian selection for the pad in the course of the four or five generations of the experiments. That this possibility was never mentioned, as far as I can remember, in all the discussion of Kammerer's work that I heard and took part in at the time, is a measure of the extraordinary change in attitude to evolutionary processes that has taken place during the past half century.

The doctoring of a specimen of *Alytes*, which Koestler suggests must have taken place shortly before Noble's visit to Vienna, was believed by Dr. Hans Przibram, director of the Biologische Versuchsanstalt where Kammerer worked, to have been done by someone, possibly with anti-Semitic motives, who wanted to discredit Kammerer. Koestler gives some reason to suspect that the suicide was as much due to the failure of a love affair as to the apparent destruction of a scientific reputation.

4. Individual Paradigms and Population Paradigms (review of Koestler), *Times Literary Supplement* 70:1309–10, 1971. This very interesting review points out that the rise of Mendelian genetics displaced the Galtonian attitude to inheritance in populations treated statistically by an emphasis on individual genomes. The population paradigm did not return strongly till the 1930s.

S. Gould, Zealous Advocates (review of Koestler), *Science* 176:623–25, 1972. This gives in greatest detail the neodarwinian interpretation of Kammerer's work on *Alytes*.

L. L. Larison (review of Koestler), *Amer. Scient.* 60:644, 1972.

One set of experiments done by Kammerer, not indicating inheritance of acquired characters, but in other ways most spectacular, appears to be acceptable.[5] In the karst country of parts of Yugoslavia, the immense and partly water-filled caverns are the home of a blind white aquatic salamander known as *Proteus anguineus* or *olm* in the local vernacular. Kammerer, when he first met Bles, announced, "You are the man who bred *Xenopus*," and Bles replied, "You are the man who bred *Proteus*," though it had been bred in captivity before Kammerer's work. Bles was particularly impressed by Kammerer's work on this animal as he had built a cellar under his laboratory in which he hoped to establish a colony, but he had had no success. It was well known that when *Proteus* was kept in an aquarium in daylight, it became very darkly pigmented; Gadow many years before had had such animals in Cambridge. Kammerer found that when the olm was reared in red light the pigment did not form. This permitted the red light to penetrate more deeply and to stimulate the development of the small larval eyes. The specimen, brought to Cambridge to demonstrate this, was very convincing, even to Hans Gadow, who did not like Kammerer's other experiments. If this work is really repeatable it should lend itself to a most interesting study of action spectra in development regulated by light.

Curiously, these seemingly acceptable results may have contributed a little to Kammerer's psychological downfall. Michael Perkins, who had played a considerable part in arranging Kammerer's visit, including being

5. P. Kammerer, Experimente über Fortpflanzung, Farbe, Augen und Körperreduktion bei Proteus angineus Lam, *Arch. Entwicklungsmech.* 33:349–461, 1912; P. Kammerer, Nachweis normaler Funktion beim herangewachsenen Lichtauge der Proteus, *Arch. ges. Physiol.* 51:1090–94, 1913.

one of three members, with J. H. Quastel and L. Harrison Matthews, to go to Harwich to welcome him to British soil, was an extremely versatile and very charming man. He had an enormous knowledge of zoology but was rather uncritical both of himself and others. Little of his early zoological work has stood the test of time. I was, however, very fond of him. He visited me in Cambridge some years later, when he had turned to medicine; he was then particularly interested in the folklore of pigs. He died of septicemia at the age of thirty-three to the great sorrow of his friends. Perkins knew a journalist working for the *Daily Express* who learnt about Kammerer and decided he would attempt a journalistic coup. Kammerer wanted no such publicity and the council of the society was unanimously opposed to any journalist being admitted to the meeting. This may have been a mistake as the apparent secrecy perhaps stimulated his curiosity. He managed to interview some people who had attended the meeting and heard of the experiments on *Proteus*. Eyes grown in sightless animals, which to too many readers must have suggested hope for the human blind, naturally got into the headlines of the *Daily Express* and from there even reached the *New York Times*. This produced a very unfavorable reaction in America, so that when Kammerer arrived for a lecture tour late in 1923 he found an atmosphere very different from that which he had met in Cambridge. This forced him into the position of popularizing a travesty of his own work as his only means of livelihood. The late Ross G. Harrison told me how distasteful he had found the propaganda used by Kammerer's agent and how skeptical of his work the American biological world had become.[6]

6. Among his few American supporters was Irving Fisher, the economist, who was always most anxious that unconventional views

One further incident, not discussed by Koestler, should I think be added, as I believe it exposes Kammerer's extraordinary naiveté, while it is consistent with his honesty. Another Viennese had claimed that by simply cutting off the heads of the large water beetles of the genus *Dytiscus*, immobilized by being placed in cardboard tubes, the heads could be exchanged, as in a folktale, and would establish full morphological relations with their new bodies.[7] Kammerer demonstrated the technique, though he was leaving Cambridge next day. He must have believed it would work, because otherwise he would have been exposing himself to full condemnation for an obvious fraud. Of course the animals all died, though actually nobody blamed Kammerer. I believe we were just puzzled and did not know what to think.

Apart from having sponsored Kammerer's appearance in England, the Cambridge Natural History Society kept a list of the fauna of Cambridgeshire and of that associated with pigeons in the space in the roof of King's College Chapel, on which A. D. Hobson and L. Harrison Matthews had published a paper.[8] We had a number of general meetings each year and at one of them I gave a talk on folklore and natural history. As the result of hearing a lecture by Grafton Eliot Smith in 1921,[9] I had become

---

have a hearing. He put up money for an honorarium for a lecture at Yale, which money was transmitted to the secretary of the university by Harrison (Yale University Archives, Ross Granville Harrison Papers, ser. no. 1, box 9, folder 662).

7. W. Finkler, Kopftransplantationen an Insekten, *Arch. mikroscop. Anat.* 99:104–33, 1923.

8. A. D. Hobson and L. H. Matthews, The Animal Ecology of King's College Chapel, Cambridge—A Preliminary Note, *Ann. Mag. Nat. Hist.* (ser. 9) 11:240–45, 1923.

9. This public lecture on the study of man, with which I had been enormously impressed, was given by Grafton Eliot Smith at the meeting of the British Association in Liverpool (see *Rep. Brit. Ass. Adv. Sci.* [Liverpool], 1923, p. xvii). It was unfortunately not published.

fascinated by his ideas on cultural diffusion and read with
avidity his works and those of his supporters, W. J. Perry,
Rendel Harris, and Wilfred Jackson. Though there can
be no doubt that at times these authors wrote pretentious
nonsense on a grand scale, they also drew attention to a
number of very interesting facts that seem to fall into
patterns. As is usual in such cases, a good many small but
rather delightful babies have now gone out with the bath-
water. My lecture dealt with some of them. Much of its
valid part, greatly developed as the result of personal
experience in Italy and Indian Tibet, turned into a piece
called "The Enchanted Voyage," which was given nearly
thirty years later as an evening lecture to an oceanographic
convocation held at Woods Hole, Massachusetts, in June
1954, at the dedication of the Laboratory of Oceanography,
established by the Office of Naval Research.[10] On this
occasion, though a majority of the audience appeared
fascinated, a vocal minority, believing sex and religion
to be immiscible with seawater, complained to the management. The theme then developed was that the sea contained a set of objects, often of great magical power, that
represented, psychologically and in folklore, things that
are found on land. One of the most potent of these was
the cowry shell; on land its equivalent was a mandrake
root. My earlier lecture was mainly about the belief of
Rendel Harris that the mandrake was the origin of the
cult of Aphrodite.[11] The plant was not only narcotic but
when worn, rather than taken internally, was believed to
promote fertility. A well-known and complicated set of
beliefs arose about these plants of the genus *Mandragora*.

10. G. E. Hutchinson, The Enchanted Voyage: a Study of the
Effect of the Ocean on Some Aspects of Human Culture, *J. Mar. Res.*
14:276–83, 1955.
11. J. Rendel Harris, *The Ascent of Olympus* (Manchester:
Manchester University Press; London and New York: Longmans
Green, 1917).

They could be black or white, female or male, and even bearded or beardless, apparently irrespective of sex. They were supposed to be very dangerous to collect and were pulled from the ground by the light of the moon, the plant being tied to a dog's tail; the dog died, the mandrake screamed, and the man in charge became possessed of a potent charm. Even with a supply of surplus dogs, mandrakes were not easy to come by as they originated from the semen of a corpse, usually of an innocent man, hung on a gibbet. Britain, anyhow, was outside their phytogeographic range, but the white bryony, *Bryonia dioica*, and the black bryony, *Tamis communis*, though unrelated plants, made acceptable substitutes. In Lincolnshire, so Geoffrey Grigson tells us, they were called Womandrake and Mandrake respectively.[12] Long after my lecture I saw a gnarled root of white bryony with arm-like branches in the Cambridge Folk Museum, the label indicating that in the Fenland, north of Cambridge, men used to vie with each other in finding roots most like the bodies of women. One put in a pigsty would insure that the sow had an extra piglet in the next litter. Done into French, mandragora became mandegloire, and this almost translates into English as hand-of-glory, the dried hand of a criminal who had been hanged. A candle was placed in the more or less clasped hand. This gave burglars, who used it instead of a flashlight, the convenient property of invisibility.

Rendel Harris was evidently an extraordinary man. He was born in 1852, the son of a house painter in Plymouth. He was educated at Plymouth Grammar School, came up to Cambridge, read mathematics, and was third wrangler, the third man in part II of the mathematical tripos. He became a fellow of Clare and taught mathe-

12. Geoffrey Grigson, *The Englishman's Flora* (London: Phoenix House, 1955).

matics but in 1882 was called to Johns Hopkins University to teach New Testament Greek. His protests against animal experimentation in the medical school there led to his resignation, but after teaching at Haverford he returned to Cambridge as lecturer in paleography. Later he directed the Friends' Settlement for Social and Religious Studies at Woodbrooke near Birmingham and was curator of manuscripts in the John Rylands Library at Manchester. Much of his earlier scholarly work is classically respectable and of great importance, but later his rather monomaniacal imagination took over uncritically for much of the time. He believed the timbers of the Mayflower formed the roof of a barn at Jordans in Buckinghamshire, close to the Friends' Cemetery in which William Penn is buried.[13] He concluded that Christ's question to Judas Iscariot in the Garden of Gethsemane, "Friend wherefore art thou come?" was a literal quotation from the rim of the cup of the Last Supper, cups with this inscription being known from the first century but adding, "Be merry." If this is true, and it carries a curious conviction, it is the ultimate in sardonic humor in any literature.[14] Before he died in 1941, Rendel Harris had found an increasing number of twins among the Twelve Apostles. His extreme diffusionism led him to derive the name of the Susquehanna River from Usquebagh, or Irish whiskey, and to identifying place names in the English Lake District with others along the Nile. In his *Ascent of Olympus*, in which he develops the equivalence of Aphrodite and the mandrake, he says little about her origin from sea foam, though

13. J. Rendel Harris, *The Finding of the "Mayflower"* (London and New York: Longmans Green, 1920).

14. J. Rendel Harris, Glass Chalices of the First Century, *Bull. John Rylands Library* 11:286–95, 1927. The credit for the observation that the remark in the Garden of Gethsemane was a quotation from a convivial inscription is given by Harris to Deissmann.

Hesiod's story that this foam collected around the genitalia of Uranos, castrated by his son Cronos, has obviously some affinity, in a marine translation, with the corpse on the gibbet and in a macabre way suggests Simone Weil's belief that Aphrodite was the Holy Ghost.

It is interesting to note that Rendel Harris equates the black and white mandrakes with a black and a white Aphrodite, the former being ancestral to the black madonnas venerated in some Mediterranean countries. He mentions also a bearded Aphrodite, dressed as a woman, but does not note Saint Wilgefortis or Uncumber, a bearded woman on a crucifix, as a possible Christian derivative.[15] She is usually supposed to be based on a misunderstanding of an early crucifixion, such as the Volto Santo at Lucca, in which the figure of Christ is robed, but she might well be older. It is hard not to conclude that some dark and partly forgotten mythology and ritual unite the hand-of-glory and the gibbet with the fruitfulness of the mandrake and the life-giving cowry shell.

Another Cambridge institution of great importance

15. "Her story has the unenviable distinction of being one of the most obviously false and preposterous of the pseudopious romances by which simple Christians have been deceived or regaled" (H. Thurston and D. Attwater, *Butler's Lives of the Saints*, vol. 4 [New York: P. J. Kenedy, 1957], p. 20).

The daughter of a pagan king of Portugal, she became a Christian along with her six or eight brothers and sisters, all produced at a single birth and all destined for martyrdom. She took a vow of virginity; her father attempted to marry her to the king of Sicily, whereupon she grew a beard and mustache. This so enraged her father that he had her crucified. As Saint Uncumber she was venerated, notably in Old Saint Paul's, London, by women who wished to be relieved of their husbands. As Saint Liberata her occasional appearances today are probably a small price to pay for the benefits of the contemporary advancement of women, on which the future of our species is likely to depend.

to me, the Biological Tea Club, was founded—or as we put it at the time convened—by Joseph Omer-Cooper. He was older than the rest of us, having been in military service and then for a few years in business and teaching in Bournemouth, before coming up to Cambridge. He was already a skillful amateur zoologist who had shared an interest in isopod Crustacea with his brother, Wilfred, killed in the First World War. He was one of the few authorities in Britain on the taxonomy of the Oniscoidea, the sowbugs or wood lice. Later he made an important expedition to Ethiopia with Hugh Scott. He was also extremely interested in white magic and alchemy, in which he believed in a subjective religious way. He had a rather narrow face with a pointed nose and habitually wore a monocle, often with a cloth cap. He was a noncollegiate student associated with Fitzwilliam Hall, but I do not think this meant very much to him. He had a remarkable talent for friendship and gathered round him a highly diverse group of young men and women.

The Tea Club was founded at a meeting convened by Omer-Cooper on Wednesday, 25 October 1922, in Thurston's Café on Regent's Street, at 4:30 P.M. The original membership consisted of the convener; Joyce Barrington, later to become Mrs. Omer-Cooper and the leading authority on the dytiscid beetles of Africa; E. J. Pearce, now Father Justin, C. R., of Mirfield, of whom I have already written; Gregory Bateson, now a most distinguished anthropologist, the Honorable Ivor G. S. Montagu, then a mammalogist but later much involved in left-wing politics and films, and myself. Later in the year, half a dozen more members were elected. I was appointed recorder. Through an initially unfortunate accident, the minute book was placed among my undergraduate lecture notebooks, where I discovered it about four years ago when I gave these notebooks to the Yale archives. I learned from my friend Paul Richards, then of Bangor, that the Tea Club still existed and he kindly offered to return the minutes to the appropriate officer of the club. Before I sent it to him, I made a Xerox copy of the contents, which has been invaluable to me. Since it is not possible to find where some members are now living, if they are still alive, in quoting directly I have taken care to limit myself to material of which I am reasonably certainly the author.

At most meetings members brought guests; some of these guests were prospective members, but among those who were not I find in the first year of activity: Joseph Needham; W. A. H. Rushton; Miss Edith R. Saunders who almost rediscovered Mendelian inheritance; Professor F. Zschokke, the Swiss limnologist and parasitologist; Dr. Hugh Scott, whom I have mentioned; Sydnie Manton; Dr. Paul Kammerer; Mr. and Mrs. E. J. Bles; a Carter who was either G. S. or H. G. Carter, and J. H. Quastel. Few zoologists will not recognize some names in this list. Among the now less well known visitors the name of Pauline Shoubersky occurs frequently. She was an aristocratic Russian émigrée, niece of Boris Anrep who did the mosaics on the floor of the Blake Room in the Tate Gallery, and of Gleb Anrep, who had been a student of Pavlov. She smiled at every man who looked at her and my parents greatly disapproved of her. As a small girl she had watched, from a gallery or the top of a staircase, an imperial ball in St. Petersburg. She had, I believe, got out of Russia with her family into Scandinavia helped by a British naval detachment aiding the White Russians; I think the young British officers gave her quite a lively time. Her parents lived in France, at first in penury, but she attended Saint Felix, one of the best boarding schools for girls, at Southwold on the east coast of England. She

told me that there was at the school a pool or small artificial lake with an island. The girls swam in the lake, but
no one might visit the island who had not been there
before. I assume that Pauline had satisfied this condition,
which has something of the sound of the Russell paradox,
in some earlier existence.

I remember going on a long walk with her, I think
about five miles, to Comberton, west of Cambridge, to
run the turf maze that then lay by the village school,
though not on its original site; it has since been wantonly
destroyed in the name of progress.

Pauline was a friend of Virginia Woolf's sister-in-law,
Karin Stephen, whose psychoanalytical and philosophical
writings interested me at the time; the tea party arranged
for me to meet her fell through on account of someone
being ill, and I never got any nearer to Bloomsbury, except
as a purely geographical entity. Pauline may have wanted
to seduce me; she was fun while our friendship lasted and
I am very glad that I knew her.

The minutes of the first meeting of the Biological Tea
Club run:

> The first part of the meeting was occupied in the
> consumption of tea. Mr. Montagu partook or pro-
> fessed to partake of nothing but dry bread and soda
> water. After tea a discussion took place in the course
> of which the aims and rules of the society were formu-
> lated to the general satisfaction of all present. Mr.
> Hutchinson was then requested to attempt putting
> them into practice and therefore proceeded to dis-
> course upon "Species."

At a purely social meeting on 20 February 1923, there
is a record that Mr. Convener had "privately reprimanded
the members for their paucity of conversation."

A list of subjects discussed at tea was appended to show that "Mr. Convener's activities have not been entirely in vain." The list included:

The Right Way of Eating Cream Buns
The Group Soul of Rats
The Sacrificial Proclivities of Dogs
The identity $59 = \dfrac{4^! + \sqrt{4}}{0.4}$

The question about cream buns arose from a belief held by some of us that at teatime nothing to be eaten should require a fork. The group soul of rats was due to Pauline Shoubersky alleging that an experiment had shown that if a number of rats are trained to a certain task and some are killed, the performance of the remainder improves. What the sacrificial proclivities of dogs may have been I have no idea. The alleged identity, which should of course be 65 not 59, is said to have "somewhat unduly excited the wrath of Mr. Convener against one of the visitors." The visitors are recorded as Miss B. K. Burn, Miss M. W. Black, and Miss P. Shoubersky. Unless one of these ladies had actually proposed that the fraction on the right came out to 59, I cannot imagine what was involved.

As a result of the conversation about the eating of cream buns, there is a note on 23 February that "Mr. Convener having omitted to obtain cream buns filled seven times more full than they are wont to be filled for Mr. Hutchinson and Mr. Bateson to eat publicly without knife, fork, spoon or any other apparatus, promised to do so at the next meeting." During tea two weeks later "Mr. Hutchinson and Mr. Bateson each devoured a well-filled bun, without other appliances than those supplied by Nature. The time relations of this phenomenon are given below

Mr. Bateson 85 seconds
Mr. Hutchinson 100 seconds.

The Convener preferred to avail himself of the apparatus provided by the tea rooms in devouring his bun of office." This meeting was attended by Professor Zschokke among other guests; I wondered at the time what he made of it all.

Each speaker was supposed to turn in an abstract of his discourse, to be incorporated in the minutes, but some failed to do so. There are also gaps in the record in the May term and part of the Michaelmas term of 1924.

The general impression of the talks is one of considerable conservatism. Five of the twenty-five contributions dealt with the natural history of insects. Extensive reviews on plankton, parasitic copepods, and arboreal animals also fall into the same general category of natural history. Behavior is treated explicitly in papers on instinct and on conditioned reflexes, and some psychoanalytic material appears in "Senescence, rejuvenescence and thoughts on death." The grand strategy of phylogenesis is considered in three or four papers.

The contemporary arguments about the inheritance of acquired characters are considered in Gregory Bateson's first contribution, in which he admits that none of the evidence in favor of the phenomenon is convincing but that all other theories of evolution fail and that in a complete explanation of the process Lamarckian phenomena as well as mutation must be involved. In his later paper on molluscan radulae he favored the idea that speciation involves geographical isolation. No abstract was submitted for his third contribution; I believe that one point that he made concerned the commonness of asymmetrical piebald patterns in domestic animals, and their very great rarity in nature.

Child's work on polarity and axial gradients appears both in Omer-Cooper on organization and in my own contribution on senescence. *Drosophila* genetics is discussed only in the abstract of Joyce Barrington's talk on sex determination. Ann Bishop, the most senior person academically when she gave her talk, obviously knew all about the contemporary American work on ciliate conjugation.

My own contribution on species, which opened the series, was summarized thus:

Ideal Definition

When two forms, meeting on equal terms, in any part of their range, do not habitually interbreed, they are to be considered as species.

In Practice

(1) The forms studied do not so meet on equal terms in many cases.

(2) It is often difficult to decide whether any two forms do or do not habitually interbreed. In such cases species must be diagnosed by inference, from their differences in life history, etc., such differences being comparable to those separating known species, i.e. those to which the ideal definition can be applied.

I am pretty sure my ideas were based primarily on Delcourt's work on the water bugs of the genus *Notonecta* in Europe.[16] The commonest species, *Notonecta g. glauca*, has brownish-yellow wing cases with darker spots along the outer margin. A slightly larger and not quite as common species, *N. o. obliqua*, has dark slate-gray wing cases with

16. A. Delcourt, Recherches sur la variabilité du genre *Notonecta*, *Bull. Biol. Fr. Belg.* 43:373–460, 1909. See also, R. Poisson, Les espèces françaises du genre *Notonecta* et leurs principales formes affines paléarctiques, *Ann. Soc. entom. Fr.* 102:317–58, 1933.

two short basal longitudinal yellow stripes. In northern Europe, the two species are quite distinct in nature though they can interbreed in captivity. In southern Europe, *N. g. glauca* is replaced by *N. g. rufescens*, which has a reddish-brown tint, while *N. o. obliqua* is represented by *N. o. meridionalis*, in which the outer basal yellow stripe is reduced but the central dark area of the wing case has a slightly mottled appearance. Where these occur together there is often much interbreeding, with specimens of an intermediate *N. × hybrida* occurring in nature. There is, however, some evidence that mating is more likely between like than between unlike individuals. Delcourt called the phenomenon that he observed regional amixia; we should probably speak of the nonoccurrence or occurrence of local introgression.

By my definition, following Delcourt's practice, *glauca* and *obliqua* are certainly valid species. I knew them well in England, where they are ordinarily quite separate, though occasional *glauca* with dark spots in the center of the wing cases may indicate a little introgression.

The genus is an interesting one, and its members are very well known to anyone who has studied pond life in Europe or North America. In the eighteenth century they were called boatflies, and in nineteenth-century England water boatmen. This term has been preempted for the water bugs of the family Corixidae in North America, where the Notonectidae are back swimmers. Due to Hungerford's extensive taxonomic studies of both groups the American usage is becoming international. The Notonectidae, as their name implies, swim on their backs, waiting at the surface for prey such as mosquito larvae, with the oar-like back legs spread out ready for a sudden stroke. Moffet (or Mouffett), who wrote the first major work on insects in England, though admittedly mainly by compiling unpublished notes of Edward Wooton,

Konrad von Gessner, and Thomas Penny, writes of these insects in the English version of his book: "We call some insects of the water *Notonecta*, which do not swim upon their bellies as the rest do, but upon their back, from whence it is probable that men learned the art of swimming upon their backs also. Some of these have eyes, shoulders and bodies all black, some are green, some are fiery-coloured, and some pitch-coloured. For you shall seldom see two of them of the same colour; nature hath so variously sported herself in adorning them."[17] The variability is rather exaggerated and perhaps suggests Gessner having experienced a southern population.

The fiery-colored species is presumably *N. maculata*, which unlike the other species in Europe lays its eggs on solid surfaces rather than in slits in pond weed. It is therefore common in Italy in the pools of fountains kept free of vegetation, where it doubtless plays a useful role in eating mosquito larvae. This species, not too well known until recently, was figured in the mysterious Cocharelli Treatise on the Vices done about 1380.[18] One illustration

17. The original Latin is in Tho. Moufeti, *Insectorum sive Minimorum Animalium Theatrum* (London: T. Coales, 1634), pp. 320–21. The translation here quoted is from the English version appended as book 2 of Topsell's Historie of Four-footed Beasts and Serpents, p. 1126.

18. Four fragments of this manuscript are in the British Library (formerly British Museum; Add. Ms. 27695, Add. Ms. 28841, Egerton 3127, Egerton 3781); there is also a single leaf of no zoological interest in the Cleveland Museum of Art. The zoology is described in A. C. Crombie, Cybo d'Hyères: A Fourteenth Century Zoological Artist, *Endeavour* 11:183–87, 1952, and more briefly in G. E. Hutchinson, Aposematic Insects and the Master of the Brussels Initials, *Amer. Scient.* 62:161–71, 1974. The attribution to the possibly nonexistent Cybo is no longer accepted. Though apparently of Genoese origin, there are strong hints of Oriental and Sicilian (Frederick II) influences in some of the illustrations. The whole work requires much more study than it has received. It is clearly a critical document to the historian of medieval natural history.

shows the wing cases open, disclosing the yellow color of the front part of the body; in the other European species this area is black, so there is no doubt about the identity of the insect. No other really good figure of *N. maculata* or, for that matter, of any other species, appears for about five hundred years.

While we speculated interminably on phylogeny, little theoretical biology of a modern kind existed. Bidder's work came closest to what we now seek in biological theory, but although I treasured it, some years passed before I was able to put it to use. I had been familiar with D'Arcy Thompson's great work "On Growth and Form" since it came out, as the author was a friend of my father's and we had the book at home.[19] Though as a piece of literature I knew it to be important, I did not see how to reconcile what I learned from it with what I knew of genetics and evolutionary biology, till much later in my career.

My own interest in theoretical constructs in biology seems to have arisen in a peculiar way. The issue of vitalism versus mechanism was hotly debated, mainly in terms of the German and American work on experimental embryology. I read avidly and more or less at random in the area without finding anything theoretically satisfying, though Harrison's work on the development of symmetries in amphibian embryos fascinated me, as it still does. The mechanistic argument that ultimate reduction to physics would always be possible seemed to postulate a false simplicity, the vitalist argument that some special property was needed to produce living beings seemed to imply a naive belief that if one could not think of a mechanistic explanation no such explanation exists. Two areas seemed to suggest profitable ways of proceeding.

19. D'A. W. Thompson, *On Growth and Form* (Cambridge: Cambridge University Press, 1917).

One way was what is now called parapsychology, which we then called psychical research. Cambridge had earlier been an important center for this sort of study; the celebrated and partly inexplicable Italian medium Eusapia Palladino had stayed there and was known to have cheated when playing croquet, though perhaps not when in full trance. When I was up, there was little activity of this sort in the university, though the subject was not dead. I had bought William McDougall's *Body and Mind* at the end of 1923 and found it both a systematic and a stimulating account of the psychophysical problem as understood at the time:[20] at a very basic level I suspect we now have mainly gained in humility rather than understanding, in spite of vast progress in our knowledge of the physiology of the brain.

My grandmother died in August 1924 and as she wished to be buried at Culgaith my parents asked me to go north to discuss the matter with the local parson while they were concerned with the necessary arrangements in Cambridge. When I got to Culgaith I learned that the tenants in our house had been sitting in the drawing room on the evening that my grandmother had her fatal stroke, and that two of them believed they had seen an elderly lady in black walk through the room and disappear. As far as I could learn, this had been discussed well before they knew of my grandmother's death. There is, of course, an enormous literature on such phantasms, which are hard to treat statistically, though they are very convincing when one is brought up against a case personally.

McDougall's book had prepared me to take psychical phenomena seriously, and the incident at Culgaith reinforced such an attitude. The few experiments that I have

20. W. McDougall, *Body and Mind, A History and Defense of Animism*, 5th ed. (London: Methuen, 1920).

tried have all been negative, as is true for most people, but I have been near enough to further spontaneous cases later in life to take the problem very seriously. Research in the area seems to me now like traveling a thorny and overgrown path full of well-disguised pitfalls, which might just possibly lead to something of enormous importance. In middle life I was greatly interested in the subject, but became discouraged when curious suggestions of fraud were discovered in S. G. Soal's experiments, which I had accepted in print as highly convincing.[21] I still feel that the history of the experiments strongly suggests real parapsychological phenomena, but the evidence that they provide is clearly not what it was supposed to be. Following the position adopted by Wald and by Braithwaite, that the tenacity with which an idea should be entertained depends both on its probability and on its importance should it be adequately confirmed, I still believe that a very great effort should be made in parapsychological research. The empirical evidence suggests that the probability of something being valid, though perhaps not as great as it once was, is not vanishingly small and the importance, should the validity be confirmed, is scientifically enormous. The investigator in this area must be very tough and immune to limitless disappointment. I have often wondered if there is not some inevitable, if unformulated, uncertainty

21. S. G. Soal, Fresh Light on Card-Guessing—Some New Effects, *Proc. Soc. Psych. Res.* 46:152–98, 1940; S. G. Soal and K. M. Goldney, Experiments in Precognitive Telepathy, *Proc. Soc. Psych. Res.* 47:21–150, 1943; S. G. Soal and F. Bakeman, with an introductory note by G. E. Hutchinson, *Modern Experiments in Telepathy* (New Haven: Yale University Press, 1954). G. E. Hutchinson, Precognition on Ash Wednesday, *Amer. Scient.* 36:291–94, 1948; C. Scott and P. Haskell, "Normal" Explanation of the Soal-Goldney Experiments in Extrasensory Perception, *Nature* 245:52–54, 1973; C. W. K. Mundle, The Soal-Goldney Experiments, *Nature* 245:54, 1973.

principle that makes really satisfactory work in this area impossible.

The other approach that seemed promising was psychoanalysis. The interest in Cambridge in various aspects of what was often called the "new psychology" was very great. W. H. R. Rivers, who had turned from sensory physiology to anthropology, returned to medicine during the First World War, working particularly with what was then called shell shock. Undoubtedly greatly influenced by Freud, but unable to accept much of the latter's teaching, Rivers developed a more physiological approach to the unconscious.[22] His theory was obviously very incomplete, but it had the attractive feature of providing a phylogenetic explanation of repression or, as Rivers called it, dissociation. He conceived of the process as having been developed to inhibit responses appropriate to aquatic existence and permit the development of terrestrial behavior in our amphibian ancestors. A little independent evidence was later published that suggested such a phenomenon, but I do not think anyone except myself has taken it seriously in recent years.

Morton Prince lectured on multiple personalities in Cambridge when I was up and made an immense impression. I was later to learn that Dame Rebecca West, who in more recent years has become a very dear friend, had been influenced in a comparable way by some of this work.

A paper on "The Significance of the Freudian

22. W. H. R. Rivers, *Instinct and the Unconscious* (Cambridge: Cambridge University Press, 1920). W. H. R. Rivers, Psychological Dissociation as a Biological Process, *Scientia* 35:331–38, 1924. Experimental evidence suggesting loss of conditioning on metamorphosis is given by S. S. Flower, Loss of Memory Accompanying Metamorphosis, *Proc. Zool. Soc. Lond.* 1927(1):155–56, 1927. See also, G. E. Hutchinson, Psychological Dissociation as a Biological Process, *Nature* 120:695, 1927.

Psychology for Evolutionary Theory," by C. C. Fagg, was published as a presidential address to the Croydon Natural History and Scientific Society in 1923.[23] It was mentioned in *Nature* and I was then led to look it up in the Cambridge University Library. Consulting it again recently, it proved rather disappointing, but merely by showing that the two subjects could be put together it had a lasting effect on me.

The most important psychoanalytic work that I encountered as an undergraduate was Freud's *Beyond the Pleasure Principle*.[24] This book was a revelation in showing me how daring speculation could be made to spring from reality. In it Freud concluded that instinctive behavior always tended to bring the organism back to an equilibrium position, being, as we should now say, homeostatic. He then concluded that such behavior could be divided into life instincts tending to preserve the organismic equilibrium intact and death instincts tending to restore a preorganic equilibrium. In the detailed analysis of the latter process Freud suggested that masochism was a primary type of death-directed behavior which became associated with the life-seeking sexual instinct and could then become inverted to produce sadism. This initially fanciful scheme suddenly made sense to me in terms of the very peculiar mating mechanisms of many terrestrial hermaphrodite snails. These animals have a calcareous dart, the *spicula amoris* or *telum veneris*, with which they wound each other during mutual insemination. There can be no question of sadism here, as there might be in higher

23. C. C. Fagg, The Significance of the Freudian Psychology for Evolution Theory, *Proc. Trans. Croydon Nat. Hist. Sci. Soc.* 9:137–64, 1923.

24. Sigmund Freud, *Beyond the Pleasure Principle*. Authorized translation from the 2d German edition by C. J. M. Hubback (London and Vienna: International Psycho-analytical Press, 1922).

mammals, for it is unreasonable to suppose that the snails have any clear idea of what they are doing. The phenomenon still seems to me to provide a possible way of starting to think about a difficult but enormously important problem, though I must admit that so far I can make no headway with this approach. A few years after reading Freud's book I wrote a short paper which appeared in the *International Journal of Psychoanalysis*.[25] This dealt not only with masochism in molluscs but also with certain apparent correlations between times of maximum growth rate and immature sexual behavior in man. My friend Lucille Ritvo who, more than anyone else, has studied Freud's biological background, believes that Freud had looked at the part of my paper dealing with growth rates. There is no evidence that anyone, except presumably Dr. Ernest Jones, then the editor of the journal, ever read the other part about the *telum veneris* of snails. It is, however, quite likely that Freud would have known of this structure early in his career. Very much later I returned to this sort of approach in a paper on evolutionary aspects of sexual behavior in man, which has made me an unwitting very minor founding father of the Gay Liberation movement.[26] I wish that in return for my pointing out that any genes promoting homosexual behavior must, if they exist, be common enough to suggest an adaptive value under some circumstances, they would give me back the original meaning of the word *gay*, which I used to use continually and for which I can find no adequate English synonym.

25. G. E. Hutchinson, Two Biological Aspects of Psychoanalysis, *Internat. J. Psychoanal.* 11:83–86, 1930.

26. G. E. Hutchinson, A Speculative Consideration of Certain Possible Forms of Sexual Selection in Man, *Amer. Natural.* 93:81–91, 1959; see also, J. A. W. Kirsh and J. E. Rodman, The Natural History of Homosexuality, *Yale Scientific Magazine* 51:7–13, 1977.

A quite different theoretical interest also occupied me during much of my time in Cambridge. J. C. Willis, a botanist with great experience of tropical lands, had concluded that the very restricted distributions of some plants which had usually been regarded as relics of a former much wider distribution, more generally indicated new species at the beginnings of their careers. He made a statistical study of the number of species per genus, finding monotypic genera to be much commoner than any others, and concluded that his observations could best be explained by assuming that species originated discontinuously each at a single focus. His ideas were presented in a well-known book *Age and Area*.[27] His investigations stimulated the eminent statistician G. Udny Yule, who concluded that the detailed properties of Willis's "hollow curve" of genera of various sizes did indeed give evidence for discontinuous evolution. Knowing of Sumner's work on subspecies of *Peromyscus*, which clearly indicated that the different local populations differed by many genes and were most unlikely therefore to have arisen discontinuously, I tried Willis's method of plotting the number of subspecies per species in the European mammal fauna and obtained a result like his. I communicated these results to Willis, whom I knew and liked greatly. They were, however, never published, I cannot remember why, though I know I had contem-

27. J. C. Willis, *Age and Area*; *a Study in Geographical Distribution and Origin of Species* (Cambridge: Cambridge University Press, 1922); see also, G. Udny Yule, A Mathematical Theory of Evolution, Based on the Conclusions of Dr. J. C. Willis, F.R.S., *Phil. Trans. Roy. Soc. London* B213:21–87, 1925.

A brief documented summary of the history of the study of the distributions expressing the commonness or rarity of species is given in G. E. Hutchinson, *An Introduction to Population Ecology* (New Haven and London: Yale University Press, 1978), p. 228, n. 41; p. 231, n. 45.

plated a letter to *Nature*. The *Age and Area* hypothesis, in its most rigid form, tended to fade away, but it appears to have influenced A. S. Corbet, a very able agricultural biochemist working in Malaya and collecting butterflies in his spare time. Corbet was led to examine the numbers of species represented by one, two, three, etc., specimens in a collection, and he concluded very roughly that if there were *n* singletons, the numbers would fall off more or less harmonically with *n* / 2 doubletons, then *n* / 3, etc. A modification of this distribution by Fisher, Corbet, and Williams became the ancestor of a number of modern treatments of collections of data of this kind, some of considerable fertility. I think Willis can be claimed as an ancestor of a quite respectable body of contemporary ecological research.

During these years at Cambridge, I continued to study water bugs and began to look into mating behavior, notably the sounds produced by the males of some of these insects. From my time at Gresham's School I had been in continuous correspondence with the leading authority on the Hemiptera-Heteroptera in Britain, a retired schoolmaster called E. A. Butler. He was writing a book that appeared in 1923 on the biology of British Hemiptera-Heteroptera, which considered, species by species, everything available about life history, food habits, and distribution of these insects.[28] I wrote to him about my observations and my remarks are incorporated, with due acknowledgment, in the book.

The singing water bugs belong to the Corixidae, now generally called water boatmen, at least in North America,

28. E. A. Butler, *A Biology of the British Hemiptera-Heteroptera* (London: Witherby, 1923); see also, G. E. Hutchinson, Hemiptera-Heteroptera. Part I Hydrobiotica and Sandaliorhyncha, in J. Stanley Gardiner, ed., *The Natural History of Wicken Fen* (Cambridge: Bowes and Bowes, 1926.)

though the name was originally applied to the Notonectidae. They are of rather elongate oval form with shiny
thorax and wing covers and very specialized legs. The
front legs are short and used by both sexes for feeding.
The middle legs, very long and thin, are used to anchor
the insect to anything that it can hold on to; since there
is a store of air carried beneath the wing covers the insect
is less dense than water and must either keep swimming
or be anchored, if it is to remain submerged. The hind
legs are admirable oars. As in all true bugs, the mouth
parts are suctorial, but they are able to draw in microscopic animals and plants, as well as pierce the walls of
filamentous algae, soft insect larvae, and small worms,
though they do not seem to suck higher plants, as terrestrial bugs regularly do. Superficially the sexes are quite
alike from above but on turning over a male he is found
to have a highly asymmetrical abdomen. The apical joint
of the front leg of the male is, moreover, highly modified
and is used for holding the female in mating. In most
species when the female is secured the male abdomen is
slid to the left and the female abdomen is held in a cleft
on the right-hand side of the male abdomen between the
sixth and seventh segment. A highly asymmetrical apparatus formed from the ninth abdominal segment can now
be directed toward the female aperture into which the
aedeagus or intromittent organ is inserted and fertilization
takes place. There is usually a strange comb-like organ,
called the *strigil*, on the right side of the sixth abdominal
segment of the male. It looks like a sound-producing organ
and certainly is so in some of these insects, but in the
largest subfamily of Corixidae no adequate evidence for
its function exists.

Apart from a peculiar primitive Australian group,
the Diaprepocorinae, there are two widely distributed
subfamilies, the Micronectinae, which are small, under

4 or 5 millimeters long, and largely Old World and tropical, and the cosmopolitan Corixinae, which are from 5 to about 16 millimeters in length. In a minority of species, notably in the genera *Corixa*, *Trichocorixa*, and *Heliocorixa*, the male abdomen is mirror-imaged, so that mating involves sliding it to the right while the strigil lies on the left. Such *situs inversus* only involves the body wall and musculature, the asymmetry of the gut, of the wing cases, and of the suctorial stylets of the mouth being unchanged. In this the inversion differs greatly from that found in some snails in which the whole of the visible structure, though not the molecular asymmetry of the biochemical constituents, is inverted in the left-handed form. In a few species of Corixinae, notably *Krizousacorixa femorata* of the lakes around Mexico City, both right- and left-handed males occur perennially in the same population. My friend Father Walter Peters, S. J., has shown that in this species the left-handed male is usually due to a dominant gene (S) that is lethal when homozygous (SS), so that the heterozygotes (Ss) which appear sinistral must have some enormous advantage over the dextral individuals (ss).[29] The whole story is very odd.

It had been known since 1845 that some species of Corixinae sing but the observations on how this was done were quite imperfect. While I was an undergraduate I kept small aquaria, inhabited by *Corixa panzeri*, on my mantel shelf, with a horizontally mounted microscope handy and was able to see that the movements accompanying the song involved rubbing an area of short spinous hairs on the femur or third joint of the front leg against the side of the head. It is now known that there is a specialized area on the latter called the *plectrum*, responsible

29. W. Peters, Inheritance of Asymmetry in a Water Boatman (*Krizousacorixa femorata*), *Nature* (London) 186:737, 1960.

for the contact that makes the sound. My observations were somewhat tentatively communicated to Butler and appear under *Corixa panzeri* in his book. Later a German investigator quite independently did an admirable study on stridulation in the Corixinae, showing how it is used to excite the female.[30] My earlier observations were forgotten, as no one seemed to consult Butler's book on this matter; if they had they would have found that in another genus, *Cymatia*, which is now put in a special tribe, the Cymatiini of the subfamily Corixinae, the mode of stridulation is quite different, apparently involving the rubbing of the apical joint of the front leg against the head. Since I was a student I have never lived for any length of time in the same place as a species of *Cymatia* and have never been able to extend my observations on singing in this insect.

The small water boatmen of the subfamily Micronectinae, often only 2 mm. long, may also sing, though the phenomenon is so far known only in three or four of the dozens of species in the genus. It occurs in one or both of the European species, *Micronecta minutissima* and *M. poweri*, which have often been confused; in the South African *M. citharistia*, which I heard singing in 1927; and in the Australian *M. batilla*, whose sound production is well described by I. M. King.[31] Here the strigil is certainly the sound-producing organ. In the Australian

30. H. von Mitis, Zur Biologie der Corixiden, Stridulation, *Zschr. Morphol. Oekol. Tiere.* 30:479–95, 1936. The following more recent paper is of particular significance: A. Janssen, Mechanisms of Sound Production and Morphology of the Stridulatory Apparatus in the Genus *Cenocorixa* (Hemiptera, Corixidae), *Ann. Zool. Fenn.* 9:120–29, 1972.

31. I. M. King, Underwater Sound Production in *Micronecta batilla* Hale (Heteroptera, Corixidae), *J. Austr. Entom. Soc.* 15:35–43, 1970.

Diaprepocoris the strigil seems to be a paired organ; possibly the left-hand strigil has moved over to lie by that on the right. One wonders if one part is moved against the other.

These most attractive insects pose a great many problems in their asymmetry and their differing modes of song, as well as in their ecology and distribution, and though during my later life I have worked with them but intermittently, they have been a continual source of interest and delight since I first met with them on Sheep's Green.

My life at Cambridge had taught me an immense amount about zoology and a great deal about other fields which proved attractive and interesting in later life. My mental sustenance was, however, that of a hunter and gatherer rather than that of someone settled in the industrious pursuit of intellectual agriculture. It led me into an enormous number of fields, none exploited very deeply or with any recognizable originality. When I started on more serious research after leaving Cambridge, I felt somewhat as though I were drifting and that my educational experience was rather inadequate. Later, as I saw more and more clearly what I wanted to do, it proved to have been the ideal preparation. Most curiously, when I look at a copy of the *American Zoologist*, such as that just published for the spring of 1977 on the subject of "Recent Advances in the Biology of Sharks,"[32] the tenor of the articles now appearing seems far more in keeping with what I knew as a student in England than with what I was later to know as a young instructor at Yale in the late 1920s. I shall return to this rather odd fact in the last chapter, as I think it has some general significance in the history of biology.

32. Recent Advances in the Biology of Sharks, *Amer. Zool.* 17, no. 2:289–515, 1977.

I was extremely fortunate to have matured in the 1920s rather than the 1930s. Politics were of little interest to most of us reading science, which ten years later would not have been true. At Gresham's School it had become clear to me that some form of guild socialism would be the only possible basis of a just and varied society. Ideally I still hold this view. The practical aspects of politics revolted me from the day that I went to hear the prospective Labour Party candidate for Cambridge making a pre-election speech. He claimed that unlike the Conservative candidate, who lived in a big house far from Cambridge, he was a genuine resident with a house on Panton Street. I happened to know that he had taken this house solely for the purpose of the campaign. The statement was technically true but in every other way misleading.

My brother, who came up two years later than I did, plunged into politics and finally succeeded Michael Ramsey as president of the Union. He was for a time the secretary of the Cambridge University Labour Club and in that capacity had to arrange a visit of Mr. Shapurji Saklatvala, a Parsi and Communist member of Parliament for North Battersea in London, who had been invited by the club to lecture.

At this time a small British Fascist movement had arisen; its members wore a metal stud bearing *BF* in their lapel buttonholes, to the great delight of the more numerous anti-Fascists. The British Fascists, or bloody fools, decided to kidnap Mr. Saklatvala as he got off his train, bind him, and leave him on Wicken Fen. My brother learned of this and arranged for him to be taken off the train, I think at Audley End, and given dinner at some inn on the way by car to Cambridge. When he arrived he was put in a gown and impersonated an Indian student outside the hall where his lecture was advertised to take place, watching the disturbance created by the Fascists. Meanwhile, the bona fide members of the Labour Club were informed by word of mouth, as they arrived, to assemble elsewhere, and when an audience had been assembled in another lecture room, Mr. Saklatvala was brought to it to give his lecture in peace. This sort of thing was no doubt an exciting foretaste of the horrors to come, but I am glad that I was able to get educated without such disturbances. I am sure I have been able to do far more good from having learned about nature in a relatively undisturbed environment.

CHAPTER SIX

VIA CARACCIOLO 14

FEW PHYSIOLOGICAL DISCOVERIES can have made so great an impression on zoologists as the demonstration by Gudernatsch in 1912 that amphibian metamorphosis could be induced prematurely in immature tadpoles by administration of thyroid tissue.[1] I know I repeated the experiments as soon as I knew of them, probably in 1921, using I think what was left over in the family medicine cabinet of the desiccated thyroid prescribed for my sister. Later, having been fascinated by the homology between the thyroid and the endostyle, an elongate ciliated and secretory groove along the floor of the pharynx in sea squirts and *Amphioxus*, some of us at Cambridge reared

1. J. F. Gudernatsch, Futterungsversuche an Amphibienlarven, *Zentralbl. Physiol.* 26:323–25, 1912; J. F. Gudernatsch, Feeding Experiments on Tadpoles, I. The Influence of Specific Organs Given as Food on Growth and Differentiation, *Arch. Entwicklungsmech.* (*Roux*) 35:457–81, 1912. The fact that neotenous axolotls could be induced to metamorphose by feeding them on thyroid gland, was discovered, apparently independently, by V. Laufberger (O Vzbuzeni Metamorfosy Axolotlů Krmenim Žlazou Štítnou, *Biolog. Listy*, 1913), and quoted by E. Babak, in whose laboratory the work was done, in Einige Gedanken über die Beziehung der Metamorphose bei den Amphibien zur inneren Sekretion, *Zentralbl. Physiol.* 27:536–41, 1913.

tadpoles on the endostyle of ascidians as food, but got no metamorphosis. I think other people did this experiment about the same time, and the negative results are probably noted somewhere in the literature. Clearly the thyroid function was not present in the endostyle of the most obvious invertebrate allies of the vertebrates.

The whole subject of sex determination was much discussed when I was an undergraduate. By that time almost everyone had accepted the chromosomal mechanism, males being XY and females XX except in birds and Lepidoptera. Much of the work showing the female to be heterogametic, or ZW, in the latter group, had been done in Cambridge by Leonard Doncaster.

There were still a few dissident voices. Cresswell Shearer—Norma Shearer's uncle—who taught embryology to a few zoology students in the department of anatomy, loved to point out that his own work had shown that in the aberrant little worm *Dinophilus* a very odd kind of sex determination occurred, perhaps not unlike that known in the honeybee.[2] It was clear that the simple XY-XX mechanism could not be universal. We were interested but did not take him too much to heart. He always spoke of *Dropsophila* and habitually described some classical experiments as involving attempted hybridization of *Antedon* with a crinoid, when we all knew that *Antedon* was a crinoid and that the attempted distant cross involved *Antedon* and a sea urchin or echinoid. Though he gave the only formal instruction in embryology then surviving in F. M. Balfour's university, by the time I took it his heart was more in thirteenth-century Capua and the architectural renaissance of the

2. C. Shearer, The Problem of Sex Determination in *Dinophilus gyrociliatus*, Quart. J. Micros. Sci. 57:329–71, 1912.

emperor Frederick II.[3] When he married late in life and was building a house near Aysthorpe, puzzled neighbors inspecting the layout of the cellar on Sunday afternoons supposed that he had included an oubliette in the design.

We were very excited by the beautiful work by Morgan and Bridges that showed how gynandromorphs, female on one side, male on the other, could be explained by the loss of an X-chromosome at a very early cell division, XX being female and XO a sterile male, in *Drosophila*.[4] The story seemed almost too good to be true.

Insects clearly did not have sex hormones which could modify secondary sexual characters by diffusing uniformly throughout the body. Vertebrates did not in general produce gynandromorphs, though at least four cases in birds had been reported.[5] There were also some puzzling cases in arthropods.[6] Perez, and after him many

3. C. Shearer, *The Renaissance of Architecture in Southern Italy; a Study of Frederick II of Hohenstaufen and the Capua Triumphator Archway and Towers* (Cambridge: Heffer, 1935).

4. T. H. Morgan and C. B. Bridges, The Origin of Gynandromorphs; *Contributions to the Genetics of Drosophila melanogaster*, Carnegie Inst. Washington Publ. 278:1–122, 1919.

5. C. J. Bond, On a Case of Unilateral Development of Secondary Male Characters in a Pheasant, with Remarks on the Influence of Hormones in the Production of Secondary Sex Characters, *J. Genet.* 3:205–16, 1914. This paper refers to the earlier work of Poll. In Bond's case the greater part of the bird was a fairly clear-cut bilateral gynandromorph, being male on the left side, but it differed from the other avian examples in that each tail feather was bisexual, the outer vane having a male pattern, the inner vane a female pattern; the tail as a whole was thus bilaterally symmetrical. The difference between the pattern of the inside and outside vanes is not great, but it is clear in Bond's photographs. No adequate explanation of this case has been forthcoming.

6. References to the early contributions to invertebrate endocrinology and related matters here discussed may be found in the

other workers, had found that bees parasitized by the most peculiar insects of the order Strepsiptera, apparently an offshoot of the beetles, were castrated and also could show modification of secondary sexual characters. The same story was elucidated by Giard in crabs parasitized by *Sacculina*, an ally of the barnacles. The Oxford zoologist Geoffrey Smith had done much work on these problems until he died tragically young in the First World War. Such cases suggested that perhaps invertebrates sometimes did have sex hormones, though other interpretations were possible. The avian gynandromorphs seemed in contrast to imply that the tissues of some birds did not react morphologically to whatever sex hormones they might have.

A few more claims to experimental evidence of invertebrate endocrine organs had been made. Harms believed the testis of the ordinary hermaphroditic earthworm to be essential for the maintenance of the clitellum, the band on the worm that forms the egg capsule, though Avel came to a different conclusion.

Harms also discovered an internephridial organ in the sipunculoid worm *Physcosoma* which appeared to be essential to life. Gaskell, working at Cambridge in the pathology department, had found chromaffine cells in the nerve cords of segmented worms, suggesting that adrenalin-like substances might be present.[7] His father, in whose garden in Shelford I had eaten my first ice cream, was a physiologist who had written a book on the

---

historically important paper: G. Koller, Die innere Sekretion bei wirbellosen Tieren, *Biol. Rev.* 4:269–306, 1929.

7. J. F. Gaskell, The Chromaffine System of Annelids and the Relation of This System to the Contractile Vascular System in the Leech *Hirudo medicinalis, Phil. Trans. Roy. Soc.* 205B:153–211, 1914. Other references are given in B. Hanstrom, *Hormones in Invertebrates* (Oxford: Clarendon Press, 1939).

ancestry of the vertebrates, which he derived from arthropods, particularly some fossil xyphosuran related to the king crab *Limulus*.[8] We used to say that the book carried enormous conviction while being read, but that the conviction had entirely evaporated by next day. I suspect the younger Gaskell had derived his interest in the physiology of invertebrates from this approach of his father.

Physiologists with largely medical interests were rapidly piling up information about vertebrate, mainly mammalian, endocrinology. It seemed as though zoologists should enter a comparable invertebrate field where, intellectually at least, the harvest might be very rich. This is what I proposed to do when I set out with a Rockefeller Higher Education Fellowship to the Stazione Zoologica in Naples in September 1925. I failed to achieve my aim, though I did get very close to a quite interesting detail in molluscan physiology. Other people, mainly using arthropods, did establish invertebrate endocrinology within the decade, but it seems likely that only in insects and crustaceans is hormonal control comparable to what is found in vertebrates. The general level of organization of the cephalopods, comparable to that of the fishes, was evidently misleading in this regard. My stay in Naples was, however, very rewarding in other ways.

I took a microscope with me, as was indeed necessary, but I had not realized how hard it would be to convince the customs officials that I was not intending to sell it. They accordingly weighed it and levied duty of a standard rate per kilo, which left me almost penniless. With the little that I had, I bought an admirable lunch basket,

8. W. H. Gaskell, *The Origin of Vertebrates* (London: Longmans Green, 1908).

complete with a small flask of Chianti, which was to be my sustenance for the next twenty-four hours. While doing this, my mackintosh was stolen. I arrived in Naples hungry and tired, in torrential rain.

I had a letter from G. P. Bidder to the current owner of Parker's Hotel. When Bidder was doing his classical work on the hydrodynamics of sponges at Naples a quarter of a century before, he had bought the hotel. In Cambridge this was believed to have taken place early one morning when the management had woken him up to make an inventory prior to a sale of the premises. He is reported to have inquired from his bed if he could buy the hotel by private treaty, then and there. On being given a price he asked for his cheque book, wrote a cheque, and went to sleep again. The story may be apocryphal, but Bidder certainly owned the hotel until Mussolini put numerous difficulties in the way of foreign proprietors of businesses in Italy. He remained on friendly terms with the Italian who had bought it and his letter enabled me to stay in this very elegant establishment for a week or two at a reduced rate, while I found more modest quarters. Feeling greatly cheered by seeing the Parker's Hotel bus at the station, I made straight for it. I can still remember how much I enjoyed my dinner that night at the hotel.

The Stazione Zoologica, which stands in a park called the Villa Nazionale, close to the seafront, was founded by the German zoologist Anton Dohrn in 1872 and was administered by his son, Reinhard Dohrn, when I was there. Reinhard Dohrn's life was made continually difficult by friction with the Italian authorities, but during my stay the laboratory still retained its strikingly international character. Dohrn and his wife were very kind, going out of their way to make life pleasant for a young stranger. Of the other workers I remember particularly Schewiakoff, working on his monograph on the Acantharia,[9] a peculiar group of marine unicellular animals that make their skeletons of strontium sulphate; a young Pole called Skowron who was most kind and helped me replace my stolen raincoat with an *impermiabile inglese*; Adolf Remane, who showed me his extraordinary sand-living gastrotrichs and other strange and small animals; and the various American visitors, notably E. Newton Harvey and his wife Ethel Browne Harvey, Paul S. Welch, who wrote some of his *Limnology* at the Stazione,[10] and G. E. Gates, the oligochaetologist from Burma. Later in the year I went with Newton Harvey and Skowron to Messina to examine the deep-sea animals brought up by the upwelling, which the Greeks called Charybdis, in the straits. Here we saw the fascinating little squid *Heteroteuthis*, which when disturbed retreats, not into a cloud of ink as most squids do, but into a ball of light.

My plan of work was to study the branchial gland of squids and octopuses, the molluscs of the class Cephalopoda. This gland is a white strap-like organ with a special blood supply, no duct, and at the time a completely unknown function, which characteristics naturally suggested an endocrine organ. I soon found that in all the cephalopods that I studied, the branchial gland had a characteristic microscopic structure. The cells stained deeply with basic dyes such as methylene blue, not only the nucleus but the cytoplasm around it taking up the color, which in most tissues does not happen. In this cytoplasm many cells had inclusions which stained

9. W. T. Schewiakoff, Fauna & Flora del Golfo di Napoli. 37 Monographia. Die Acantharia der Golfes von Neapel (Rome and Berlin).

10. P. S. Welch, *Limnology* (New York and London: McGraw-Hill, 1935).

bright red with eosin. The doubly stained preparations were spectacular as well as characteristic. The blood of cephalopods contains a protein called hemocyanin, rich in copper, which is used in the same sort of way as we use our hemoglobin, rich in iron. The coagulated blood stained red with eosin and this led me naively to think that I had found the organ in which the hemocyanin was made. I then set about to do some operative removal of the gland but ran into difficulties. The only cephalopod that can be used for such work at Naples is *Octopus*. Other available species die under the least anesthesia or have inaccessible branchial glands or will not live in aquaria. I asked for *Octopus* and after some days one came. I managed to remove the gland on one side in a few animals before the supply dried up completely. Prolonged study of the sociology of this situation showed me the cause of my troubles. A very beautiful young woman from Holland was working in another part of the laboratory on the effect of various standard drugs used in vertebrate physiology and in medical practice on the visceral muscles of *Octopus*. Every day an *Octopus* arrived for her at ten o'clock, she made her muscle preparations, recorded the effect of the drug of the day on a smoked drum, as physiologists do, and was through work in the afternoon in time to dress for a *thé dansant*. I suspect, however, that the wholesale diversion of *Octopus* in her direction was as much due to hunger as to sex. Most of her animal was freshly dead, highly edible, and left to be cleared away. The laboratory attendant doubtless got a good if monotonous set of dinners from her activities.

I was never able to get enough material to do adequate experiments. I published a letter in *Nature* indicating that on ablation of the organ on one side there was striking compensatory hypertrophy on the other and that the blood of such animals showed a normal hemocyanin content.[11] In 1974 Messenger, Muzii, Nardi, and Steinberg conclusively demonstrated that the branchial gland does produce hemocyanin.[12] So much for my hope of establishing invertebrate endocrinology.

About a week after arriving in Naples, I learned at the laboratory of a *pensione* called Alexandra House, run by a Signorina Winifred Allen, on the Via Caracciolo, which went along the seafront, west of the Villa Nazionale. I found I could get a modest room there at a very modest price, and soon settled in. This was one of the most fortunate things that ever happened to me.

I was asked out to dinner by several of the members of the English colony in Naples, a group that still had a curious social cohesion and which was largely centered around the English church. One of my earliest invitations was from Lady Holden. She proved to be a most charming and intelligent woman, I think in her late seventies, living with her daughter, the Honorable Mary Palk, who was a zoologist and worked part-time at the Stazione Zoologica on the Bryozoa collected by the Scottish Antarctic Expedition. Lady Holden introduced me to Sacheverell Sitwell's *Southern Baroque Art*.[13] As my Ruskinian background had not indicated to me that such art existed, let alone could be enjoyed, even though I was surrounded by it on all sides, this introduction came just at the right moment. The Guglia della Concezione, a graceful eighteenth-century column bearing a figure

11. The Branchial Gland of the Cephalopoda: a Possible Endocrine Organ, *Nature* (London) 121:674, 1928.

12. J. B. Messenger, E. O. Muzii, G. Nardi, and H. Steinberg, Haemocyanin Synthesis and the Branchial Gland of *Octopus*, *Nature* (*London*) 250:154–55, 1974.

13. Sacheverell Sitwell, *Southern Baroque Art* (London: Grant Richards, 1924).

of the Virgin of the Immaculate Conception, standing in the Piazza Obedan, rapidly became one of my favorite Neapolitan monuments and was still as lovely as ever, in spite of some bullet marks, when I saw it again in 1949.

Lady Holden also showed me a number of Neapolitan silver charms, the fascination of which started immediately to grow on me.

She unfortunately fell ill shortly after my meeting with her. She returned to England with her daughter and I never saw them again. A few years ago I happened to pick up a copy of the autobiography of "Spy," the Victorian and Edwardian caricaturist; my wife was reading the book at the time.[14] I opened it at a plate showing an absurd young man in tailcoat, white waistcoat and tie, and monocle, with the most triumphantly vacuous face that could be imagined. This picture represented "Piggy" Palk, as his friends called him, who became the second Lord Holden, husband of my charming and learned hostess and father of the expert on Bryozoa. A little research with Debrett indicated that he had managed to go bankrupt, which did not surprise me. His son, the third lord, married Mlle Miska, a French musical comedy actress, who prior to being Mrs. Drew had started life as Liliane Amelia Crezencia Maichlé, the daughter of a Russian colonel. My mother assured me, when I mentioned Lady Holden to her, that she understood her son was not very satisfactory. I was puzzled as to how she knew anything about him, until it dawned on me that she was thinking of J. B. S. Haldane, whose run-in, as the corespondent in a divorce case, with the university court called the *sex viri*, had shaken Cambridge to its foundations. I am still incredulous that Lady Holden was the widow of "Spy's" model "Piggy" Palk.

14. Leslie Ward, *Forty Years of "Spy"* (London: Chatto and Windus, 1915); see pp. 137–39.

A little later, when I was having dinner at the *pensione*, I was seated next to Miss Allen at the top of the table and began asking her about the charms that Lady Holden had shown me. I soon found that I was sitting by a lady of extraordinary erudition who was willing to share her knowledge of Naples with anyone who wanted to learn. We soon became friends and went to various festivals together. As many people of varied intellectual interests, some connected with the Stazione and some independent writers and archaeologists, often stayed at Alexandra House, Miss Allen was continually being helpful. I am sure she was too modest to realize it, but she must have played a significant part in the intellectual growth of many visitors to Naples. I am very happy to be able to pay a tribute to the memory of a wonderful teacher. Much of the rest of this chapter recounts what she taught me.

She was of the third generation of her family to live in Naples. The pregnant English women of the colony all went to Malta for the births of their children to insure that they produced British subjects even though some had never visited Britain. The original Allen had come out as the Royal Coachman to Ferdinand II, or "Bomba," the last but one Bourbon king of the Two Sicilies. In every Italian court in the middle nineteenth-century, it was de rigueur that the head coachman should be English. His son became an accountant at the Cantiere Armstrong at Pozzuoli, an armament factory, originally a British subsidiary of Vickers Armstrong, Ltd., but later taken over by the Italian government. He and his wife had two daughters; the elder ran the *pensione*, the younger married B. W. Tucker, the well-known Oxford ornithologist.

Though I attempted to do all that I could on the branchial gland, the irremedial lack of material furthered my Neapolitan studies. Merely going out into the street provided opportunities for wonder and speculation. Almost everything, except the motor bicycles of the

Fascisti, was horse-drawn, and the harness of the draft horses ordinarily included an elaborate saddle. This bore a tall upright piece, the top of which was edged with wolf skin as a charm against werewolves. The upright carried a female figure, presumably Parthenope, and below it, in over half the saddles, a horse with or without a fish's tail. In a minority of saddles, however, the horse was replaced by a figure of a boy with an annulated conical cap, holding up his robe to show his genitalia, which were, however, unmutilated. This gesture, though certainly

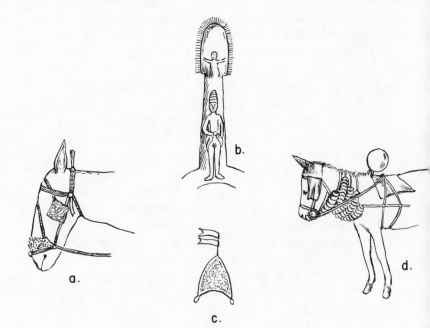

FIGURE 10   *a.* Horse with strip of wolf's skin across its face. *b.* Attis-like figure on saddle. *c.* Mitre-shaped saddle. *d.* Donkey with strings of *taralli* and a balloon (Virginia Simon, from photographs).

apotropaic, also apparently characterizes the figure as Attis (figure 10b). Below the horse or the boy there might be a small figure, presumably Atlas, holding up a globe. An alternative type of saddle was miter-shaped with a metal flag on the top (figure 10c); I was told that such flags were formerly also used on the top of the wolf skin–trimmed upright of the large saddle. Sometimes the wolf skin was worn as a simple band across the lower half of the head of the horse (figure 10a). Another type of saddle ornament was a mere projection bearing a snake's head or a few bells. One of these was noticed swathed in black on Maundy Thursday as if it had been an image in a church. By 1949, the streets were full of cars and almost all of these horse trappings had disappeared, gone no doubt with most of the mythological evils that they were believed to contain.

Early in 1927, Miss Allen wrote to me:

Many werewolves still exist in Naples. Had I known last year we would have gone to seek for one. Two old English ladies told me they heard one years ago. Miss Robertson (did you meet her?) said one night at Posillipo she was roused by violent scratching on the blinds (she lives on the ground floor). The dog whined and "was wet with perspiration" (!!!) and his hair standing on end. She could not think what it was and next morning heard that the "lupo mannaro" had been on the premises. This is a man born on Xmas night; when it is a stormy night or a bright full moon the "destiny" gets hold of him and at midnight he *must* go out. He runs along barking and causing all the dogs in the neighbourhood to howl, his eyes are vicious, his nails become long claws and some say he has long hairs all over. He dashes along and tears anyone to bits so the only salvation is to put one's arms out forming a + for then he is harmless. He cannot go beyond a road crossing. At 12.30 he becomes a man again. The only thing to deliver him is to prick him and cause at least one drop of blood to come out, while he is a werewolf. One man stood on one of those very low balconies at Mergellina with a hat pin stuck to a long fishing rod, as the werewolf passed he pricked him and the man was delivered. One woman told me of her constant anxiety, while expecting to be a mother, that her child might be born on *that* night and then the terror when *that* evening she did not feel well and had to call the midwife and they all listened to the striking hours and twelve approached and passed and the babe was not born yet! The Lord has been merciful to this particular woman and her son was and is only rather "selvaggio," could never bear any clothes round his neck, tore his shirts open always! There is a man somewhere in the vicinity who is a werewolf and the baker (now dead) in the Vico behind St. Anna Church was one. Of course it is a form of epilepsy.

As well as protection against werewolves, charms against various aspects of the evil eye were commonly in use, though the more elaborate ones were less prevalent than formerly. I have written elsewhere on the *cimaruta* (figures 11a, b), an elaborate silver charm used to protect pregnant women.[15] Women who could not afford a silver amulet are said to have stuffed actual rue leaves into their nostrils. Though called a sprig of rue, there can be little doubt that ultimately the charm is derived from a branch of coral (figure 11e). At least one prehistoric prototypic bronze charm clearly imitating coral is known (figure 11c),

15. G. E. Hutchinson, The Enchanted Voyage, *J. Mar. Res.* 14:276–83, 1955; reprinted in *The Enchanted Voyage*, pp. 1–11.

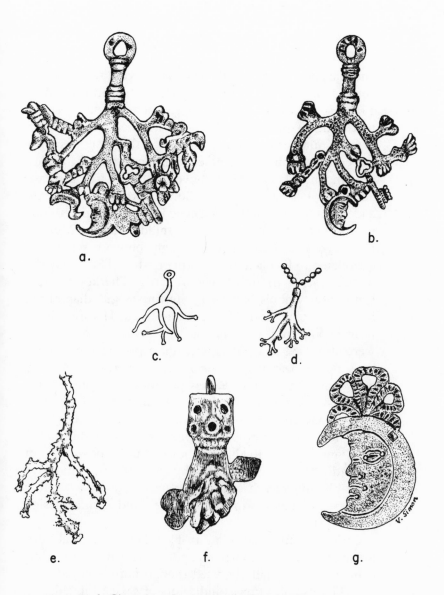

FIGURE 11 *a, b. Cimarute. c.* Iron-age prototype of a *cimaruta* in the form of a piece of coral, made in bronze (Bologna Museum, after Elworthy, *The Evil Eye*). *d.* Coral ornament on necklace of the Christ child, in Piero della Francesca's Madonna and Angels, Ducal Palace, Urbino. *e. Corallium rubrum*, branch. *f. Mano a fico* with dagger, Naples. *g.* Crescent moon, Naples (Virginia Simon).

and the general form of the *cimaruta* is very similar to the coral (figure 11d) worn by the Christ child in Piero della Francesca's Madonna and Angels, now happily restored to the ducal palace at Urbino. The *cimaruta*, however, bears a number of symbols added to the basic design of the coral branch, the complete complement being a crescent moon, a key, a heart converted into a trefoil by the addition of an extra lobe, a flower, two different birds, and several *mano a fico*, clenched fists with the thumb placed between the index and middle finger. Most of these symbols, some of which might be worn separately, are related to Diana in some form or other. This is obvious in the case of the moon (figure 11g). The key and the trefoil are symbols of Diana Tifertina as guardian of the infernal region and of the three-faced Hecate. Silver frogs, connected with her as the goddess of swamps, were also used as amulets, but this aspect of the goddess does not appear on the *cimaruta*. The *mano a fico*, an obviously phallic gesture, was part of an ancient Roman charm, the *res turpicula*, or shameful thing, of which it formed one end, the other being explicitly phallic. Such an object was supposed to draw off malign influences, involving at least to the psychoanalyst the possibility of castration, from the Roman baby who wore it. A modern, probably nineteenth-century, example shows a slightly more respectable form of the same fundamental design (figure 11f).

Very often, even today in New Haven, a coral horn is used for the same purpose, and an explicit coral phallus may still occasionally be used though not displayed.

The use of horns as indicators of sexual infidelity is, of course, very widespread. In Naples *cornuto* or *cornuta* meant not only the husband or wife of an unfaithful spouse, but also the brother or sister of someone so misbehaving. Saint Martin was regarded as the patron

saint of cuckolds. He is said to have had a bad sister who
fell ill. When her brother tried to move her to a more
comfortable bed, he found that she had become too heavy
to lift. Saint Martin then realized that he was growing
horns and was in fact *cornuto*. Old Mr. Allen said that in
former years a mock procession was organized by the
employees of the Cantiere Armstrong on Saint Martin's
Day, November 11. It consisted of a man dressed as a
bishop, men with horns on poles, pretended relics, an
image of Saint Martin, and flags. The procession went
to the doors of the offices of any members of the staff
whose morals were supposed to be questionable and said
prayers there. There was a band and fireworks afterwards.

The Neapolitan populace took a fairly tolerant
attitude to premarital love affairs, and a girl who had an
illegitimate baby quickly got married, for the baby's
existence guaranteed a certain degree of high spirits and
amorousness in its mother.

A girl in a shop near the Villa Nazionale had an
affair with a man who ran the shop, while he was on leave
during the First World War. He promised marriage but
kept putting it off. One day she told him that she was
pregnant and that he had better hurry up and marry her.
He said he was tired of her and that he was going away.
She immediately produced a revolver, shot him dead,
and gave herself up to the police. The baby was born in
prison before her trial, at which she was acquitted as
temporarily deranged mentally at the time. The exultant
populace put her in a carriage decked with flowers which
was dragged along the Via Caracciolo to her home, the
girl showing off her baby at intervals to the admiring
crowd. Soon after, she succumbed to the charms of one
of her numerous suitors and was married.

Bachelors, when ill or in difficulties, often vowed to
marry a prostitute when they recovered their health or

wealth, so reclaiming her and returning her to respectable society. A child from the foundling hospital when adopted might, as "a child of the Madonna," be given preferential treatment over the rest of the family. In these practices one feels not only Christian charity but something at work that is much more ancient.

Miss Allen took me to see, in the Gothic church of San Giovanni a Mare, a popular cult relating to a skull that had acquired the name of Pasquale, locally abbreviated to Pascà.[16] The skull lay at the top of a pile in a hole in front of a shrine to the Madonna and Child, with many *ex voto*s to the right of the high altar of the church (figure 12a). It was ordinarily covered by a flagstone, but this was removed after the mass for the dead, traditionally said every Monday morning. Around the hole on a railing were set numerous candles. Pascà was the only skull in the pile with a full set of teeth; he also wore a coronet of artificial flowers. His soul was believed to be in purgatory and so in need of prayers.

Every Monday morning small shrines were placed in the streets, containing a crucifix, an image of the Blessed Virgin, and a number of naked human figures surrounded by purgatorial flames. Each shrine had a money box into which the charitable could drop a coin toward providing masses for the dead. It was believed that souls in purgatory, in gratitude for the prayers of those on earth, could slip in some terrestrial requests to the Virgin, who would pass them on to her Son. The iconography of the *purgatorio* encouraged this view (figure 12b). The custom must have been widespread in Roman Catholic Mediterranean countries and I have seen an example of a *purgatorio* from the Philippines.

16. G. E. Hutchinson, Pascà: a Note on the Veneration of Souls in Purgatory, in *The Enchanted Voyage*, pp. 12–19.

FIGURE 12   *a*. Pascà. *b*. Purgatorio.

A group of about fifteen women had collected around Pascà. The church was dark save for numerous flickering candles, and the moving lights and shadows on their faces produced remarkable effects. I was told that in a chapel decorated with bones, I think in the main cemetery in Naples, the shadows cast by such moving candleflames gave useful hints as to lucky numbers to play in the lottery. The congregation were led in prayer by a middle-aged woman in a black skirt, white blouse, and pink knitted jacket; she held a rosary. Between prayers the leader kept up a running conversation with Pascà, moving her hands slightly as she spoke. Some of her companions joined in the talk, speaking much as one would to a rather refractory child. They scolded and brought their troubles to the skull, and between these conversations and prayers engaged in gossip. Some believed that Pascà had visited them in dreams.

Many years later I learned of the Sicilian cult of the *anime sante dei corpi decollati*, or souls of executed criminals, also associated with an altar dedicated to Saint John the Baptist, who, like Pascà, was obviously *decollato*. The Sicilian souls were capable of giving all sorts of help if one knew how to interpret their replies correctly. In general, in a land that had suffered continual foreign rule, the *anime sante* were against the authorities. They helped fight the Bourbon army in 1860 and could always be counted on to assist innocent victims.

Subsequently I read in M. A. R. Tucker and Hope Malleson's *Rome* that in the Campagna, if anyone wanted to do well in the lottery, he should say the *Kyrie Eleison* and thirteen *Aves* to thirteen different madonnas.[17] Having then invoked the three wise men, he should go, without replying to anything said to him on his way, to the church of San Giovanni Decollato, where executed criminals were formerly buried. At the church anything striking or unusual was to be noticed. A book existed, known as the *smòrfia* or "grimace" in Naples, in which practically every object or contingency was translated into numbers. Whatever was noticed in the church thus provided a lucky number for the lottery.

At this point, fortune or perhaps the *anime sante* themselves favored me because quite by accident I ran

17. M. A. R. Tucker and H. Malleson, *Rome, Painted by Alberto Pisa* (London: A. & C. Black, 1905); see pp. 85–86.

upon the βιαιοθάνατοι, the souls of those who have died violently, and who to the ancient Greek populace provided, when suitably propitiated, the best of luck in gambling transactions and the like.[18] I think now that it is almost certain that the three cults that I have discussed are derived from that of the βιαιοθάνατοι, slightly different aspects being emphasized in different places. Political retribution plays a part in Sicily, domesticity in Naples, sheer practicality in the Roman Campagna. It would be very interesting to have many more examples, and to trace how far the modern cults are found north of the boundaries of Magna Graecia. It is, as a last word on the matter, fascinating to realize that martyrs are, by definition, *biaiothanatoi*.

Another very picturesque festivity that I enjoyed may also have had some overtones of pagan antiquity. On the festival of Saint Antonio Abbate on 17 January, horses and donkeys were brought to be blessed at the church of the saint. After a pontifical high mass, people drove up horses and carriages, the horses being blessed by a priest and sprinkled with holy water. The horses were nearly all decorated with festoons of *taralli*, little ring-shaped loaves or bagels, colored paper, and balloons (figure 10d). After the blessing they were driven along the seafront to be admired. In the evening the *taralli* were eaten by the owners of the horses and their families. Some, if not all, of the *taralli* on sale in stalls by the church had been made by the bakeress nuns known as *sacramentine*, members of an enclosed order wearing scarlet habits who made the wafers for the mass, as well as sweets and cakes

18. H. J. R[ose], Greek Religion, *Encyclopaedia Britannica* 14th ed. Most general accounts of Greek religion have nothing to say about the *biaiothanatoi*; I stumbled on Rose's article by pure chance, consulting the volume for something quite different.

FIGURE 13 *Left*, boy dressed as a Franciscan; *right*, boy in western Tibet, dressed in a short version of a lama's dull-red robe, with his mother and small brother.

for sale. The *taralli* might be blessed before being tied to decorate the horses.

Children in the crowd played at horse and coachman, and the horse children had their decoration of *taralli* and colored paper.

In the crowd I also noticed a small boy dressed as a Franciscan friar; this was done in fulfillment of a vow, in this case to Saint Francis of Assisi, made by his mother when the child was sick (figure 13, left). Later I saw a precise parallel in small boys dressed as lamas in Indian Tibet (figure 13, right). In marked contrast to this attitude of respect, a man in the same crowd was selling toys that represented a monk who when a string was pulled lifted to his mouth a wine bottle, marked "My penance," as his cowl fell off his head.

In the evening of the festival bonfires were traditionally lit in the streets, though this had recently been forbidden as too dangerous. A few fires still were made in the suburbs. Burning old furniture was supposed to insure that it would be replaced during the course of the year. Saint Antonio is elsewhere associated with pigs, butchers, and animal husbandry in general, but here his feast seems to be a displaced solsticial fire festival; perhaps the *taralli* are solar discs associated with the horses and chariot of the sun. New Year's Eve was traditionally celebrated by throwing crockery out of the window in the same spirit as the furniture was burnt. A very popular film actress called Leda Gys, who lived next door to the *pensione*, kept up this custom with considerable abandon on New Year's Eve 1925.

On the Wednesday of Holy Week in 1926, I heard Tenebrae sung in Santa Chiara. The interior of this enormous church at that time looked like a magnificent sacred baroque ballroom. Frightful damage in the Second World War left it a Gothic skeleton, very impressive,

though, when I saw it, somewhat bare. On the eve of
Maundy Thursday the church was fairly dark, with the
six dark tapers on the altar and fourteen, with a fifteenth
white one in the middle, on the triangular frame termed
a "Tenebrae hearse," on the Epistle or south side of the
altar. There are fourteen psalms sung in the service and
a dark candle is extinguished after each. The dark candles
of the altar are put out after each of the last six verses of
the Benedictus. The single white candle is now placed
behind the altar. All lights, except in Naples a few at the
back to prevent theft, are extinguished. The choir sings
the psalm *Miserere mei*. A noise, the *streptacula*, is made
by banging pieces of wood, such as chairs, together or
on the floor. The light is brought from behind the altar
and placed at the top of the hearse for a few minutes before
being put out. The choir leaves silently and the congregation disperses. The chanting of the choir, the tolling of
the Angelus as night begins, the *streptacula* and the sounds
of the crowd leaving, old men shuffling, young women
clicking their high heels, everyone making slight noises
but no one talking, made an auditory ceremony in the
darkness as impressive as the play with the lights.

Much of the ceremonial of Holy Week combined
Christian and pagan observance in a fascinating way. On
Maundy Thursday the archbishop celebrated mass in the
cathedral and blessed a supply of oil and chrism for
extreme unction and baptisms throughout the diocese
during the coming year. He then placed the reserved
Sacrament in the Easter sepulcher or altar of repose in
one of the chapels. Here the Sacrament was venerated
and later used for the Mass of the Presanctified on Good
Friday. The chapel used for this purpose was usually
festooned with red and gold hangings, and the altar was
decorated not only with flowers and candles but also
with etiolated wheat growing in pots. This is the most

extraordinary pagan survival, as pots of wheat and other plants were used to make the gardens of Adonis where this young god was symbolically mourned.[19] Traditionally a crucifix was put on the ground in front of the reserved Sacrament so that it could be kissed by the worshipper. In 1925, so many of the more fashionable ladies turned up in dresses with deeply cut necklines that the priests in charge were disturbed and hurriedly placed the crucifixes on adjacent walls. In 1926, strict rules about dress were enforced but not all the crucifixes were back on the floor. One worshipper, a layman of about fifty, came as close to looking like a saint in ecstasy as anyone whom I have ever seen; I suspect that, indeed, he may well have been such a one.

The archbishop then went to the old cathedral of Santa Restituta to wash the feet, said to have been well scrubbed ahead of time, of twelve old men from a poorhouse. They wore long white coats and round white caps. Each old man was given a ring-shaped loaf with a bunch of flowers in it; one was hungry enough to bite a piece out then and there. The flowers mostly went to weeping or smiling relations standing behind the old men.

On Maundy Thursday afternoon, the Via Roma, formerly, under the Bourbon kings, the Via Toledo, a major street forming the north-south axis of the city, was closed to all wheeled traffic "because our Lord is in the ground." In past times it had been customary for the court to walk down this street on their way to the churches where they watched before the Sacrament. All the ladies wore new black silk dresses, so the practice was known as *lo struscio* or "the rustle." The shops in the street put out

19. J. G. Frazer gives a very full discussion of the gardens of Adonis and their modern descendants in chapter 33 of *The Golden Bough* (abridged ed. [London: MacMillan, 1925]).

a great display of spring fashions and a large crowd paraded up and down.

The sequence of these Holy Week customs led to the events of Good Friday and Easter Day being put forward by a day. The Easter Eve mass took place on the morning of Easter Saturday, and at 10:00 A.M., officially, as the singing of the *Gloria in Excelsis* began, everything in Naples that could make a noise was turned on for ten minutes to celebrate the Resurrection.

On Easter Sunday the most interesting ceremonial took place in a piazza on the Vomero, the hill that rises behind the western part of Naples. Crowds collected throughout the morning as tramload after tramload of people arrived. Young men with canes and patent leather shoes seemed to predominate, there were lots of children, some boys had a live Easter lamb with them, few old people, but a number of middle-aged women with elaborate coiffures and lovely shawls, and girls in silk dresses with brightly colored combs. There were stalls laden with sweets, lemonade and granite, and men selling balloons and whirligig propellers on sticks. By just after midday, movement was not easy, but I saw all heads turn in one direction. Finally a large banner appeared, and a band with some inevitable Fascisti; and then three towering images, the central Madonna covered with a black silk sheet flanked by Maria Maddalena and Maria Cleofa. They stop in the middle of the piazza, and then Maria Maddalena goes back round the corner, looking for the Risen Christ. She returns, finding nothing, bows to Maria Vergine, and then goes off with Maria Cleofa for a second search. They return and wait a moment before taking their original places. The Virgin now moves forward, the veil falls from her, the Risen Christ appears from around the corner. There is much shouting and waving of hands, fireworks are set off, and a bird is let out of a cage. Then all the images go back in procession to the church nearby. It is usually supposed that this ceremonial is based on Demeter's search for Persephone.

The most celebrated and most exciting religious festivals held in Naples are those of the liquefaction of the blood of Saint Januarius. These festivals seem to have no explicit pagan precursor.

Saint Januarius, bishop of Benevento, was martyred, supposedly on 19 September 305, in the Forum of Vulcan near the Solfatara, a volcanic vent outside Pozzuoli.[20] A number of other Christians, some of them prominent men in Puteoli, were martyred with him. His severed head and his body subsequently underwent several translations but have been in Naples since the Middle Ages.

Though it is not impossible that vials filled with his blood were preserved after his martyrdom, as such a practice was not unknown in early Christian times, there is no hint of a blood relic existing until the seventh century and no record of its liquefaction until 1389, when an anonymous historian of the Kingdom of Sicily wrote:

20. The literature on the liquefaction of the blood of Saint Januarius is enormous. I have used as a main source, other than my own observations: G. B. Alfano and A. Amitrano, *Il miracolo di S. Gennaro: documentazione storica e scientifica*, 2d ed. (Naples: Arti Grafiche Vincenzo Scarpati, 1950). In the bibliography of this work prepared by G. B. Alfano and A. Bellucci, 1470 works are cited. Though the authors accept the miraculous nature of the liquefaction, the historical material that they have assembled is treated quite critically and they give a fair presentation of the views of their opponents. Of these by far the most important was the English Jesuit Herbert Thurston, S. J., whose conclusions are summarized in Januarius, Saint, *Catholic Encyclopedia*. Thurston also wrote a series of articles on the blood miracles of Naples in *The Month*, Jan.–Mar. 1927, 751–53. These I most unfortunately have not been able to consult, though their contents are quite apparent from the summary of Thurston's views given by Alfano and Amitrano.

"A great procession was made on the seventeenth day of August on account of the miracle that our Lord Jesus Christ had manifested in relation to the blood of the blessed Januarius, which was in an ampoule and then was liquefied just as if it had flown that day from the body."[21] The date given is not one of the feasts of the saint;

21. The following references, among others, to early accounts of the liquefaction are given by Alfano and Amitrano: Josephus de Blasiis, Chronicon Siculum incerti auctoris ab anno 1340 ad annum 1396 in forma diarii ex inedito codice ottoboniano vaticano, Soc. Napol. Storia Patria, Monumenti Storici, ser. 1 (Cronache), (Naples: Giannini, 1887).

The text of the account of the first liquefaction is as follows (p. 85):

> Sequenti die xvii augusti [anno 1389] facta fuit maxima processio propter miraculum quod ostendidit Dominus noster Jesus Christus de sanguine beati Januarii quod erat in pulla et tunc erat liquefactum tamquam si eo die exisset de corpore beati Januarii.

The account by Aeneas Sylvius is in *In libros Antonii Panormitae Poetae, de dictis et factis Alphonsi Regis memorabilibus commentarius*, and may be found in *Aeneae Sylvii Piccolominei Senensis, qui post adeptum pontificatum Pius eius nominis secundus appelatus est, opera quae extant omnia*... (Basileae; ex officina Henricpetrina [1571], p. 483). It is not an eyewitness account: "Et quinto loco si quis audire petierit, sacrum illum divi Januarii cruorem, quem modo concretum, modo liquatum ostendunt."

Pico della Mirandola's account is in *Theoremata numero XXV de Fide et Ordine Credendi*, to be found in *Opera omnia Ioannis Francesci Pici, Mirandulae Domini. Tomus Secundus* (Basileae; ex officina Henricpetrina [1573], p. 240). It is a long and important discussion.

> Adservantur Neapoli in Campania Januarii Martiris reliquiae: adservatur et in vase sanguis post eius trucidationem pie collectus, qui e regione membrorum positus, ebullire quodammodo incipit et liquefieri, atque ad pristinam veri sanguinis speciem redire, remotus autem et alio collocatus in densum cruorem coit, coagulaturque eam retinens formam, quae cruori multis saeculis effuso conveniat, donec iterum reliquiis ipsis, argentea theca

it is not clear whether this was the first occurrence of the miracle, though from the context it seems possible. During the fifteenth and sixteenth centuries a number of accounts of the phenomenon were written including those by Aeneas Sylvius Piccolomini in 1456, who has appeared in another guise earlier in this book, and by the Neo-platonist Giovanni Francesco Pico della Mirandola in 1504. Subsequently nearly everyone writing about Naples has mentioned *Il miracolo*.

The blood is preserved in a glass bottle about sixty milliliters in volume; this and another much smaller bottle, on the inner surface of which are some small lumps that might be blood clots, are mounted in a circular silver ring with clear glass windows front and back. The two vessels appear to be sealed up and attached to the ring by some resinous material. Ordinarily the reliquary is set in a monstrance and is kept locked up in a tabernacle behind the high altar of the chapel of Saint Januarius, or *tesòro*, on the south side of the cathedral.

The nearly empty vial is ordinarily supposed to have contained a relic of the blood that was taken to Madrid, supposedly as a gift from Carlo III in 1759, when the throne of the Kingdom of the Two Sicilies passed to Spain. This, however, cannot be true, as the smaller vial is known to have been almost empty in 1575. Though popularly supposed to liquefy simultaneously with the relic in Naples, the only time, 19 September 1912, that

---

reconditis ex adverso opponatur, nec id quoque semper evenit.

Nam dum regionibus illis aliquid imminet malum vel turbatio impendit, minime liquefit, sua illa quiete vexationem portendens. Ita incolae longa experientia didicere. Ego meis oculis cruorem illum qui concretus et teter sua natura manet, objecta capitis rubescere liquere, et ebullire vidi.

The current belief in the prognostic significance of the miracle obviously existed when Pico wrote.

this was properly checked, the relic in Madrid did not liquefy, while that in Naples did. The Madrid relic seems to be of no importance and its exposition probably only exists in Neapolitan folklore.

Three times a year there is an exposition of the relic in Naples, on the saint's festival on 19 September, on 16 December, and on the Saturday before the first Sunday in May. The December exposition originated in an occasion when the saint was supposed to have saved Naples from destruction by Vesuvius on that day in 1631; the May exposition commemorates the first translation of the relics from Pozzuoli to the Catacomb of Saint Januarius in Naples.

The May exposition took place in the Church of Santa Chiara after a procession from the cathedral. After 1943, when great damage was done to Santa Chiara by bombing, this practice was abandoned and not immediately renewed. The December exposition is a formality which it was regarded as rather bad form to attend; it is considered unfortunate if the blood liquefies. At the other two liquefactions, the quicker the miracle happens, the better.

The older accounts seem to suggest the belief that the proximity of the blood to the relic of the saint's head on the altar is a necessary condition for the liquefaction.

At the December exposition in 1925, when we arrived about 8:15 A.M., a number of busts, each of a saint with a parish church in Naples and a patron of the city, were being removed from the treasury chapel where they were ordinarily kept and arranged around the choir of the cathedral on a shelf. About eighteen of these busts were large and important and it was said that each parish had to post security with the governor of the treasury chapel if its bust was to leave the latter. The governor, of a ducal family, was a layman who wore dress clothes on this occasion. A number of old women from the slums, known as "le zie di San Gennaro," the aunts, or perhaps more generally the relations of Saint Januarius, were in the treasury chapel. They have last say on all proceedings connected with the exposition. A sacristan put stools for the officiating clergy in front of the altar. *Le zie* made him take them away lest they interfere with the saint when he came down into the cathedral. The officiating clergy came with the governor and opened the tabernacle behind the altar, taking from it the head reliquary, in the form of a bust of the saint, and the blood. The head is a fine medieval work but it was covered almost immediately with a cope and miter so that its details were hard to see.

The relics were placed side by side on the altar and some prayers were said. The officiant, presumably the monsignor who is prelate of the treasury, inverted the reliquary to show that the contents of the larger bottle were solid. The solid material seemed to tremble a little, like a jelly. This inversion was repeated at intervals. The lay officials kept consulting their watches and seemed anxious for the proceedings to stop. This went on for about twenty minutes. The officiant then decided that the miracle had been given a good trial and had not happened. *Le zie* examined the reliquary and evidently agreed. As it rarely occurs in much under an hour at the other expositions, the lack of a miracle was not entirely unexpected. Everyone present was given an opportunity to kiss the reliquary of the blood, which made a close examination possible. Later the two relics were taken to the high altar of the cathedral and a mass was sung, the archbishop being present. The relics were then taken outside in procession with all the choir and clergy and circumambulated the church (figure 14a).

On the morning of the exposition on 1 May 1926, the reliquary of the head was taken in procession to Santa Chiara, accompanied by the Neapolitan nobility responsible for the care of the treasury. About 5 : 30 P.M. a large procession left the cathedral. Twenty-six of the busts of the patron saints were carried through the streets, followed by the reliquary with the miraculous blood under a canopy.

In the sixteenth to eighteenth centuries the relics were transported in large cars or catafalques, and cantatas by composers such as Pergolesi and Paesiello were sung.

The dignity of the occasion was somewhat reduced by the fact that some lights over the west door of the cathedral had to be fixed and the ladder got in the way. Two important-looking people had a row with the ceremonarius. The canons thought it might rain and carried umbrellas under their arms. On leaving the church they blew out their candles and put them, too, under their arms with the umbrellas. The liquefying blood under its canopy was cheered and pelted with confetti from the windows all along the way to Santa Chiara. A sedan chair accompanied the procession but was empty. It may have represented the archbishop, who being in figure *bellissimo*, as one man put it to me with a forward sweep of his hand, would not have been able to get into it.

Once arrived at Santa Chiara, each of the patron saints paused before Saint Januarius on the high altar before taking a place in the choir. The reliquary of the blood was then put on the high altar and inspected. Prayers were said and the reliquary was inverted with a candle behind it, but nothing happened. This was repeated, but, again, nothing happened. On the third trial, when the bottle was held upside down, suddenly the blood, or at least the greater part of it, liquefied. A bell was rung and the reliquary held up on its side with a light behind it, so that the whole immense congregation could see and applaud (figure 14b). The reliquary was then examined by the clergy and other people around the high altar and

FIGURE 14 *a*. Relics of Saint Januarius in procession. *b. Il miracolo.*

v·s. E·H. **b.**

shown to the congregation again, with more applause. Watches were consulted as the time at which liquefaction occurs gives a valuable number for playing the lottery. I find I have no note of how long we had to wait on this occasion, but my memory suggests fifty-five minutes. Anything over an hour is regarded as unsatisfactory, and a prolonged delay of several hours is ominous. Occasionally, as quite recently in May 1976, the miracle does not happen.

In September and May the miracle is repeated daily throughout the octave. Unfortunately, I got a septic sore on my foot and after having walked quickly to Santa Chiara from the cathedral as the procession left the latter church, to work my way forward to get a place within thirty feet of the high altar, I was in no state for further study of the miracle. I had intended to go to one of these later expositions because there is a persistent belief that

the blood in the bottle, which usually fills it by about
two-thirds, may increase in volume during the octave in
May and decrease again in September.[22] Sometimes the
entire bottle appears to be full; drawings purporting to
show this phenomenon have been published, though they
are not very satisfactory. Much more extraordinary claims
were made early in this century by G. Sperindeo and P.
Silva, who were able to weigh the reliquary with its relic
on what was described as a sensitive balance, in both 1902
and 1904. In the first of these years the mass was found to
be 1015 grams on 12 May after the May exposition, and
987 grams on 26 September after the September exposition. In 1904 the mass was 1015 grams on 19 September
at the beginning of the octave, falling to 1004 grams on
21 September, and rising irregularly to 1011 grams on
26 September. At the beginning of the octave the bottle
appeared full, but the volume of the blood decreased
throughout the period in spite of both a decrease and an
increase in mass. These changes are most peculiar. Though
I cannot help suspecting incompetence in weighing, the

22. The material on the changes in volume and mass and the
spectral properties of the edge of the clot were published in P. Silva,
Il miracolo di S. G., *Civ. Catt. e Riv. Sci. Lett.* (Naples) 12:157–58,
1905; G. Sperindeo, Un altra osservazione sul miracolo, Ibid. 12:160,
1905; G. Sperindeo, *Il miracolo di S. Gennaro* (Naples, 1903), pp. 70–
71. There were a number of other publications by this author, but I
have only been able to consult the account given by Alfano and Amitrano. Sperindeo was apparently advised by a Professor Gennaro when
doing his spectroscopic work; the identities of these investigators seem
not to have been questioned in spite of their names, which to the
unbeliever might suggest a hoax. I attempted to obtain some of the
literature when in Naples in 1925–26, but I was told that whenever anything was published about *il miracolo*, pro or con, the opposing side
bought up and burnt all the copies that they could lay their hands on.
    An account of the failure of the miracle appeared in the *New
Haven Register* on 10 May 1976.

alleged results could obviously be claimed as miraculous by those believing in the miracle and as indicating continual tampering with the relic to those accepting a naturalistic interpretation. Outside Naples I imagine that few educated Roman Catholics accept the miracle at face value. The idea that the event is fraudulently staged anew at each exposition is, however, no more attractive intellectually than it is morally. Any systematic fraud would involve a number of persons in a completely guarded secret over a period just short of six hundred years. It would be extraordinary if all the people who have been involved officially and who must mostly have been good, if sometimes limited, men, would be by training and temperament automatically willing to become impostors. However much one may consider the Roman Church, for better or for worse, to be monolithic, it is inconceivable that some cracks would not show. The governor of the treasury chapel is an aristocratic layman, and the risk of some anticlericalism among people close to the relic cannot always be negligible.

The most intelligent and learned Roman Catholic critic of the miracle, the late Father Herbert Thurston, S. J. who probably knew more than anyone else in his lifetime about the odder physical phenomena associated with sanctity, has pointed out the very curious fact that though other liquefying blood relics are known, they appear to be disproportionately abundant in Naples and its vicinity. At least the following are recorded in the treasuries of churches in the city:

> Saint John the Baptist in San Gregorio Armeno (two relics)
> Saint Stephen in Santa Chiara, and in San Gregorio Armeno
> Saint Lawrence in San Gregorio Armeno

Saint Patricia in San Gregorio Armeno
Saint Luigi Gonzaga in Gesù Vecchio
Saint Alfonso dei Liguori in Santa Maria
    della Redenzione dei Cattivi

The relic of the blood of Saint John the Baptist was brought from France by Charles I of Anjou; it is said to have come from the Orient in the sixth century. It was divided into two portions, one going to San Arcangelo a Baiano, where it liquefied for the first time on 29 August 1554, the other to San Giovanni a Carbonari, which portion seems to have been lost. When San Arcangelo was suppressed in 1577 the relic was again divided; one part went directly to San Gregorio Armeno, the other reached that church in the nineteenth century. Both liquefy, but the first sample does so quite regularly, the second only at long intervals. The same sort of story is told of the blood of Saint Stephen, the relic in Santa Chiara liquefying regularly, though not completely, on 3 August, that at San Gregorio Armeno now only at long intervals, though it seems to have been more regular in the fifteenth and sixteenth centuries.

The blood of Saint Luigi Gonzaga, who died in 1591, long after the relic of Saint Januarius is reliably known to have liquefied, did not show the phenomenon until 1841, when it liquefied in the hands of the Venerable Don Placido Baccher, who was popularly believed to be a saint, though he has not been beatified.

The blood of Saint Alfonso dei Liguori, who died in 1787, liquefied on 1 August 1851, in the church which he had consecrated. It is evident that the origination of liquefying blood relics has occurred in Naples at least from 1389 to 1851. The last two relics, of Saint Luigi Gonzaga and Saint Alfonso dei Liguori, could be genuine, though the origin of the first of them may be doubtful. That of Saint

Januarius just conceivably might be genuine also, though Father Thurston is very doubtful. The relics of Saint John the Baptist and Saint Stephen are doubtless spurious and that of the very dubious Saint Patricia likewise.

Two blood relics of Saint Pantaleo, in San Gregorio Armeno in Naples and Santa Maria in Vallicella in Rome, are always liquid, but a third at Ravello liquefies and is believed there to provide a more convincing *miracolo* than does the blood of Saint Januarius.[23]

The various less famous liquefying blood relics in Naples, none of which are of more than parochial importance, are even less likely to have been deliberately manufactured than that of Saint Januarius. If a secret recipe exists, it would have to have been known not only in the *tesòro* of the cathedral, but all over the central part of the city, without ever having been publicly divulged in the past half millennium. If one does not want to accept a series of rather sportive miracles, a naturalistic explanation not involving intentional production of a liquefying blood relic would seem likely. The simplest hypothetical suggestion, basically that of Father Thurston, and one that in the course of years would be testable, is that a human blood clot, sealed up in a vial under the right, but very easily realizable, conditions, slowly undergoes a series of chemical changes that result in a substance easily liquefying when certain external conditions are fulfilled. Father Thurston thought the stimulus to be photochemical; an increase in the light flux on the relic must usually accompany liquefaction. Slight mechanical disturbances may be involved, as is known of the liquefaction of various thixotropic colloids. The fact that on twelve of the

---

23. G. P. Bidder, personal communication. It was claimed that the exposition at Ravello did not allow so great a possibility of heating by candle flames as may have occurred in Naples.

twenty occasions when the reliquary of Saint Januarius's blood has been repaired the blood liquefied, is in line with this.

Admittedly this suggestion is supported by no evidence except that of the relics themselves. I am unable to make any guess on biochemical grounds as to what the probability of such a change might be. The suggestion, though vague, is in accord with all the evidence except the very dubious changes in the mass of the reliquary. It would receive some support from the alleged observations of the absorption spectrum of hemoglobin in the thin meniscus or margin of the clot if this occurrence is ever confirmed; the published evidence does not seem to me adequate. Vastly better nondestructive methods of analysis could be applied today without injuring the relic or its reliquary in any way. Whatever happens in the reliquary, Saint Januarius offers his devotees much excitement, and some pleasure comes from him to a number of successful lottery winners, as well as to those who are simply fascinated by what happens. Viva San Gennaro.

Vesuvius appeared to me as an old friend as soon as the rain stopped on the day of my arrival in Naples; I once saw it blow a smoke ring. I loved wandering through the Phlegraean Fields, the region of former intense volcanic activity to the west of Naples, in which a remarkable explosion crater, Monte Nuovo, was formed on 30 September 1538. Nearby lies Lake Avernus, apparently lifeless in antiquity but now with a reasonable lacustrine fauna. I spent many weekends exploring this region. One Sunday I decided to see what is visible of the grotto of the Cumaean sibyl. The easiest way seemed to be to follow the tunnel that was excavated for Agrippa but is usually called the Grotta della Pace after Pietro della Pace, who explored it in 1507. It is about three-quarters of a mile long, running from Avernus northwest to Cumae. A series of shafts give light from above, and there are a number of small chambers cut in the wall. When I was halfway along a man stepped out of a chamber. I said "Buon giorno" and walked on. I suppose my pace quickened; I was ultimately very glad to be in daylight again.

From Naples, I went on several short excursions. I have already mentioned *Heteroteuthis* in Messina. Apart from the fruits of Charybdis, Messina was a depressing place, for after seventeen years it was still suffering from the earthquake that wrecked the city in 1908. It did, however, have a good marionette theater playing with great bravura the classical cycle of Orlando. I remember also a café where we had coffee and rolls for breakfast. All but one of the patrons were men. The single woman who frequented it was about thirty-five years old, dressed in a very smart but very masculine suit and felt hat, and carried a walking stick. Though I am sure she had a status and a role, she seemed to be waiting for an author to make clear what that status and that role might be.

From Messina I went by train to Palermo. This was the great artistic experience of my first Italian visit. I found the Byzantine beauty of the Capella Palatina completely overwhelming. When I saw it again nearly fifty years later, it had just the same effect. In most of the great buildings I know, one feels that one is inside something very beautiful but the beauty resides in the walls, the pillars, and the various ornaments. In the Capella Palatina it seems to fill the empty spaces between the walls so that the air itself is subtly golden.

When I first visited this marvelous palace chapel, a man came up to me and, addressing me in English, said merely, "Are you interested in these things?" I replied in great surprise, "Yes—very." He said: "We are going to Cefalù this afternoon. Will you come to lunch with us at the Hotel Las Palmas and drive there with us?" Astonished, I accepted with avidity, for I had otherwise little hope of getting there. During the course of the lunch, I discovered that the party consisted of my interlocutor, Matthew Prichard, who was a Byzantinist, an English architect called Borree or Borrea, who was a baroque enthusiast, which Prichard found frivolous, a Mrs. Chadbourne, an American lady who proved to be the sister-in-law of Frank Lilley, a very well known biologist at the University of Chicago, with her companion, a Miss Lamotte. Mrs. Chadbourne, who was very rich, evidently employed the two English experts as ciceroni. Prichard believed that there were three major sets of works of art, that made by the ancient Greeks, that made by the Byzantine Greeks, and that made by El Greco. He admitted that the mosaics on the roof of the very ancient baptistry adjacent to the old cathedral of Santa Restituta in Naples had some merit; he had had a stepladder brought to make his examination of them more thorough and was glad that I knew them. The rest of Naples seemed to have no interest for him. Rome, he felt, contained Keats's tomb but otherwise was not worth a visit. He believed the Christos Pantocrator, the universal judge, in the apse of Cefalù to be the highest point in the second great period of Byzantine art, and in his presence it certainly seemed to be.

The next day I met the party again at Monreale. The cathedral there does not have the magical glow of the Capella Palatina and nothing equals the majesty of the apse at Cefalù. When, however, it is the site of a pontifical high mass, as it was on a much later visit, the narrative decoration of its walls comes to life and it is fascinatingly beautiful.

Prichard would have none of it. The oriental elegance of the cloisters particularly upset him. He said he wanted to write obscene remarks on the marble. He was under the impression that the whole work was an Italian imitation of the real thing. It is now practically certain that the craftsmen involved had come from Byzantium. I have often wondered what he would have thought of Monreale if he had known that it was Greek.

More than twenty years later, when staying at Ibstone with Dame Rebecca West and her late husband Henry Maxwell Andrews, I found that Henry had known Prichard well as they had both been interned in the notorious concentration camp at Ruhleben during the First World War, where Prichard had lectured on Byzantine art. Later, I learned more of him from Walter Muir Whitehill, who had come across him in his study of the history of the Boston Museum of Fine Arts, where Prichard had been assistant director from 1902 to 1905. Mr. Whitehill believes that in those days he was less rigid and intellectually exclusive than when I met him. As a host he was most considerate and thoughtful.

I visited Benevento, but unhappily my extensive notes on this city were much eaten by mice in later years. I doubt they contained anything not available in guidebooks. Benevento had a great reputation as a gathering place for witches.[24] Apart from the bronze doors of the

---

24. The witches were supposed to ride through the air,

Sotte aqua e sotte viento
Alla noce di Beneviento,

a nut tree where their rites took place. The nut tree was destroyed in the middle of the seventh century by Saint Barbatus, who was disturbed by the paganism of the place. The inhabitants are said to have held a festival which ended by archers shooting over their shoulders at a skin of a wild animal hanging from the tree. When I heard of this skin it made a great impression on me because I was familiar with the practice of gamekeepers in England who hung up stoats and weasels on a gibbet, usually a beam of wood attached to a tree, ostensibly to warn off other predators. The Benevento witches and Saint Barbatus suggested something older and more magical in this practice.

cathedral and a good deal of nice Romanesque sculpture, my most vivid memory is of an old crone with a brazier going at night into a house built in the ruins of the Roman amphitheater. She looked as though she might well have been in the place to attend a meeting of her coven, though the famous nut tree under which the witches met was long ago cut down. She was most polite in wishing me good night.

I also spent a few days in Rome at the time of the carnival, but though the weather was good the masked revelers in carriages had been forbidden to appear on the streets by Mussolini, who had issued an order outlawing all covering of the face in public. This, incidentally, prohibited the members of the *archiconfraternite*, or burial societies, from wearing the white-hooded robes with eye slits which had been borrowed by the Ku Klux Klan, though the prohibition was at first lightly enforced near Naples and I saw such a funeral at Pozzuoli the first time I went there.

I saw all the things that one was supposed to see in Rome but they nearly all had to be seen again after thirty years before I could feel properly what fell on my retina.

There were two great exceptions to this. One was the archaic Greek stone seat known as the Ludovici Throne, the back carved with a relief of the birth of Aphrodite, where the figure of the goddess is flanked by two girls, one a nude playing flutes. The other exception was the Church of Santa Prassede, into which I stumbled during the singing of a plainsong requiem mass. The motif of the white sheep coming out of Bethlehem and of Jerusalem, which can be seen on either side of the apses of the most ancient churches in Rome, suddenly made sense to me when I was lecturing in the Zoological Institute of the University of Rome many years later. The pitch of the auditorium was very steep and, just before I was introduced, the whole staff, mostly young women, in white coats, entered ceremonially from either end of the front row.

On the afternoon of the last Sunday before Lent I went by bus to the Porta San Sebastiano to visit the Catacombs of Saint Calixtus and after having seen them started walking southeast along the old Appian Way, looking at the various Roman tombs and other remains.

A young woman who had been on the bus and had also visited the catacombs was walking behind me; then she passed me as I examined some ancient fragment; then I passed her. We arrived at the tomb of Cecilia Metella together. Here an old guide assured us that everything to be seen was *la piu bella del mondo fuorchè la signorina*. This delighted the young woman, who, though tall and attractive, must have known she was not outstandingly beautiful. We walked on together, she finding that I was English, I finding that she was French, a governess to a family, on her last afternoon off before they left Rome next day. We went on walking, agreeing to speak each other's language on the way out, our own on the return journey. She had been in London and had found the idea of sheep in Hyde Park extremely amusing. We talked about pictures; on Manet's *Olympia* she was outspoken and conservative.

The part of the Appian Way along which we were walking was still quite rural, with shepherds in the fields by the road. They were playing the concertina and not the flute, but still they gave to the scene a faintly Virgilian feeling. We flirted just a little while consulting my guide-book and turned back so that she would not miss her bus. She stopped to pray at the Church of Domine Quo Vadis?, near where Christ is said to have appeared to Saint Peter, fleeing from persecution, telling him that he came to Rome to be crucified anew. We reached the end of our walk and said good-bye, without ever knowing each other's names. "Desine Maenalios, jam desine, tibia, versus."[25]

25. "Cease, O my pipe, now cease your Maenalian measures." Maenalos was a pine-covered mountain in Greece sacred to Pan (Virgil, *Bucolics*, *ecl.* 8, l. 61).

CHAPTER SEVEN

NO CERTAIN ADDRESS

EARLY IN 1926 AN ADVERTISEMENT of the position of senior lecturer in zoology at the University of the Witwatersrand appeared in *Nature*. I decided to apply.

I wrote to tell my parents what I was doing and received a very discouraging reply. They had made inquiries in Cambridge, particularly discussing the matter with my uncle, and had learned that Professor H. B. Fantham was an extremely difficult man, whom I should avoid. However, even in British zoological circles, it seems not then to have been known that the vacancy existed because the previous incumbent had been physically ejected from the zoological laboratory of the university.

Against what I heard of this, I set the experience of an entirely new fauna. I was young enough to be extremely pigheaded about other people's opinions. My wife tells me I still am. My scientific judgment and everyone else's human judgment both proved to be right. I was appointed to the position; perhaps I was the only applicant. I had an awful time. I emerged from it with an intellectual vista stretching out in front of me which obviously would take more than a lifetime to explore. This chapter deals with my realization of that vista. The misery that accompanied the realization is mostly commonplace and uninteresting. The account will, therefore, be more strictly scientific than is the rest of my story. I hope I have treasured just enough beautiful or pleasantly outrageous human memories of this time to encourage the unscientific reader to reach the end of the chapter.

Having to take up my duties in Johannesburg at the end of July after the southern winter vacation meant leaving Naples earlier than I had intended. My foot was still suffering from an infection and when I arrived in England on the cross-channel steamer I found that the first and only general strike in British history was in full swing. The docks were manned by undergraduates and the transportation system of the country had been taken over by an extraordinary number of amateur engine drivers. The situation could have been viewed as the prelude to a revolution or as the climax of a picnic. The latter view proved correct. I cannot remember how I managed to get to Dulwich, where my medical uncle examined my foot and pronounced it out of danger. I can only recall my mother's relief when I got through to her later that evening over the telephone.

By the time that I was to sail for Cape Town, the strike was over. My journey was extremely pleasant. My father had taught an undergraduate called G. W. Grabham, who had become government geologist in the Sudan. He had been born in Madeira, where his father, Dr. Michael Comport Grabham, had settled in 1861 as a consulting physician to the British colony in Funchal. The elder Grabham was a skilled organist and had invented an early type of electrical control for his instrument. He had also become interested in various meteorological problems, notably the relation of health to climate, meteoric dust, and particularly atmospheric electricity. He collaborated with Lord Kelvin on the last-named subject. He married a daughter of one of the English families on the island, and later, the first Lady Kelvin having died, Lord Kelvin married Mrs. Grabham's sister.

At the time of my visit, Dr. Grabham was eighty-six, and had largely turned to horticulture. He later published a book on the cultivated plants that were grown in Madeira. Having been, through his son, in touch with my father, he sent a message down to the ship when she had docked at Funchal for the day, asking me to lunch and requesting me to tell the bearer the year of my birth.

I spent the morning looking at the little town; the close connection with England was early apparent, as there is an English monumental brass in the attractive Manueline cathedral. The whole place had a spic-and-span look that I later learned to associate with Portuguese territories. I walked into the country and did a little collecting, finding the endemic earthworm *Allolobophora möbii*, in which the clitellum, or band that secretes the egg cocoon, a structure known to every gardener who has upturned a mature worm, lies further back than in any other species. It is just about in the middle of the worm, so that in comparison with other kinds it looks as though it might, in the course of evolution, slide off the tail of the worm completely.

I then went to Dr. Grabham's house for lunch. He said in his biography in *Who's Who* that his recreations were "teasing chiefly . . . ," but if he teased me it was very gentle. The lunch was delicious, the main dish being bear-crab, or *Scyllarus*, a flat relative of the *langouste*, or rock lobster. With this most edible crustacean I learned why he had inquired the date of my birth; the Madeira that we drank was a 1903.

My great delight on the voyage, as we entered tropical waters, was the continual sight of flying fish. I met a young South African who had read classics at Oxford; he assured

me that though there were some good people in South
Africa, all of them were black. He was no doubt anxious
to shock, but also to prepare me for the disastrous course
that he felt his country was pursuing.

Almost the first experience that I had on landing was
of demonstrations by the Cape Coloured people against the
new South African flag, in the design of which the Union
Jack had no part. Though it was natural to hear that there
had been much feeling about this in Natal, where the
white population was mainly of British descent, the Cape
Town demonstrations needed more explanation.

The Cape Coloured are a group of people mainly of
Hottentot and European ancestry, with admixtures from
slaves of Malagasy origin and from Indonesians condemned
as criminals in the early days of the Dutch East Indian
empire to banishment in South Africa. They form an
economically important social class in the southwestern
part of the country. After the abolition of the much-hated
pass system in 1828 and of slavery in 1833, the Cape
Coloured regarded Britain as their friend.

The complexity of the problems that arise in South
Africa, a lovely land with a surfeit of the wrong sort of
history, is apparent when it is realized that the same kind
of people in Britain who were against the pass system and
slavery in the early nineteenth century and are now strongly
opposed to most of the contemporary policy of the South
African government, would largely have been pro-Boer
at the time of the Boer War.

I shall say little more directly about such matters, save
the recollection that both the universities that I knew, Cape
Town and the Witwatersrand, had liberal and humane
faculties. They still appear to be firmly committed to
academic freedom, however difficult such a commitment
may have become today.

I stayed for a short time near Cape Town and was

introduced to the incredible flora of the coastal region of the southwestern tip of Africa. This I first met, to my intense delight, in the botanic gardens at Kirstenbosch, with Table Mountain as a backdrop. Meeting proteas and the sunbirds that fed on their flowers was like traveling into a plate of some sumptuous hand-colored monograph from the middle of the nineteenth century.

My first great zoological excitement in South Africa was seeing *Peripatopsis capensis* in rotting wood beside a shady trail going up Table Mountain (figure 15a). This animal is a member of a group called the Onychophora; zoologists often use the name peripatus as a common noun to denote any of the species. The first one was found on Saint Vincent by the Reverend L. Guilding, a missionary who had worked in the Guianas and Caribbean Islands, and was described by him in 1826. He thought the strange animal that he had discovered must be a slug with legs.[1] He named it *Peripatus*, because as a legged animal it is peripatetic, as someone once wrote in an examination.

Professor Adam Sedgwick, who did not like the mistress of Girton or her importunate students, as we have seen, wrote of the Onychophora, particularly of the South African species, the embryology of which he had studied, as if he had been seduced by a harem of voluptuous women; "The exquisite sensitiveness and constantly changing form of the antennae, the well-rounded plump body, the eyes set like small diamonds on the side of the head, the delicate feet, and, above all, the rich colouring and velvety texture of the skin, all combine to give these animals an aspect of quite exceptional beauty."[2] He was

1. L. Guilding, Mollusca Caribbaeana: An Account of a New Genus of Mollusca, *Zool. J.* 2:443, 1826; reprinted *Isis* 21:158, 1828.

2. A. Sedgwick, Peripatus, *in* S. F. Harmer and A. E. Shipley, eds., *The Cambridge Natural History* (London: Macmillan), vol. 5, *Peripatus; Myriapods, Insects Part I*, 1895; see p. 5.

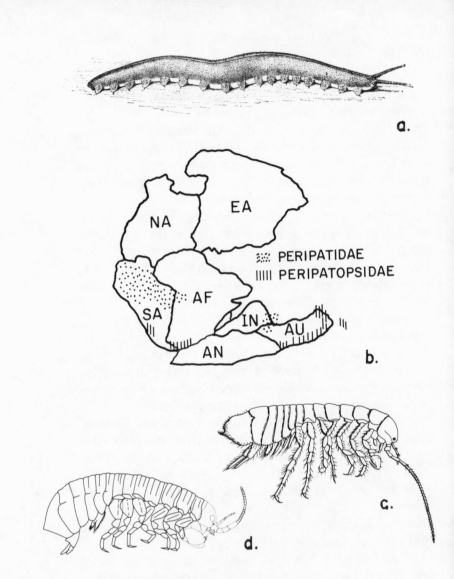

FIGURE 15 *a. Peripatopsis capensis* (from Shipley, after Sedgwick).
b. Distribution of the two families of Onychophora drawn approximately on a
map of the original single continent, Pangaea, which broke up into Eurasia
(EA), North America (NA), South America (SA), Africa (AF), Antarctica
(AN), Australia (AU), and India (IN). *c. Mesamphisopus capensis*, from Table
Mountain, a member of a group widely spread in Australia and New Zealand
and known in underground water in India (from Hutchinson after Barnard).
d. Protamphisopus wianamattensis, a fossil relative from Australia (from
Hutchinson after Nicholls).

most enamoured of the dark-green form of *P. capensis* and the comparable looking *P. balfouri*. Since his day, a brownish-rose species, *Opisthopatus roseus*, has been discovered in a very restricted area in the eastern Cape Province; this might have displaced *P. capensis* and *P. balfouri* in his admiration.

The seventy-odd species now known fall into two families distinguished by various technical anatomical details.[3] Usually the Peripatidae of the humid tropics have more than twenty-five legs, while the Peripatopsidae of the damp parts of the South Temperate Zone have a smaller and, within a species, less variable number of legs. If the present distributions of the two families are drawn on a map showing all the continents up against each other as they are now believed to have been at the end of the Paleozic era, about 225 million years ago, the possible significance of the distribution becomes apparent, though

3. The standard taxonomic treatment is E. L. Bouvier, Monographie des Onychophores, *Ann. Sci. Natur.* (ser. 9) 2:1–383, 1905; (ser 9) 5:61–318, 1907.

For later taxonomic and zoogeographical information, see G. E. Hutchinson, Observations on South African Onychophora, *Ann. S. Afr. Mus.* 25:337–40, 1929; R. F. Lawrence, A New Peripatopsid from the Table Mountain Caves, *Ann. S. Afr. Mus.* 30:101–07, 1931; S. M. Manton, Studies on the Onychophora V. Onychophora Found in Cape Colony, *Ann. Mag. Nat. Hist.* (ser. 11) 1:476–80, 1938; R. F. Lawrence, Note on a New Species of *Opisthopatus* (Onychophora), *Ann. Natal Mus.* 11:165–68, 1947. P. Brinck, Onychophora, *South African Animal Life. Results of the Lund University Expedition in 1950–1951*, ed. B. Hanstrom, P. Brinck, and G. Rudebeck (Stockholm: Almqvist Wiksell), vol. 4:7–32, 1956. Brinck points out that the stag beetles of the subfamily Lampriminae have a distribution today very like that of the Peripatopsidae but are represented by a fossil genus in the Baltic amber. He feels that this makes the distribution of the Onychophora by continental drift unconvincing. To me the zonal distribution of the two families, if they are genuine taxonomic entities, is highly suggestive.

not all zoologists accept this explanation unequivocally (figure 15b).

Peripatus lives in rotting wood and soil, feeding on insects, mites, and the like. It can squeeze, or perhaps more accurately flow, through very narrow cracks as the body-wall muscles in one part of the animal contract, putting pressure on the fluid contents of the uncontracted part.[4]

As a carnivore capable of hunting in very narrow passages, it has some similarity to a weasel. Like a weasel, it has to pay for this capacity. In the mammalian passage-hunter the long, narrow form is a very poor one for conserving heat in cold winter weather. In the invertebrate the extreme softness of the pliant body wall and lack of any kind of external skeleton makes water conservation a problem; at least the South African species require a relative humidity of 80 percent to remain alive. The areas where the animals live must have been quite humid ever since the continents began to drift apart. This continuous history of damp temperate conditions is also doubtless partly the cause of the extraordinary diversity of the Cape flora.

Morphologically the Onychophora evidently are not too far distant from the remote ancestors of insects, centipedes and millipedes, in some ways connecting these animals with segmented worms. There is a fossil form

4. For mode of locomotion in relation to habitat, see S. M. Manton, The Evolution of Arthropodan Locomotory Mechanisms. Part I. The Locomotion of *Peripatus*, *J. Linn. Soc. Lond.* (*Zool.*) 51:529–70, 1950. For the water relations, see S. M. Manton and A. Ramsay, Studies on the Onychophora 3. On the Control of Water Loss in *Peripatopsis*. *J. Exp. Biol.* 14:470–72. Though no one educated in zoology in Cambridge in my time could have failed to respond to the tradition of Balfour and Sedgwick, only Manton surpassed them in the study of the Onychophora.

Aysheaia pedunculata from ancient rocks in Canada which seems to me very clearly to be allied to the Onychophora.[5] It must have been marine, and it is clearly much more primitive than the modern species. In spite of the excellence of the fossils there is still argument about this animal and some people have rejected my interpretation of its structure and affinities.

It is easy to understand the excitement any zoologist acquainted with the structure, distribution, and mode of life of this strange animal would have when first meeting it in nature. There seem to be twelve species of Onychophora in South Africa, but two have never been fully described. One species, *Peripatopsis leonina*, used to live on the Lion's Head, a small peak near Table Mountain, but appeared extinct in 1927, when all possible localities in its old home had been burnt or cleared. One species is known from a single poorly preserved specimen from a place called Montagu about a hundred miles east of Cape Town; the specimen had been lying unexamined in the collections of the South African Museum and I described it as far as its poor state of preservation permitted. It must have a very limited range, and like *P. leonina* conceivably may be extinct. Most of the dozen South African members of the group are to some extent endangered.

There is a blind white species, *P. alba*, found in a cave on Table Mountain. It presumably squeezes through small cracks in the sandstone of the mountain, doubtless feeding on mites, springtails, and other minute insects. On a later visit to Cape Town with several other naturalists, I visited the cave, but we found nothing, missing not only

5. G. E. Hutchinson, A Restudy of Some Burgess Shale Fossils, *Proc. U.S. Nat. Mus.* 78, Art. 2, 1930; G. E. Hutchinson, *Aysheaia* and the General Morphology of the Onychophora, *Amer. J. Sci.* 267: 1062–66, 1969.

the then-undiscovered *P. alba* but also an extraordinary crustacean *Spelaeogriphus lepidops*, put in its own order, the Spelaeogriphaceae, which was found there still later.[6]

Table Mountain is also the home of another most peculiar aquatic crustacean called *Mesamphisopus capensis* (figure 15c), which lives in the flat valleys of the table top of the mountain. These valleys are believed to have been formed late in the Mesozoic era and have probably been wet ever since. *Mesamphisopus* is a distant aquatic relative of the sowbugs or wood lice, living in waterlogged moss on Table Mountain and some of the mountains to the east of the Cape Peninsula. Its close relatives are all found in Australia and New Zealand, and it has more distant affinities to a subterranean Indian form. An Australian fossil form is also known (figure 15d). It clearly belongs with the South African Peripatopsidae as a faunal element most easily distributed by continental drift. It has survived because its habitats have been wet and mossy since the end of the Cretaceous period about sixty million years ago, their main change having been a gradual elevation from a little above sea level to about one thousand meters today. All this time they provided habitats not only for *Mesamphisopus*, but for a curious earthworm which has allied species on the mountains further east and is very characteristic of this type of locality.[7]

It is most peculiar that Lückhoff's lovely book on Table Mountain, in which the flora is described and beautifully illustrated, pays no attention to the small but

6. I. Gordon, On *Spelaeogriphus*, a New Cavernicolous Crustacean from South Africa, *Bull. Brit. Mus. Nat. Hist. Zool.* 5:31–47, 1957.

7. K. H. Barnard, A Study of the Fresh Water Isopodan and Amphipodan Crustacea of South Africa, *Trans. R. Soc. S. Afr.* 14:139–215, 1927.

intellectually rewarding invertebrates of the mountain.[8]

Of my first journey nine hundred miles northwest I remember little save the Inselbergen, or flat-topped hills, in the most desert part of the route, the Great Karroo. Again, so far as inanimate nature was concerned, the nineteenth-century illustrators seemed convincing, but when they saw the country it was alive with antelope and quagga or zebra. Although I spent most of my vacations traveling, the places I visited were at first always those in which aquatic insects could be found. Water being the limiting factor for man in much of the country, aquatic localities tended to occur near settlements and I was never able to see any of the larger mammals except baboons. In Knysna Forest a small herd of elephants survived; their footprints were visible, but the nature of the forest made observation of the animals themselves impossible.

The birds delighted me as soon as I landed and continued to do so for the whole of my two-year sojourn in the country. Very soon after settling in Johannesburg I find that I wrote, in a letter to my parents, about the strange behavior of the redknobbed or crested coot, *Fulica cristata*. The letter, recently found by my sister, is imperfect; it is dated in my mother's hand 7 September 1926, in the southern spring, but gives no hint as to where the observations were made. I suspect, however, that the birds were at Florida Lake, an artificial body of water a little to the west of Johannesburg; this lake had a splendid avifauna in the rich marginal vegetation. Nest-building by the coots is said to have been almost complete. One bird would rush at another and in doing so make a great noise. This attracted other coots and they all started rushing at each other in a heap. This happened three times during a period of an

8. C. A. Lückhoff, *Table Mountain. Our National Heritage after Three Hundred Years* (Cape Town: A. A. Balkem, 1951).

hour and a half one afternoon. Two birds were also observed rising up opposite each other in the water, throwing themselves backwards so that they formed a broad V, and then dispersing.

In another letter, of 19 April 1927, I described the game or dance of the hamerkop, scientifically *Scopus umbretta*, a peculiar ally of the storks. The bird is brown with a large, backwardly directed crest on its head. A few days before I wrote, three of these birds had flown down on to some stones by the river at a place called Waterval Boven in the eastern Transvaal, a town above a small but spectacular waterfall about 150 feet high. Two hamerkops then started a performance, taking turns standing on each other's back. The individual on top flapped its wings while the one below raised its tail while depressing its head (figure 16a).

Though at the time I was told that such behavior was known in the bird, it was apparently not properly described till much more recently.[9] The male getting up on to the female and standing on her back a number of times is a normal prelude to copulation. The reversal of position which I had observed, in what is now usually called reciprocal false mounting, seems to occur mainly when there are other hamerkops around, as if it were a method of indicating that the couple engaging in the dance is a mated pair. Nothing of this was known at the time of my letter, so I merely added, "From the attitude I imagine that it is a highly symbolised mating act, which would be called a sublimation in human psychology." My interest

9. R. F. Stowell, A Note on the Behaviour of *Scopus umbretta*, *Ibis* 96:150–51, 1954; C. F. Goodfellow, Display in the Hamerkop, *Scopus umbretta*, *Ostrich* 29:1–4, 1958; M. P. Kahl, Observations on the Behaviour of the Hamerkop *Scopus umbretta* in Uganda, *Ibis* 109:25–32, 1967; A. S. Cheke, Copulation in the Hammerkop *Scopus umbretta*, *Ibis* 110:201–03, 1968.

in psychoanalysis, developed in Cambridge, was clearly continuing in South Africa.

Once in Johannesburg I discovered that my duties were to run the elementary lab and to give a course on contemporary problems in biology. This sounded nice enough. I also learned that there were three junior lecturers in the department, all women, one Afrikaner, one English, and one Jewish, which again sounded reasonable. When I got to know these ladies better, I discovered that they were essentially readers, in the medieval sense of the word. They read lectures prepared by the professor. The departmental library, which constituted the entire collection of zoological books and periodicals in the university, was kept in the professor's room, which did not make for easy access. My course at first was not good, but it would have been better if it had not been attended by the professor. I gradually came to realize that I was not wanted, and during my second year this was made clear by my being suspended from all teaching duties. Unlike my predecessor, I was not physically thrown out.

Early in 1977 a graduate students' laboratory in the zoology department of the University of the Witwatersrand was named the G. Evelyn Hutchinson Research Laboratory.[10]

Even if I had been properly employed as a teacher, I should have had ample time for research, as my function was largely to give prestige to a department which was quite well supplied with additional outlets for the professor's words.

I had been much impressed by a paper by C. C. Hurst on the genus *Rosa*, a reprint of which, given by the

10. I owe this charming act of restitution, which took place on 18 July 1977, to the present professor of zoology, Hugh E. Paterson, and the vice-chancellor of the university, Professor G. R. Bozzoli.

author to my father, I had read on the voyage out.[11] I began to wonder if animal genera with lots of species would resemble or differ from what Hurst had found. Suspecting from what was already known of the taxonomy of African water bugs that large genera would occur, I decided that a study of taxonomy, distribution, cytology, and ecology over a wide area on one or two such genera would be rewarding. It was first necessary to get the taxonomy in order. Anyone whom I knew or met was asked to collect and they were all extremely kind. I traveled widely in the vacations. Most of what I set out to do has not yet been done, though we know now that the cytology would have been rather uninformative. In spite of Hurst on *Rosa* I had already suspected this from Ethel Browne Harvey's work on the chromosomes of American species of *Notonecta*, which we had discussed together in Naples.

What I did do was to bring some degree of order into the systematics of the Notonectidae, the tiny family Pleidae, which was put with the latter until recently, and the Corixidae of South Africa.[12] When I started work, there were eight species of Notonectidae, one of Pleidae, and five of Corixidae known south of the Zambezi. When I

11. C. C. Hurst, Chromosomes and Characters in *Rosa* and their Significance in the Origin of Species, *Experiments in Genetics* (Cambridge University Press) 38:534–50, 1925.

12. G. E. Hutchinson, A Revision of the Notonectidae and Corixidae of South Africa. *Ann. S. Afr. Mus.* 25:359–474, 1929. Perhaps the most interesting observation in this paper relates to the existence of several color morphs in *Micronecta dimidiata* (sub *piccanim*) in the coastal part of the western Cape Province. The typical unmarked form occurs throughout most of this area and indeed is distributed widely in central Africa, but in the coastal belt a regularly arranged series of well-marked forms, starting with *audax* in the west, then *variegata*, and finally, eastward, *nigroclavata* with the heaviest dark markings, form a conspicuous cline, even though *dimidiata* is present and invariant. The adaptive meaning of such a case is very obscure.

finished my big paper on the group, just before I left Johannesburg, it included eighteen species of Notonectidae, two of Pleidae, and twenty of Corixidae, though of the last-named family two or three species are probably synonyms of two of the others. A few of the species added were already known from central Africa, but most were new. Though I would have described them better today, all seem to have proved recognizable to other workers. With the apparent exception of one endemic species of small back swimmer, *Anisops hypatia*, which is certainly not of Australian origin, none of the water bugs showed an African distribution like the Onychophora, the earthworms, the Crustacea of Austral affinities, or for that matter the wonderful flowering bushes of the family Proteaceae. The other water bugs fell into two groups. One contained those living in temperate South Africa, from the Cape north and east; high altitude compensated for low latitude as one approached the Transvaal. In contrast to these insects were the species coming from tropical central Africa down the low-lying east coast, through Natal. Some of these seemed to stop short of the southern tip of South Africa as if they had not yet had time to get there. The two types of distribution (figure 16b) seem reasonable and can, of course, be paralleled in other animals. The temperate South African group, however, would primarily be expected to consist of aquatic animals with fairly good power of dispersal but definite ranges of temperature tolerance. For a terrestrial animal the environments near the coast and far inland are very different, but if an aquatic form can find its medium, it is not directly

---

For problems of distribution, see The Zoogeography of the African Aquatic Hemiptera in Relation to Past Climatic Change, *Int. Rev. gesamten Hydrobiol. Hydrogr.* 28:436–68, 1933 (the case of *Glaenocorixa* reported here is spurious).

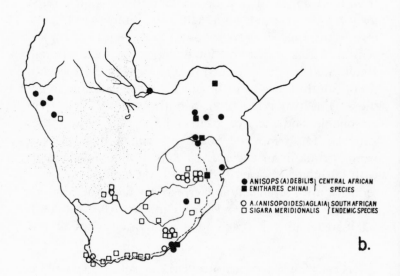

FIGURE 16 *a*. A pair of hamerkops, *Scopus umbretta*, engaged in reciprocal false mounting. *b*. Typical South African distributions of water bugs; the broken line delineates the limit of the frostless coastal zone in South Africa, down which central African species seem to move.

influenced by the humidity of air or soil. As I was working with aquatic insects the distinction that I observed probably appeared simpler and sharper than it would have had I been concerned with some other group.

As it became known that I was studying South African water bugs, many people sent me material from other parts of Africa. There was much exploration of central African waters going on at the time, and I was asked to determine specimens from Ethiopia, Uganda, and Kenya. The most exciting thing to turn up in this work was the presence of occasional species allied to European corixids in the higher parts of central Africa. In the genus *Corixa* itself, which occurs in Europe, western Asia, and Africa north of the Sahara, a new species *C. mirandella* was taken in Lake Naivasha in Kenya. Moreover, two female specimens, which lacked most of the best discriminant characters, but were clearly referable to the same genus, were present in the collections of Scott and Omer-Cooper, from a locality high in the mountains of Ethiopia. The two seemed different from each other and are now obviously referable to *C. frigidae* and *C. monticola*, more recently described by Linnavuori, from this region.[13]

When I was working on these distributional problems the study of early man in Africa was just beginning. R. A. Dart was professor of anatomy at the University of the Witwatersrand and he was extremely kind to me. The memory of having the original *Australopithecus* skull in my hands still thrills me. This discovery of R. B. Young, who obtained the skull from a mine manager, and of Dart, who described it, was, of course, followed by the lasting activity of Robert Broom in South Africa and L. S. B.

13. R. Linnavuori, Hemiptera of the Sudan, with Remarks on Some Species of the Adjacent Countries. The Aquatic and Subaquatic Families, *Ann. Zool. Fenn.* 8:340–66, 1971.

and Mary Leakey in central Africa. Along with the paleontological investigations, there was great activity in stratigraphic geology. Clear evidence of periods of very high water levels in the basins and of glaciation on the mountains of central Africa was soon forthcoming. Although the correlation between high lake levels and glaciations which was first postulated is now known to be only partially valid, it was natural at first to suppose that the ancestors of *Corixa mirandella* and some other species had moved from the Mediterranean lands down the Nile Valley in a cool wet time; this idea can, in fact, be traced back to what Darwin knew of the montane flora of tropical lands when he wrote the *Origin of Species*.

Broom, who was to contribute so much to human paleobiology after the period of which I am writing, was a most strange man. His original interest was in the homologies of the vomer, a bone in the roof of the mouth in lower vertebrates. He had a medical degree, and for a time after a dispute with the University of Stellenbosch— one of the trustees is said to have claimed that Broom was too interested in his daughter—he practiced medicine in a remote country district. He made a large collection of Permo-triassic fossils which he apparently sold to the American Museum of Natural History and then got a grant to travel to New York to study there. This outraged some people in Africa. Broom replied by calculating the number of Permo-triassic fossils naturally exposed each year and destroyed by weathering because they were not collected. His collection was minuscule compared to this.

He once gave a lecture at Yale, drawing on the board, with a single unbroken line, the whole skeleton of the fossil reptile *Pareiasaurus*. He spoke only of the anatomy and phylogeny of his fossils during the lecture, with no hint of his views on evolutionary mechanisms. At that time there was a superintendent of a block of apartments in New Haven who looked like a Byzantine icon of Saint Paul and who spent his free time attending public lectures. In the discussion he tried to bait Broom on the religious aspects of evolution, assuming the lecturer to be an agnostic. Broom then remarked that his private belief was that every evolutionary line was entrusted by God to an angel or archeus, but unfortunately some of the angels were fallen. This rather Gnostic concept so outraged one paleontologist of eminence who was present that he insisted that Broom had devoted his lecture, rather than an aside in the discussion, to this somewhat unusual view, and in so doing had insulted the intelligence of his audience.

Though I traveled over a large part of the damper portion of the western Cape Province and visited Rhodesia and the Linyanti River, on the banks of which most bushes seemed to harbor a gorgeous roller or bee eater, the most interesting part of the country in retrospect was the Zoutpansberg Mountains, a range running east and west across the northern part of the Transvaal, a little south of the Limpopo River. The range produces a rain shadow, with a wet southern slope and a dry area to the north. Standing high on the southern side one can look down on a humid subtropical forest, with a great diversity of species, each tree looking like a bubble of a different shade of green.

The region was inhabited by a tribe called the Bavenda, who appear to have come from central Africa within historical times.[14] They were very conscious of their

---

14. The standard work on the Bavenda is H. A. Stayt, *The Bavenda* (Oxford, 1931; reprinted F. Cass, 1968). Though I was fairly sure that I had been told about the xylophones either by Mr. Stayt, Professor Lestrade, or Mrs. Hoernlé, I can find nothing in this book to support my memory, which therefore may be a fantasy. The great dignity and beauty of the young woman may in part reflect the fact that women apparently played a greater social and religious role in Bavenda culture than was usual among other Bantu peoples.

culture; I was told that they kept a standard xylophone against which ordinary instruments were tuned. Once when I was in this region I wandered off by myself, leaving the rest of a small party from the University of the Witwatersrand; I came accidentally into a Bavenda village, a group of round huts, scrupulously neat and clean, but all apparently empty. Then, as I walked through the settlement, I saw a young woman bathing a small baby in a metal basin. Rather embarrassed, I asked her the way to Louis Trichardt, the little town where we were staying, at the base of the mountains. She stood up, naked above the waist, with some bracelets and a leather skirt, raised her arm, and slowly swung it round pointing in the direction that I was to go. In the few seconds that this took I was given a vision of human dignity so lasting that whenever I hear these two words, rather overworked in political contexts as they are, their meaning is always that young Bavenda woman.

In 1927, Lancelot Hogben was appointed professor of zoology at the University of Cape Town. He had heard of me from Nancy Southward, the former wife of a music master at Gresham's. She had later been a great friend of my biology teacher "P." Lancelot Hogben knew that I was in difficulties with Fantham and thought at first that he would offer me a position. He asked me to work in his lab in the southern summer of 1927–28. It was then evident to both of us that I was not the kind of person he wanted. He did, however, suggest that I write to Yale, which suggestion proved critical to the material development of my career. He also was responsible for my finding what I really wanted to do. For these two things I am deeply grateful to him.

Lancelot looked like the self-portrait of Aubrey Beardsley in the Tate Gallery, though no one seemed to have noticed this. He was brought up in a very strict

Protestant sect, I think the Straighter Plymouth Brethren. He had become a Marxist but did not fully realize how much of his personality was invariant under this transformation. When I knew him, he sometimes gave the impression of much disliking nature. He had, with Marx, ultimately little use for an explanation that was not the basis for a change.

Like Oscar Wilde, he tended to believe that one's first duty in life was to be as artificial as possible, but for Lancelot Hogben the artificiality could, in fact should, be mass-produced. I think he was intensely unhappy in Cape Town. He was extremely able intellectually and initially, as a lecturer at the Imperial College of Science in South Kensington, had done beautiful work on the pigmentary effector system and other aspects of the endocrinology of the lower vertebrates. When I knew him, he seemed to have lost all sense of scientific direction. Later, he came into his own as one of the most skillful writers on mathematics, science, and linguistics for the intelligent general reader that the century has produced. *Mathematics for the Million* was literally what its title proclaimed it to be. In Cape Town this side of his mind had hardly begun to show. He wrote a little rather desperate but technically skillful poetry, some of which was published under a pseudonym in *Voorslag*, the short-lived literary magazine that had Roy Campbell among its founders, though he rapidly resigned from its staff.[15]

15. Lancelot Hogben's most important early works are *The Pigmentary Effector System: A Review of the Physiology of Colour Response* (Edinburgh and London: Oliver Boyd, 1924) and *The Comparative Physiology of Internal Secretion* (Cambridge: Cambridge University Press, 1927). His most widely known later works are probably *Mathematics for the Million; a Popular Self Educator* (London: Allen & Unwin, 1936, and numerous subsequent editions and translations); *Science for the Citizen: A Self Educator Based on the Social Background*

Lancelot Hogben was married to Enid Charles, who was a mathematician by training. She gave me the most peculiar impression of being a harmonious mixture of the most improbably diverse elements. She was usually very reserved in speech, though never in an unfriendly manner. Though highly intelligent in an abstract way, I can remember nothing that she ever said. She was physically very attractive and occasionally quite provocative. I think at such times she enjoyed disturbing men and trusted them to enjoy being disturbed by her, with no thought of anything further. I once knew her to streak through a crowded room, the occupants all male, when she had been having a bath at one end of the house and all the bath towels were in a cupboard at the other end; she rightly judged her figure to be up to the occasion. She usually wore four or

---

of *Scientific Discovery* (London: Allen & Unwin, 1938, and numerous subsequent editions and translations); and *From Cave Painting to Comic Strip*: *A Kaleidoscope of Human Communication* (London: M. Parrish, 1949). Early in life he rather improbably wrote *Alfred Russel Wallace, the Story of a Great Discoverer* (London: Society for Promoting Christian Knowledge, 1918).

As well as numerous other scientific expository works he published *Exiles of the Snow, and other Poems* (London: A. C. Fifield, 1918). Neither these poems nor the brief work on Wallace have been available to me. The poems mentioned in the text are probably to be identified with Philip Page, Seven Sonnets, *Voorslag 1*, no. 11, 3–9, 1927. I am reasonably certain that I validly remember line eleven of the second sonnet, "Illness and household tasks and debt and rent," as belonging in a poem, part of a series, that a mutual friend told me had been written by Lancelot Hogben. If I am right about this, the sequence celebrating a lost love, though slightly Marxian in that poverty is the root of tragedy, is curiously romantic. The two lines quoted are from the beginning of sonnet 7. *Voorslag* was founded by a group that included Roy Campbell, who, however, resigned with "much pleasure," as is noted in the third issue. This issue, nevertheless, contains an article of his and an important poem, "To a young man with pink eyes."

five immense silver rings and possibly smoked more cigarettes in a quite long life than anyone else had ever done. She had clearly taken delight in childbearing and was an admirable mother to her four. She wrote a book called *The Twilight of Parenthood*, which lamented the decline of the specific fertility rate of women during the twentieth century and expressed a most improbable fear that it might approach zero.[16] I think she enjoyed everything she did and was the only reason that her husband survived this period of his life. Later, she became an important demographer working in Southeast Asia. "And now as evening closes on our laughter / I brood on her tranquility again."

Hogben had become interested temporarily in chemical oceanography and did a study on the pH of the water on either side of the discontinuity separating the water masses of the Atlantic and Indian oceans, south of the Cape of Good Hope. Having discovered that I was much more the old-fashioned naturalist and much less *le dernier cri*, or the coming man, than Nancy Southward, who anyhow hardly knew me, had led him to believe, he suggested that, with one or two other people, I have a look at the chemistry and biology of the *vleis*, or shallow lakes, near Cape Town.

The Cape Peninsula is separated from the mainland by a flat, broad, sandy isthmus called the Cape Flats. On this there are several coastal lakes lying in shallow dammed valleys, the most important being Zeekoe, Ronde, and Princess Vleis. They are eutrophic, slightly saline and alkaline, and have a qualitatively rich fauna and flora. In complete contrast to these are several reservoirs on Table Mountain, very dilute, with brown water and little

16. Enid Charles, *The Twilight of Parenthood* (New York: Norton, 1934), also published as *The Menace of Under-population, a Biological Study of the Decline of Population Growth* (London: Watts, 1936).

phytoplankton. I knew some of these places from my water bug work. Having got started, I realized that at last I had found what I wanted to do.

Back in Johannesburg, I was relieved of all teaching, for which I was deemed incompetent. Professor J. A. Wilkinson, the professor of inorganic chemistry at the University of the Witwatersrand, had been a student of my father's and offered to make some space available for limnological chemistry in his department.

By great good fortune, H. W. Harvey's *The Biological Chemistry and Physics of Sea Water* was published in 1928.[17] I suspect I ordered it from Heffer's, the Cambridge book shop, where I have had an account for fifty-five years. Without this admirable book and the *Standard Methods of Water Analysis* of the American Public Health Association,[18] the best-equipped laboratory would have been useless.

Another former student of my father's, Dr. A. W. Rogers, had become director of the Geological Survey of the Union of South Africa. He was much interested in the past climates of southern Africa and in this connection had studied the saucer-shaped depressions that occur throughout the southeastern Transvaal and some other parts of the country, and which are usually called pans.[19] These depressions were clearly formed under more arid conditions than exist in many of the areas in which they occur today. They were certainly primarily due to deflation or wind erosion, but insofar as they might have contained a little water, at least at some times of the year, they were

17. H. W. Harvey, *The Biological Chemistry and Physics of Sea Water* (Cambridge: Cambridge University Press, 1928).

18. American Public Health Association, *Standard Methods for the Examination of Water and Sewage*, 5th ed. (New York, 1923).

19. A. W. Rogers, Post-Cretaceous Climates of South Africa, *S. Afr. J. Sci.* 19:1–31, 1922.

doubtless visited by vast herds of ungulates which probably carried away mud on their hooves and so contributed to the excavation. Comparable basins occur in Texas.

A group of very large pans, most of which are now perennially filled with water, is found in the Ermelo district of the Transvaal. This group consists of Lake Chrissie, Lake Banagher, Magdalenasmeer, Eilandspan, the Blaauwater Pans, and some others. They looked particularly attractive and several of us from the university visited them in February and May of 1928. A number of smaller pans nearer Johannesburg were also studied. Though we had makeshift equipment and no boat, except on Lake Chrissie, it was possible to learn a great deal about these extraordinary basins.

They varied in an astonishing manner. One basin contained fresh, soft water with a rich flora of desmids; at the other extreme there was saline eutrophic water, soupy with the blue-green alga *Nodularia*. Most typically the lakes were slightly saline and alkaline and were either very turbid with suspended mud and colloidal silica or had sepia-colored water, apparently due to the accumulation of a peaty extract of decomposing wind-blown grass. Nothing like the last-named type of lake had been described in the limnological literature; of this I knew nothing at the time.

One invertebrate zoologist had visited the area, an English amateur called P. A. Methuen,[20] who had gone there in 1908 with Colonel Richard Meinertzhagen, the well-known ornithologist. Methuen had described an extraordinary looking water flea, *Daphnia gibba*, which proved to be common; it was accompanied by two other crustaceans, both diaptomid copepods, the smaller *Para-*

20. P. A. Methuen, On a Collection of Fresh Water Crustacea from the Transvaal, *Proc. Zool. Soc.* (London), 1910, 148–66.

diaptomus transvaalensis and the larger *Lovenula excellens*. Later work has shown that in semiarid regions this kind of association is common. The ideas of my friend John L. Brooks, who has given much thought to such cases, suggest that the association develops in lakes to which fish have no access, so that no upper limit to the size of the small crustacea is placed by predators picking off the big ones.[21]

When I returned to Cambridge on my way to America, Penelope Jenkin, whom I had known as a student, and who has since done most beautiful work on the limnological aspects of flamingos,[22] showed me August Thienemann's newly published *Die Binnengewässer Mitteleuropas*.[23] Reading this, I learned how the Lake Chrissie pans fitted, as new categories, into the scheme of lake classification that was being developed in Europe. I also came to see, reading this book after Elton's *Animal Ecology*, how all the ways of looking at nature that I had acquired in a random, disorganized way could be focused together on lakes as microcosms.[24] I had, in fact, become a limnologist.

21. J. L. Brooks and S. I. Dodson, Predation, Body Size, and Composition of Plankton, *Science* 150:28–35, 1965; J. L. Brooks, The Effects of Prey Size Selection by Lake Planktivores, *System. Zool.* 17:273–91, 1968.

22. P. M. Jenkin, The Filter-Feeding and Food of Flamingoes (Phoenicopteri), *Phil. Trans. Roy. Soc. B.* 240:401–93, 1957.

23. A. Thienemann, *Die Binnengewässer*. Vol. 1, *Die Binnengewässer Mitteleuropas* (Stuttgart: Schweizerbart'sche Verlagsbuchhandlung, 1925).

24. C. S. Elton, *Animal Ecology* (London: Sidgwick & Jackson, 1927).

CHAPTER EIGHT

NEW ENGLAND MORAL
TO ADORN THE TALE

LANCELOT HOGBEN MOST KINDLY WROTE a very laudatory letter to Professor Ross G. Harrison, recommending me for anything that happened to be available. Harrison was in Naples on sabbatical leave, but the letter ultimately reached Professor L. L. Woodruff, who was acting chairman of the zoology department at Yale, and from him I received a Sterling Fellowship application form. The deadline for such a fellowship had passed by March 31, but I decided, nevertheless, to cable my qualifications to Woodruff, using the numbers of the application blank. The overseas telegram cost five pounds; I felt rather as though I had placed a large bet on an improbable horse; it was in fact the only thing I could do. Shortly after this, Harold Kirby, who was well known for his work on the curious flagellates that live in the guts of termites and assist in the digestion of wood, received an excellent offer from the University of California late in the academic year and so was leaving Yale rather unexpectedly. As a result of this, Woodruff cabled me on May 17, offering me an instructorship, and I immediately accepted.[1] I later learned

1. All the extant documents relating to my initial appointment at Yale are in the Yale University Archives, Sterling Memorial Library, Ross Granville Harrison Papers, ser. no. 4, box 45, folder 213.

that the sheer improbability of receiving an application by transatlantic cable from the Southern Hemisphere had worked strongly in my favor.

My final academic appearance at the University of the Witwatersrand was before a committee or court of inquiry called to examine my dismissal. Fantham had given notice that my services were no longer required in November 1927, and had asked for and received my resignation. My friend Professor H. Stephen, an eminent organic chemist who had come to Johannesburg about the same time as I had, told me that it was believed that in not trying me out for a whole two years Fantham was acting illegally. The Lecturers' Association, which looked after the interests of the nonprofessorial faculty, wanted to demand an inquiry on these grounds. The principal of the university, H. R. Raikes, agreed to try to get my resignation withdrawn and so reopen the question of my dismissal, provided that the Lecturers' Association remained discreetly in the background. Both he and I felt that if they did not, they would received a bad snub and I should not get any consideration from the senior faculty because many of the professors were afraid of the Lecturers' Association and took every available opportunity to oppose it.

The principal, whose early career had been in the Royal Air Force, was hardly an academic type, but he was a most fair-minded and sensible man. Incidentally, his connection with the air force enabled him to have an aerial photograph of a pan near Johannesburg made for me, a very nice and useful parting present, now published several times.

The inquiry took place on 25 April. The Bishop of Johannesburg, the Right Reverend A. B. L. Karney, was in the chair, smoking a long and thin cigar. The other members of the committee were Sir Robert Kotze, a distinguished mining engineer, Professor R. B. Young, through whom the type of *Australopithecus africanus* came from Taungs to Professor Dart's laboratory, O. K. Williamson, the professor of medicine, and the registrar of the university.

On arriving I discovered that Fantham and I were to give our evidence in each other's presence, which, perhaps naively, I had not expected. Fortunately I had very carefully written out, and so could read, everything that I wanted to say. I wish I still had this statement. Almost all that is now available about the inquiry is contained in part of a letter to my parents which my sister found while I was writing this book, and which I have copied almost verbatim.

The proceedings were opened by a representative of the Lecturers' Association formally presenting the case. Fantham was then called and started by attempting to discredit the association; this was ruled *ultra vires* by the bishop. Fantham then gave an account of my career which developed into a series of personal attacks, delivered without any reference to the chronological sequence of events, and culminating with the glorious indictment that I had shown myself unwilling to listen to the ends of his conversations. Since such conversations were often vituperative monologues about other faculty members, which might last for up to an hour and a half, I was not surprised that faint wry smiles were detectable on the faces of some members of the committee.

My turn then came. I began by thanking the Fanthams for certain kindnesses when I was ill during my first term. I then pointed out that the sequence of events was hardly considered in Fantham's presentation. I read the account of all my activities in relation to Fantham, the students, and the research of the department. This document contained certain statements that Fantham, in his rebuttal, claimed to be false, though some members of the committee already knew them to be true. The committee then began its private deliberations, while Fantham and I were left, waiting to be recalled, walking around on a lawn in front of the building where the committee was meeting. He tried to be affable, I tried to reciprocate.

It was, of course, perfectly obvious that I could not continue to teach in Fantham's department. All that I asked was that the pension premiums that I had paid not be forfeited and that the debt that I legally owed the university on my passage money to South Africa be remitted. After a short deliberation by the committee we were called back and I was informed that my requests were granted. I was, moreover, told privately that although Fantham could not be removed for his actions, all the committee's sympathy was for me. I suspect that whatever the merits of my case may or may not have been, Fantham's extreme incompetence in presenting his was enough to insure that a favorable decision on my requests was handed me on a silver platter.

I was succeeded by C. J. van der Horst, a Dutch zoologist of great distinction who had done important work on the nervous systems of fishes and on the acorn worms or Enteropneusta, a group of peculiar marine animals with seemingly vertebrate affinities.

As the result of some unfathomable process, Fantham was appointed, in 1932, to the chair of zoology at McGill University in Montreal; van der Horst succeeded him at the Witwatersrand. The new professor immediately wrote to tell me that the departmental library was no longer housed in his personal laboratory.

Fantham died in 1937. According to his obituary in *Nature*, at his death the students of McGill "mourned the loss of a friend."[2] Evidently, there were aspects of his character that I failed to appreciate.

2. Professor H. B. Fantham, *Nature* (London) 140:1001, 1937.

My appointment having ended just before the southern winter vacation gave me a couple of months to get to New Haven. My memories of the journey are vague except for one incident. On reaching New York I discovered that any tourist passengers from South Africa had to go to Ellis Island. This was due to a somewhat stricter medical examination being imposed on lower-class than on first-class immigrants, which the consulate in Johannesburg was not authorized to arrange and which could not be given in London because I had started from Johannesburg. Ellis Island was, however, closed when finally the immigration authorities got to tourist aliens. This meant spending the night on the *Mauretania*. As the tourist accommodation was cleaned and tidied for the return trip before the rest of the ship, being no doubt dirtier and untidier, the few detained passengers were transferred to first-class accommodation. My main memory of this was encountering my first hemipterous insect within the geographical boundaries of the New World, a specimen of *Cimex lectularius*, the common bedbug, in the washbasin of the first-class cabin.

The architectural beauties of Ellis Island were not entirely lost on me, and it gave a fine view of the Statue of Liberty, as has often been observed. What did perplex me was the way of writing practiced by all the minor civil servants; they attacked the initial letter of each word with a series of limbering-up movements, like a golfer preparing for a stroke, before the pen was actually committed to paper. This enormously increased the time that had to be spent on each immigrant and so no doubt the number of immigration officials employed. When I think of these little men and then of the courteous and efficient immigration officers of more recent years, any temptation to *laus temporis acti* evaporates. Finally the formalities were completed, the few immigrants to New England being escorted to a train in Grand Central Station in New York by a guide or guardian provided by the Immigration Service.

The Yale into which I then entered consisted for me, for several years, of the Osborn Zoological Laboratory. There was no college system then, and even when it was established, in the early 1930s, practically no scientists were taken in as fellows of colleges. Harrison was not made an associate fellow of Trumbull College until his retirement. We were clearly contaminant and dangerous, so that for quite a long time there was almost no way of knowing anyone outside the laboratory.

Since I had been a student at Cambridge, I was, of course, familiar with the names of the two most respected members of the department of zoology at Yale, Professor Ross Granville Harrison and Professor Lorande Loss Woodruff. Both proved initially somewhat reserved but kind men, though in most other ways they were quite different. I slowly became well acquainted with both of them.

Harrison was the greatest scientist whom I have known continuously, week by week, over a long period of time (figure 17).[3] In age, I fitted into the span of his own family, who became friends, and I think I saw all sides of his character. He probably represented as well as or better than any other of his immediate predecessors or contemporaries, the spirit of American biology in the first third of this century.

It was often said, as for instance at the time of the first public awareness of the Manhattan Project and later at the establishment of the National Science Foundation, that American science had been largely applied, dependent

3. R. G. Harrison, *Organization and Development of the Embryo*, Silliman Lectures, vol. 42, ed. Sally Wilens (New Haven and London: Yale University Press, 1969).

FIGURE 17 Ross Granville Harrison, from a drawing by Joseph
Oppenheim in the Osborn Memorial Laboratories, Yale University
(by permission of the Department of Biology, Yale University).

on Europe for its fundamental basis. This may have been partly true of the easily applicable sciences. So far as much of biology went, the charge was completely ridiculous. In the contiguous fields of genetics, cytology, and embryology, the last two now unnecessarily lengthened, prior to acronymization, into cell biology and developmental biology, the names of T. H. Morgan, E. B. Wilson, E. G. Conklin, and R. G. Harrison were venerated throughout the scientific world. Germany might have been in the same class and indeed provided the early inspiration to America, but no other country could approach the achievements of these four men. They were all students of W. K. Brooks of Johns Hopkins, whose portrait, that of a somewhat ungainly man, hung in Harrison's laboratory.[4] Brooks must have been the greatest advanced teacher of biology that the New World has produced, rivaling, or I suspect surpassing, the Swiss-born Louis Agassiz. Brooks was a classical descriptive embryologist who did important work on the development of various marine invertebrates. He also wrote, late in life, a philosophical work, *The Foundations of Zoology*. Though his embryological interests obviously set the stage for the later scientific activities of his students, there was little in the details of his researches or in the direction of his philosophical speculations to suggest what his students were going to do. He used to say that one of his greatest pleasures was to see a student outstrip him. Good as he was as a scientist, he must have quite often experienced this pleasure.

Brooks clearly loved teaching, he loved his students much as he loved his enormous dog Tige, and by this

4. The best account of W. K. Brooks still seems to be E. G. Conklin, William Keith Brooks, *Biograph. Mem. Nat. Acad. Sci.* 7:25–88, 1910. For Brooks's philosophical position, see *The Foundations of Zoology*, Columbia University Biological Series no. 5 (New York and London: Macmillan, 1899).

love he brought out latent capacities that might not otherwise have appeared. I once heard Hindemith do this for
an hour and a half with largely amateur singers in a quite
incredible concert of medieval music.

The four that I have mentioned—Morgan, Wilson,
Conklin, and Harrison—were far from being Brooks's
only distinguished students. In his case a single man seems
to have unwittingly determined the development of an
important branch of science, possibly in directions of which
he would not himself have approved. Although one cannot
know this, I firmly believe that without him scientific
history would have been different, at least for some decades.

Harrison made two major sets of discoveries, though
his researches extended well beyond either of them. The
first was to give a clear demonstration that in the development of the nervous system of vertebrates the motor nerves
grow out from the rudiments of the brain and spinal cord,
finding their way ineluctably to the correct muscles. How
this happens is not fully understood. In showing that it
does happen, and in disposing of alternative ideas that had
been suggested, Harrison invented the technique of tissue
culture, which has had innumerable applications in biology
and medicine.

Harrison's second major discovery, the ramifications
of which occupied most of the later part of his working
life, was the very unexpected fact that in the development
of any organ in vertebrates—in the first instance in the
eggs of salamanders—the three spatial axes are determined
separately. When an area in the embryo is set aside to
form a limb, it is first fixed that the front and back of the
area shall form the appropriate parts of the limb, it is
later fixed that the top and bottom shall be so determined,
and lastly that the left and right sides shall be developed
as such. This all happens before any trace of differentiation
of limb structure is visible. This implies that if the two

front limb areas are interchanged early, keeping the front to the front, normal limbs of the correct handedness are produced, even though a reversal of axis has inevitably taken place in the transplantation. If the process takes place late enough, though before any limb structure is apparent, the left limb will be on the right, the right on the left. At intermediate times the results can be quite complex, depending on whether the dorsal-ventral axis is yet determined.

Harrison showed this also to be true of the ear, and other workers, mainly his students, completed the demonstration for other organs. Joseph Needham suggested that these results could be explained by some hypothesis involving the lining-up of linear molecules in liquid crystals,[5] and Harrison, with my father's former associate Astbury, made a valiant attempt to find such a pattern by x-ray crystallography.[6] Though they did not succeed in this, as has no one else, their work marks the beginning of an attempt to interpret the visible structure of organisms in molecular terms.

The whole of Harrison's extraordinary work on organic symmetry and the spatial axes of organisms is an invitation to cultivate an open field for anyone perspicacious enough to do so. So far, such perspicacity seems not to have arisen. When it does, Harrison's greatness will again be fully appreciated.

Harrison was chairman of the department of zoology and also had the title of director of the Osborn Zoological Laboratory, though I never could learn where one function ended and the other began. He was an excellent chairman, tolerant on small and unimportant matters, adamant on

5. J. Needham, *Order and Life* (New Haven: Yale University Press, 1936).

6. R. G. Harrison, W. T. Astbury, and K. M. Rudall, An Attempt at an X-ray Analysis of Embryonic Processes, *J. Exp. Zool.* 85: 339–63, 1940.

matters of principle. As in all departments of any size, there were potential sources of jealousy and distrust. He managed to keep these sufficiently under control that even after his retirement and in the face of fairly catastrophic human problems, his standards persisted enough to give us a reputation for peaceful and reasonable conduct.

In those days, the chairman performed the function of director of graduate studies, which in Yale is now usually a separate office; later I was to hold it for seventeen years. In 1928, the number of graduate students was small. Only three Ph.D. degrees were awarded in 1929, and only one of the candidates, Victor C. Twitty, had been in residence during the previous year. Twitty was one of Harrison's most eminent students and many years after, in a book called *Of Scientists and Salamanders*, gave the best existing account of Harrison's way of work in the Osborn Laboratory.[7] Over my first ten years, the mean number of Ph.D.'s per year was about five, which, allowing for those who dropped out, would correspond to about twenty-five students being in residence at any one time. About half of these students were working with Harrison, and about a fifth with Woodruff. The other three-tenths would be working with the remaining senior members of the faculty, who seldom had more than one student at a time and often none.

The whole calendar of the department, whatever the views of the university, was set by the reproductive behavior of the salamanders of the genus *Ambystoma* used by Harrison and his students in their research.[8] The "operating season," when experiments could be done,

7. V. C. Twitty, *Of Scientists and Salamanders* (San Francisco and London: W. H. Freeman, 1966).

8. Harrison always insisted on *Amblystoma*, meaning wide-mouthed, rather than *Ambystoma*, which appears to have priority and is now the officially accepted name of the genus of salamanders on the eggs of which he worked.

began in March with the arrival of eggs from the southern states and ended around midsummer, when eggs from northern New England were available. The intervening period was a hectic one for Harrison and everyone associated with him. "The Chief," as he was always called, worked far into every night when eggs of the right stages of development were on hand, and at least all his more devoted students did likewise. Toward the end of the season, strawberries were appearing in the market and sometimes a night's work was capped by a feast of strawberries and cream. Since graduate examinations obviously could not be held at this time, the zoology department was unique among those in Yale in holding such examinations at the beginning of the academic year, in September.

During the years of prohibition, a second seasonal event, the ripening of grapes, greatly affected Harrison. He was one of a small but distinguished group of wine-makers among the Yale faculty. Some, I believe, aspired to champagne and Professor Selden Rose wrote a book on wine-making which was printed by the great typographer Carl Rollins and is now a collector's rarity.[9] Harrison was content with a good Chianti-like *vin ordinaire*, which afforded great pleasure in a world of bathtub gin or nothing at all.

Harrison's scientific attitude was basically that of the generation reacting to the great emphasis that had been placed on descriptive morphology and embryology following in the wake of a general recognition of the validity of the theory of evolution. Biological classification, the status of which in preevolutionary days was always prob-

9. R. Selden Rose, *Wine Making for the Amateur* (New Haven, Printed for members of the Bacchus Club, Type-set by Carl Purlington Rollins at the sign of the Chorobates, 515 copies, 1930).

lematic, had now become an expression of family relationships, much more distant than any recognized by human
genealogists, but no less real. Morphology, because it was
immediately apparent, naturally provided an initial guide
to these relationships; embryology, because it seemed to
show how the morphology might have come into existence,
could be used to validate or question the more obvious
evidence of adult structure. By about 1890, a reasonably
good understanding of the affinities of the various branches
of the animal kingdom was available; there are still lots of
questionable details but many of the ablest of the younger
generation felt it was time to pass on to something else.
The initial change came in the 1880s in Germany. The
results were at first confusing, but as the new data began
to fit together, developmental mechanics became a very
exciting area, attracting most of the best young American
zoologists. A deliberate effort was made by Brooks and his
British physiological colleague, H. Newell Martin, to send
students to Germany. Harrison went to Bonn to work with
Moritz Nussbaum. The new movement, when contrasted
with the taxonomically oriented insistence on problems of
descent, certainly involved a new paradigm in Thomas
Kuhn's sense. As in all such movements, enthusiasm may
carry the proponents of the new idea to unreasonable
lengths. Everything that was descriptive became outmoded. Museums were absurdly expensive ways of providing preserved material which could be studied more
cheaply, and fresh, by the simple process of travel, as
Brooks pointed out, contrasting Johns Hopkins with
Harvard, and by implication himself with the two Agas-
sizes. Among the generation to which Harrison belonged
experiment was the road to truth. I remember his once
saying to me that he did not believe the study of evolution
could be regarded as a truly scientific activity as it could
not be the subject of an experimental investigation. I

reminded him of astrophysics, which was at that time burgeoning.

He did not make the mistake that Morgan made when he wrote: "That the fundamental aspects of heredity should have turned out to be so extraordinarily simple supports us in the hope that nature may, after all, be entirely approachable. Her much advertised inscrutability has once more been found to be an illusion due to our ignorance."[10] Though part of the inscrutability of most recent contributions to the study of heredity is due to the growing incapacity of authors to write, the continued fragmentation of all branches of science is a testimony to the enormous, if not limitless, complexity of nature. Donna Haraway, in a deep overall study of the historic aspects of these problems, sees Harrison as a nonvitalistic organicist rather than a mechanist.[11] This seems also to have been Brooks's attitude, set forth in *The Foundations of Zoology*, though he believed that the organicist point of view had been established once and for all by Aristotle. Harrison would have been less interested in these philosophical aspects of development than was Brooks before him or Needham after him. He might even have felt that too much consideration of such things would keep him away from his laboratory. He did not, however, in any way scorn mathematical as opposed to philosophical theory

10. T. H. Morgan, *The Physical Basis of Heredity* (Philadelphia and London: J. B. Lippincott, 1919), p. 15.

11. D. J. Haraway, *Crystals, Fabrics and Fields*: *Metaphors of Organicism in Twentieth-Century Developmental Biology* (New Haven and London: Yale University Press, 1976). Haraway's paradigm change from mechanism to organicism, though contemporaneous with mine from descriptive to experimental, really refers to a rather different field. She is thinking about physiology in its widest sense, while I am concerned with zoology as it was ordinarily understood. Parts of one area are superposable on parts of the other so that the major changes give a complicated pattern.

and once told me that he believed that ultimately work might be done in purely theoretical biology as it was in theoretical physics. My own limnological studies were, of course, primarily observational, though I used such mathematics as were within my grasp. After his retirement, in 1944, when I was being considered for a professorship, Harrison wrote: "I say these things all the more cordially because he has worked in a field far removed from my own special interest—a field which I have learned to respect mainly through what I have seen of Hutchinson's work."[12] I was first shown this letter long after Harrison's death and value it as much as any tribute that I have received.

In one respect, Harrison had a direct influence on ecological thought. Late in life he became interested in allometric growth, the process by which different parts of an organism grow at different rates. It is usual to find that the size x of some organ is related to some standard measure y, such as the length or weight of the whole, by an expression of the form $x = by^k$.

If k is unity x and y will be strictly proportional, but with any other value of k, growth is allometric and the organism is changing its shape. Joseph Needham had emphasized that the measures x and y could be chemical rather than morphological, so expressing situations, very common in development, in which the overall chemical composition of an embryo is changing with age.

About this time, in the late 1930s and early 1940s, Edward S. Deevey and, a little later, Raymond Lindeman, were working on lake sediments and on food cycles in lakes. Deevey had been a graduate student and both were postdoctoral fellows in the Osborn Zoological Laboratory;

12. Yale University Archives, Ross Granville Harrison Papers, ser. no. 1, box B, folder 952, 1944.

they ate sandwich lunches in the attic of the building, Harrison presiding at the lunch club. There was, from time to time, considerable discussion of allometric growth at these gatherings. A study of Deevey's and Lindeman's papers shows how ecological thought was being influenced by such discussion.[13] Deevey in particular found evidence that the populations of animals might change over time in a way suggesting an allometric relationship to their resources.

Lorande Loss Woodruff[14] was a complementary antithesis to Harrison. He was greatly concerned with undergraduate teaching, was conventionally conservative in his political and religious loyalties, and had never ventured across the Atlantic. He was, however, a very well read man. Early after my appointment, he took me to a most moving performance, in the fraternity house of AΔK, of Thomas Dekker's *The Honest Whore*, directed by the eccentric John Berdan and acted, of course, entirely by young men. This was my first intimation of the artistic riches that might lurk behind neo-Gothic details in New Haven.

Woodruff's main research had been on the problem of the immortality of cell lines in one-celled animals, particularly various species of the slipper-animalcule *Paramecium*. It is obvious that if an organism reproduces itself by dividing in half, its lineage must be potentially

13. E. S. Deevey, Studies on Connecticut Lake Sediments III. The biostratonomy of Linsley Pond, *Amer. J. Sci.* 240:239–64, 313–38, 1942; R. L. Lindeman, The Trophic-Dynamic Aspect of Ecology, *Ecology* 23:399–418, 1942. The genesis and problems of publication of this seminal paper are discussed by R. E. Cook, Raymond Lindeman and the Trophic-Dynamic Concept in Ecology, *Science* 198:22–26, 1977.

14. A more detailed account of Woodruff is in press and will appear shortly in the *Biographical Memoirs* of the National Academy of Sciences.

immortal, though, of course, the immortality is only potential, overcrowding and starvation intervening to remove most lines. A belief had grown up, largely as the result of studies by Maupas in France, that the immortality depended on a process of conjugation, presumably analogous to fertilization in sexual reproduction, taking place between cells from time to time.

In the years between 1905 and 1914, Woodruff showed that with proper feeding *Paramecium* could be cultivated for an enormous number of generations without conjugation occurring. In the most critical experiment, a population persisted for 5,000 generations without conjugation, and in another, under somewhat less rigorous conditions, for over 24,000 generations, conjugation being almost certainly absent. Evidently this apparently sexual process was not needed to maintain a line. However, a curious fluctuation in division rate persisted in such cultures, even under the best conditions.

In 1914, Woodruff and Rhoda Erdmann found that this fluctuation corresponded to an internal nuclear reorganization in the *Paramecium* cell, which reorganization they paradoxically called *endomixis*, though they believed that no nuclear fusion or *mixis* occurred during the internal process. In this they proved to have been wrong. The small nuclei divide three times in the course of the process; all but two daughters degenerate and these two fuse to produce the nuclei of the next dozen or so generations. All this work made a great impression on the biological world. In the late 1920s, Woodruff was as well known in Europe as was Harrison. The ciliates such as *Paramecium* at that time seemed more primitive than we now believe them to be, and the processes by which they maintain the integrity of what is essentially a mass of somatic chromatin dividing in a rather untidy way, now appear less fundamental than they did in 1914. There was almost a feeling then that Maupas, having overemphasized the life-giving properties of sexuality, was being corrected in Puritan New England. The later discovery of mating-types by Sonnerborn, and Diller's correction of Woodruff and Erdmann's account of the solitary autogamic process by which the nuclei of *Paramecium* are reorganized, reduced Woodruff's position in the biological world before he was ready to pass into history. He undoubtedly felt this deeply. When his wife died in 1946, he was unable to weather the shock.

Woodruff was extremely interested in the history of biology and, from 1909 until he ceased teaching, he gave a course on the subject which must have been one of the earliest of its kind in an American university. He had a fine collection of the seventeenth- and eighteenth-century classics, and specialized in the life and work of the peculiar author of the name *Paramecium*, Sir John Hill. Though his knighthood was Swedish, given to him for introducing the work of Linnaeus to the British world of science, Hill was a versatile, indeed Figaroesque Englishman who had been a pharmacist, physician, actor, dramatist, botanist, zoologist, journalist, translator, and man-about-town. Some of his work, notably his introduction of staining techniques into microscopy and his studies on the anatomy of wood, proved ultimately to be of importance, but this was little appreciated during his lifetime. His publishers, and no doubt Hill himself, would have greatly liked the increased sales that might have been expected if F.R.S. could have appeared after his name on a title page. The Royal Society not being cooperative, Hill retaliated with *Lucina sine Concubitu*.[15] This work was a parody, a mock

15. Abraham Johnson [pseud. "Sir" John Hill], *Lucina Sine Concubitu*. A Letter Humbly Addressed to the Royal Society ... (London: M. Cooper, 1750, 48 pp.). The first edition is very rare and is

communication to the Royal Society, suggested by some lines in Virgil's *Georgics* which Dryden has neatly translated:

> The mares to cliffs of rugged rocks repair
> And, with wide nostrils, sniff the western air
> When (wondrous to relate) the parent wind,
> Without the stallion, propagates the kind.

In Hill's fantasy he concentrates material from the air with "a wonderful, cylindrical, catoptrical, rotundo-concavo-convex machine" electrified at one end; microscopic examination of the concentrate shows the presence of homunculi; these taken orally prove capable of getting a well-isolated chambermaid with child. Though in private Woodruff was able to enjoy this work on potential anemophily in *Homo sapiens*, and was delighted when he received a copy of a limited edition put out by the Golden Cockerell Press in 1930, no one would have supposed that had he not been elected to the National Academy in 1924 he would

---

not included in the British Library Catalogue of Printed Books; there appear to be copies at Cornell University, the University of Chicago, and the College of Physicians in Philadelphia. Four editions appeared in 1750 and it was reprinted in *Fugitive Pieces on Various Subjects. By Several Authors*, vol. 1 (London: R. and J. Dodsley, 1761) pp. 141–70 (this is probably the most accessible edition); by Edmund Goldsmid, Edinburgh, privately printed, 1885; and by the Golden Cockerell Press, Waltham St. Lawrence, 1930.

Two French translations seem to have appeared in 1750, one in London (trans. E. G. Colombe[?]), the other without place of publication. A further French edition (London: J. Wilcox, 1776), has appended *Concubitus sine Lucina*, attributed to Richard Roe. This is another, but rather verbose and feeble, hoax and is of no particular interest to students of the history of contraception. A reprint (Paris: Bibliothèque des Curieux), contains an "essai bibliographique par B. de Villeneuve." A Dutch version (The Hague: H. H. van Drecht), was issued as a second edition in 1779.

have responded with a delightfully bawdy tract. Few two men could have been more unlike than Woodruff and Hill.

It always seemed to me sad that Woodruff's timidity prevented him from visiting the places that his heroes had known. He may, however, have preferred them to have lived in a space as remote and inaccessible as the time that they inhabited.

My first teaching assignment was to the beginning course, Biology 10. Woodruff was in charge; either he or G. A. Baitsell gave a lecture a week to each of three lecture divisions, two meeting on Friday and one on Saturday, while there were, I think, nine laboratory divisions to which the rest of the staff lectured twice a week. I had two such divisions. These lectures were devoted primarily to the material to be studied practically. The textbooks used were Woodruff's *Foundations of Biology* and Baitsell's *Manual of Biological Forms*. Woodruff's textbook was a very good one; it is said to have been ascribed to Aristotle, Theophrastus, Vesalius, Hales, Buffon, Lamarck, and Wordsworth by various students taking an examination in another New England college. Actually, since Woodruff was a very literate man, all these authors had no doubt contributed to it indirectly.

I was, however, greatly disturbed by two aspects of this and other courses in Yale; the disturbance to some extent still persists. The first was the use of a required textbook with assigned readings; the second was the continual succession of tests and the correlative idea that one could become educated by piling up credits for a given number of courses.

I know that at Cambridge I was exceptionally lucky in having a father who could advise me from inside so that I could easily and fairly safely take my education into my own hands. I also realize that for many students this could be quite dangerous, though not as dangerous as many responsible senior people might believe. The absolute impossibility of getting self-educated at Yale worried me; the impossibility is now less absolute but it still worries me. I once had to advise a Yale freshman student, rather as a friend than in an official connection, about planning his courses. He intended to go into biology and is now a member of the National Academy of Sciences. I told him to go on taking one or two mathematics courses each year until he got a D. I think actually he survived with a C in Advanced Differential Equations in his junior year. Today, when a computer doesn't know one D from another, one could hardly give such advice, but in the 1930s it payed off handsomely.

The Yale into which I was trying to fit myself, as far as possible by modifying my immediate surroundings rather than myself, was very different from the present institution. Intellectual excellence was far less important than social position among the undergraduates. The teaching assistants and junior faculty in fact appeared to me to be like highly intelligent Greek slaves serving young Roman patricians. On a short visit to Ithaca just before my second Christmas vacation in America I wrote to my parents: "I like . . . Cornell for its greater insistence on essentials. Good workers, good collections, and good libraries rather than endless mock gothic palazzi. We are more fortunate at Yale than any other department in having so eminent and tactful a head as Harrison. The other departments must be intolerable." This was doubtless the extreme and unfair estimate of an expatriate youth, but looking back I know exactly what I meant. Self-education, for the undergraduates that I had been teaching, would have been well-nigh impossible. Of course at Cambridge there were a number of aristocratic and rich young men, but if they were not intellectually inclined, they took a pass degree which did not interfere either with their

athletics or other diversions at Newmarket and in the
Hawks Club, or with the quality of the education given
to the honors men.

There were, in addition to Harrison and Woodruff,
two other full professors in the department, Wesley
Roswell Coe and Alexander Petrunkevitch. Both were
invertebrate zoologists but in every other way they differed
greatly.

Coe was born in Connecticut and became a student of
A. E. Verrill. He was thus the remaining link at Yale with
the first great expansion of zoology in America, fundamentally due to Louis Agassiz, with whom Verrill had
studied. Verrill did not remake the tradition; he was
fundamentally a systematist and a museum man, and Coe
started off in the same way. He became the leading student
of the pelagic nemertean worms, a curious and rather rare
group of invertebrates collected in small numbers by
many deep-sea expeditions. He also became much concerned with sex changes in molluscs and with the feeding
ecology of bivalves. None of these fields of specialization
evoked much enthusiasm in his colleagues, and I think he
felt apologetic about them. It is curious that in the seventh
edition of *American Men of Science* experimental zoology
is listed both at the beginning and the end of his areas of
research. He taught histology and genetics; the former
was a rigorous laboratory course, but the latter was mainly
illustrated with stuffed pigeons, chickens, and rabbits.
He had had very few graduate students. One, Stanley C.
Ball, was the curator of zoology in the Peabody Museum
when I arrived; Coe himself had earlier filled the position.
Another of his students, Victor Loosanoff, later became
a very important figure in the applied biology of oysters
and clams. He gave Coe a panel on which were mounted
shells of Connecticut oysters from the spat to a ten-year-
old individual. This exhibit of growth hung on Coe's

office wall and when I inherited the room I took care that it still should hang there. After Coe's retirement he moved to California and did admirable work on the role of detritus, largely derived from kelp, in the nutrition of marine invertebrates.

Some of Verrill's family went to California and were impeccable citizens of that state, where I hope and believe that they flourished, though not I think in science. One of Verrill's sons wrote well-illustrated if perhaps overly romantic popular books on natural history. There were in addition people around who claimed to be Verrills, and one of Coe's minor functions was to warn newcomers like myself against anyone trying to solicit subscriptions to an unpublished, and indeed probably unwritten, life of A. E. Verrill. There were also curious rumors of someone using the name in giving lectures, to temperance societies, on the experience of being rescued from the gutter and reformed. As in the case of Saint Hyacintha Mariscotti, whose sin was pride and whose feast is on my birthday, the fall from grace and the redemption appear to have occurred more than once. There was also a hint of a party given for the chorus of a musical show at the Shubert Theater in New Haven and paid for in an unconventional way by currency removed at Christmastime from registered letters. Coe's warnings were insistent but I was never approached nor tempted to become involved.

Of Petrunkevitch, I have written extensively elsewhere.[16] He came of an aristocratic but very liberal family and had been forced out of Russia for protesting the way in which students had been treated after disturbances in 1899. He had then gone to Germany to work

16. A biographical memoir will shortly be published by the National Academy of Sciences. See also, G. E. Hutchinson, Alexander Petrunkevitch. An Appreciation of his Scientific Works and a List of his Published Writings, *Trans. Conn. Acad. Arts Sci.* 36:9–24, 1945.

with August Weismann. In his Ph.D. thesis he gave the first statistically adequate demonstration of the truth of Dzierzon's hypothesis that drone bees are produced from unfertilized, and worker and queen bees from fertilized, eggs.

Petrunkevitch came to America in 1903, where he started his work in arachnology, at first as a private scholar, but after 1910 as a member of the Yale faculty. He was equally at home with the anatomy, physiology, and behavior of spiders, but his most significant work was no doubt contained in a long series of paleontological memoirs which dealt both with Paleozoic arachnids of all kinds and with spiders fossilized in amber. The latter specimens always fascinated him as they did the numerous students, including experimental embryologists and comparative physiologists, who attended "Pete's Tea" every Monday at 4:30 P.M. in his laboratory. In this way, he had a considerable influence in maintaining an interest in unfashionable phylogenetic and zoogeographic problems, though he often misunderstood his colleagues and they him. He never expressed any hint of an apology for the areas of science to which he was devoted.

Petrunkevitch had, early in his career in Moscow University, worked with the great geochemist V. I. Vernadsky, whose son, George Vernadsky, the eminent historian of Russia, was later to join the Yale faculty. Petrunkevitch as a student nearly lost his life with the elder Vernadsky when they were being taken down a mine, to see a mineral deposit, by an official of the mining company. An anarchist workman, thinking that this provided a fine chance to get rid of the official, cut the cable on the cage. Fortunately, the latter tilted and jammed in the shaft very close to an adit, through which the occupants were rescued.

Petrunkevitch published many of his most important works in the *Transactions of the Connecticut Academy of*

Arts and Sciences, a journal that had earlier been immortalized by J. Willard Gibbs. During the 1930s he was president of the Connecticut Academy, and the meetings, with the rere-suppers that followed them, became a great gathering place for intellectual émigré Russians. They were also one of the few occasions where the new and unimportant could meet interesting people outside their own departments.

Learning about V. I. Vernadsky from Petrunkevitch and from George Vernadsky, I became much interested in some of his ideas, notably his conclusion that each species of animal or plant had an elementary chemical composition, varying around a mean characteristic of the species. Later, I was able to study this possibility rather extensively among the club mosses or Lycopodiaceae, where such a situation is more or less true of the aluminum content; *L. flabelliforme*, from which Christmas wreaths are often made, contains 0.6 to 1.25 percent of the metal in the dry leaf. These fascinating plants also show great variation from species to species in their alkaloids, and at least three classifications, one based on morphology, one on aluminum content, and one on alkaloids, should be possible. Though the chemistry is still not fully known, the three approaches clearly suggest the same general kind of taxonomy.

Vernadsky had a strong influence on other aspects of my research, and I did my best to help Petrunkevitch and George Vernadsky make his ideas about the biosphere better known in English-speaking countries. Though I came to biogeochemistry through Vernadsky, I soon realized the great importance to biology of the concepts introduced by my father's friend Viktor M. Goldschmidt. Putting these two together in an ecological context I think did something to further the more chemical aspects of ecology.

The associate professors in the zoology department

in 1928 were G. A. Baitsell and J. S. Nicholas. The latter had worked with Harrison, on salamander eggs, but had also developed operative procedures that permitted the methods of experimental embryology to be applied to mammals. However, he never utilized his methods to their full capacity and later in life became too much engrossed with worldly power to continue as an effective scientist, which distressed all who knew him at all well.

Baitsell is still an enigma to me, though I owe him a great deal. He had been a student of Woodruff, but later he became interested in Harrison's approach and did work on the genesis of connective tissue fibers in tissue culture. He was, however, temperamentally much closer to Woodruff than to Harrison, a Republican Masonic Baptist and an ardent prohibitionist, but with a strong sympathy for the sons of wealthy alumni who might make great gifts to Yale. Later when I came to understand the rigors of his early life and of that of the pioneer Iowa family from which he sprang, the differences in our outlooks seemed unimportant. In the 1930s he became mainly a teacher and administrator. But he was clearly mulling over his earlier scientific work, for when in 1938 he came to give an address to the symposium arranged by the American Association for the Advancement of Science, marking the centennial of the cell theory, he seems to have been the first person to use the expression "molecular biology."[17] Although he considered the cell, as the smallest complete functional unit in biology, to be in a sense a single molecule, his ideas were in many ways strikingly modern. During his later career he became the secretary of the Society of Sigma Xi and played an enormous part in reviving the society and in estab-

17. G. A. Baitsell, The Cell as a Structural Unit, *Amer. Natural.* 74:5–24, 1940; reprinted *Amer. Scient.* 43:133–41, 147, 1955.

lishing the *American Scientist* as a unique periodical. Although initially I must have represented much of what someone of his background would dislike in an English intellectual, he realized that there might be something that I could bring to his journalistic venture. The result was a partnership that gave me a unique opportunity to try out ideas under the heading of "Marginalia."

Though sometimes greatly disturbed by the attire of the young women who worked in the laboratory, he was a strong believer in the freedom of the press, even if it involved, as it once did in one of my pieces, a naked bride with a garland of roses round her waist trespassing from the inside of a fifteenth-century *cassone* lid on to one of his pages. I think he was badly shocked, but I felt that the lady made my point perfectly and there she has remained.

The Peabody Museum began to play a great part in my life as soon as I stepped into it. In those days, there was a Foucault pendulum hanging suspended from high in the tower over the entrance. Every morning it was set swinging in a plane defined by a protractor lying below the bob. As no other significant force acted on it, it swang backwards and forwards in the same direction in space. The earth, however, was rotating, so the path of the pendulum appeared to move. Though I had been brought up from infancy to accept the rotation of the earth, seeing it demonstrated in this way for the first time was curiously exciting, something intellectually so simple and obvious, yet so unexpected to the purely practical part of a human being.

The museum had been founded by George Peabody of London and its first building was opened in 1876. It acquired enormous collections in vertebrate paleontology from Professor Othniel C. Marsh, the founder's nephew, and of marine invertebrates collected by A. E. Verrill for the United States Fish Commission. A very rich anthropological and archaeological collection was also built up, initially also largely by Marsh. The museum originally stood at Elm and High Streets, near the center of New Haven. This building was demolished in 1917 and the collections were largely inaccessible until 1925, when the present building was opened. In 1928, though the new building was complete, apart from the caulking of numerous leaks, the largest specimen that it contained, the reconstructed skeleton of *Brontosaurus*, was only partly mounted. The neck vertebrae were, I think, being put in place when I first saw it; illuminated by a powerful floodlight, the rigidly geometrical curvature of the back and uncompleted neck gave the whole scene a constructivist theatrical quality. Many years later, this theatrical quality momentarily reappeared at a dinner celebrating the opening of the first, though very small, American exhibition of King Tutankhamun's treasure. There was a belly dancer to entertain us, and she danced along the entire length of the skeleton between performances at either end of the Hall of Reptiles, where the dinner was held. Seen below the enormous, geometrical, static, reptilian skeleton of uncertain sex, the same basic tetrapod structure repeated in the small, living, and moving feminine human body of the dancer provided one of the most beautiful contrasts I have ever seen.

Near the *Brontosaurus* is a case containing the skeletal remains of the remarkable toothed, but apparently secondarily flightless, bird *Hesperornis regalis*, described by Marsh, the Cretaceous ecological equivalent of our penguins. When the great German ornithologist Erwin Stresemann came to Yale and went to see these fossils, he was apparently so surprised by their perfection that his eyebrows raised automatically and his monocle crashed on the cement floor.

When I first knew the museum, the great murals of the Age of Reptiles and the Age of Mammals, painted by Rudolf Zallinger, had not been begun, nor had the lovely habitat groups by the great museum artist J. Perry Wilson, illustrating the ecology of southern New England and some of the larger North American mammals in their natural habitats. These works, though in a sense applied, and certainly outside the mainstream of twentieth-century art as ordinarily understood, ultimately may prove to have far greater aesthetic significance than most critics would concede to them today.

In 1928 the intellectual significance of the museum was considered primarily to reside in the department of geology. Richard Swann Lull, a superb mammalian paleontologist, and a very popular undergraduate teacher, was director, and the most powerful mind associated with the collections was that of Charles Schuchert, a largely self-taught invertebrate paleontologist and stratigrapher. Schuchert's work led to important conclusions about Central American paleogeography. He was regarded as authoritative and was intellectually somewhat unbending, perhaps on account of his youthful struggle to become a scientist. He greatly disapproved of Alfred Wegener's theory of continental drift and imposed his disapproval on others so effectively that mention of the moving continents in geological circles in Yale induced a deeply silent response comparable to what might be elicited by a grossly obscene remark at a church supper. Coming from South Africa, where A. L. du Toit had expounded the theory so ably, this seemed to me extremely odd.

An excessive authoritarianism was perhaps a little too prevalent among the geologists and paleontologists of the time. In 1932 G. E. Lewis, then a young paleontologist on the Yale North India Expedition, collected from Tertiary beds in the Siwalik Hills, now in Pakistan, a fragment of the upper jawbone of a primate which he described as *Ramapithecus brevirostris*.[18] He pointed out that though there was little enough of the fossil, the animal that it represented must have had a smaller canine, a less parallel set of premolar and molar teeth, and a shorter muzzle than any Tertiary primate then known. All three of these features are man-like. He accordingly, and to me quite convincingly, concluded that *Ramapithecus* was allied to the ape-men then being described by Dart and by Broom as *Australopithecus*. Its age made it the oldest member of our own family, Hominidae, to which the African fossils were generally ascribed. Authorities in America rather pointedly ignored Lewis's claim and the fossil was largely unappreciated for a quarter of a century. Although it is now known that teeth of the same species had earlier been described as *Dryopithecus punjabicus*, the validity of Lewis's claim is now universally admitted and, as *Ramapithecus punjabicus*, it has an honorable place in our family tree. I am proud of the fact that in many lectures to elementary biology classes on the evolution of man I always showed a slide of this little Yale specimen as a relic of our oldest known ancestor, long before Elwyn Simons fully rehabilitated it.

In 1928 the status of zoology at the Peabody was at a low ebb. The curator, S. C. Ball, was an excellent field naturalist, with wide experience in the Pacific. He was at his best in the planning of the hall of southern New England natural history that I have mentioned. The design and placing of organisms in the diorama was so good that I had no difficulty in writing a pamphlet on the

18. G. E. Lewis, Preliminary Notice of New Man-Like Apes from India, *Amer. J. Sci.* (ser. 5) 27:161–79, 1934; E. L. Simons, The Phyletic Position of *Ramapithecus. Postilla* 57, 1961; E. L. Simons, On the Mandible of *Ramapithecus. Proc. Nat. Acad. Sci., Wash.* 51:528–36, 1964.

ecological principles easily seen in the exhibits, though I do not think Ball had any idea what I was writing about. He was admirable as a popularizer but had no capacity to appreciate the interests of advanced students engaged in research. He was, moreover, better at refusing than accepting collections, to our great loss.

The process of rebuilding zoology in the museum, where in the nineteenth century Verrill had done so much, bringing it up to the level of paleontology, was in a sense begun by Albert Eide Parr in the Bingham Oceanographic Laboratory, affiliated to the Peabody, in the late 1920s; but its real flowering was due to S. Dillon Ripley and in a quieter way to Willard Hartman. As all are happily alive and working, they only qualify for brief though very affectionate mention in this book.

The historical problem of the decline and restoration of museum zoology during this century is probably a general one and not merely something related to a single institution and resulting from local circumstances. The causes actually are not far to seek. The production of mathematical models of natural selection in the late 1920s and early 1930s gave grounds for believing that evolution could be studied scientifically, if not experimentally, and evoked, in the "New Systematics," a study of the nature of the barriers that developed between species and of the nature of the variation within them. Meanwhile, the rise of population genetics and of ecology, with the realization of the species, in the sense of an interbreeding population, as the real unit, put a premium on systematic work that it had not had since the early exploration of the biota of the earth in the eighteenth and beginning of the nineteenth centuries. The astonishing growth of zoology in the Peabody Museum was certainly part of this historic trend, which could probably be noted in many parts of the world. One aspect of the trend is of some interest, though it does not seem to have been much discussed. In the nineteenth century, when George Peabody was founding our museum, right on through the early part of this century, the development of natural history museums was a favorite aim of private charity. Now it depends very largely, though until recently not entirely, as the Coe and Bingham addition to the Peabody testify, on the National Science Foundation. It is interesting to inquire, and the answer might be of great practical import, if donations to natural history museums have decreased proportionately to other charities and why this should be the case. In this connection it is worth bearing in mind not only the purely scientific work of the museums but the extraordinary number of school children, many from the inner city, who may, as a friend teaching them once said to me, have their first truly intellectual experience in such an environment.

The second year I was at Yale I was asked to give a course on freshwater biology in the second term, Albert Parr having initiated the teaching of oceanography in the first term of 1929–30. In preparing my lectures I distinctly remember having the outline of a book on limnology in mind.

During my first year I had given a departmental seminar—always called a journal club in those days—on my research. I talked about the pans of the Transvaal. The whole approach, based primarily on Thienemann's point of view, was, I suspect, utterly unlike anything that had hitherto been presented to the department, though I think its respectable German origin probably appealed to Harrison. To the limnological community of North America, had any of its members been present, it would have given the same impression as a Dominican or Jesuit sermon would have done to a seventeenth-century Puritan congregation. The only professed ecologist in Yale at that time was G. E. Nichols, chairman of the department of botany, but though botany and zoology shared a common library and both contributed to the elementary course in biology, there was a great gulf artificially fixed between the two disciplines; this could not be crossed officially during working hours.

My own research was largely still involved with Africa as there was much to be done in writing up the work on the pans. I did try out unsuccessfully an idea that had been rattling around in my mind for a year or two, attempting to establish a conditioned reflex with a time lag in a poikilothermous or cold-blooded animal, such as a salamander, in order to see what its temperature characteristic might be. During the period of which I write, following the work of Crozier, such a determination would have seemed much more interesting than it would now appear to be.

Failing in this, I started an investigation of the supposed effects of magnesium salts on Cladocera, effects which were supposed to keep this group of crustacea out of Lake Tanganyika. As I wrote on 18 November 1929 to my parents: "I have several families of the most sensitive species in water 6 times more concentrated than the lake swimming about here in this room. Hydrobiology satisfies both my physiological interests and naturalist's instincts more than any other branch of zoology; I can get more work done in this field than any other for that reason. So far it has been the dumping ground for inferior off-scourings of the profession of zoologists. . . . All the best things are missed save by a few men like old Birge." I am pretty sure that my arrogant remarks about hydrobiologists were meant to apply primarily to those of the English-speaking world; even for such a subset they were grossly unfair. It took me some time to realize where the difficulties that I seemed to encounter, and which I was later to share with Ray Lindeman, actually lay.

Embryology had been taught for several years by J. W. Buchanan, a general physiologist who had worked with C. M. Child at Chicago and was, therefore, regarded as slightly heretical, though tolerated in the interests of free speech. Buchanan got a good offer and left, and I was asked to take the undergraduate embryology course that he gave. On paper this was ridiculous for someone whose only formal instruction in the matter had been Shearer's fragmentary and inaccurate course in the Cambridge department of anatomy. The fact that I was asked to give the course in a department famous throughout the world for its embryological research really made my situation quite ludicrous. Fortunately, I was pretty well self-educated in mammalian development and had followed Needham's early work in chemical embryology ever since I had met him in Sydney Cole's laboratory. I soon found that I was looking at embryos in what Needham called cleiodic, or shut-up, eggs as self-contained systems like so many South African lakes. At times I was terrified, but with Miss Pelham's hand metaphorically on my shoulder, I think the course soon went well; I hope at least some of the students learned almost as much from it as I did.

Though in those days it was regarded as very dangerous to let women take undergraduate courses, an exception was made to allow a lady called Dorothy Benton to take embryology. She had worked on *Biological Abstracts* in the early days and had many friends in biological circles in Philadelphia. Her husband had, for a few years, an instructorship in mathematics at Yale and was also a keen naturalist. I got to know them both quite well, and we had extensive conversations about population biology and mathematics.

About this time Volterra's work on competition and on prey-predator relations was becoming known. Volterra, who was one of the great mathematicians of the early twentieth century, had become interested in population mechanics, as a result of his daughter Luisa, who was a limnological zoologist, marrying Umberto d'Ancona, a fisheries biologist of great insight. D'Ancona had noticed that the limitation of fishing in parts of the Mediterranean during the First World War had apparently produced a change in the proportions of the various species of fish caught commercially. He asked his father-in-law about the possibility of constructing a theory to explain this kind of phenomenon. Though Volterra's initially best known results concerned cyclical oscillations due to predation of one species on another, he showed at the beginning of his most important paper, in 1926, that two species feeding in unrestricted competition on precisely the same food under the same conditions could not coexist indefinitely as equilibrium populations, unless their relevant properties were identical, which is most unlikely in validly separable species. J. B. S. Haldane had actually published the same result in 1924, but none of us realized its significance. The result now sounds a little obvious, but it is actually the theoretical basis of a very large part of modern ecology. In 1934, G. F. Gause stated it in the form that "as a result of competition two similar species scarcely ever occupy similar niches, but displace each other in such a manner that each takes possession of certain peculiar kinds of food and modes of life in which it has an advantage over its competitors." This conclusion is now generally denoted by G. Hardin's term, the "principle of competitive exclusion."

The whole history of this simple, powerful, but sometimes incorrect generalization is most curious and bears greatly on the state of biology at the time of which I am writing. It is now known that statements equivalent to the principle had been made, sometimes very casually, sometimes quite formally, by at least six zoologists and one botanist between 1857 and 1924.[19] Of these, Joseph Grinnell of the University of California at Berkeley was the most important. He had developed the idea quite fully in 1904 and had used the word *niche* since 1914 to express that space, in an unconsciously abstract sense, in which two closely allied species did not co-occur. Grinnell was an extremely active and well-known student of the mammals and birds of western North America, but his interests lay so far from those of the greater number of intellectually significant biologists of the time, that no one in the biological establishment realized that he had something to say of great theoretical importance. Most of his colleagues in vertebrate taxonomy and ecology were unprepared for any deep theory, and, in fact, at least the ecologists were deeply suspicious of any generalizations other than those implied in classificatory schemes. Although Grinnell was recognized as an outstanding student of birds by the British Ornithological Union, he received no honor in his own country for having made major contributions to the general understanding of the ways in which populations of more than one species might interact. It was not until the publication of Volterra's mathematics, with the comparable contributions of A. J. Lotka, and of Gause's experimental confirmation of their results, that what had seemed obvious to Grinnell and his students came to be regarded as a basic part of biological science.

Raymond Pearl of Johns Hopkins undoubtedly played a major part in making these advances possible, though I think that in his own experimental researches he kept

19. Most of the available material on the history of the concepts of competitive exclusion and the ecological niche is summarized in G. E. Hutchinson, *An Introduction to Population Ecology* (New Haven and London: Yale University Press, 1978).

to single-species populations. W. W. Alpatov, who taught Gause in Moscow, had been a student of Pearl; Pearl himself had studied with Karl Pearson, one of the founding fathers of modern statistics, in London. Gause's famous little book *The Struggle for Existence* had a foreword by Pearl and was published by Williams and Wilkins, who did the *Quarterly Review of Biology*, which Pearl edited.

I only met Pearl once, but he had greatly influenced O. W. Richards, a student of population growth in yeast, who was a colleague of mine at Yale during the thirties. We eagerly discussed Gause's work together and I then came to feel the beneficial influence of Pearl. He was well known for his wit, and as editor of the *Quarterly Review of Biology* invented a character called Reginald the Office Boy, who occasionally reviewed second-rate books on sex. He also, on at least one occasion, used the expression "There is no index" as the whole of one of his own reviews. Pearl, as a very good statistician, was highly acceptable to the biological establishment and probably played a greater part in bringing together disparate areas of biology than anyone else at that time.

Quite apart from the concept of competitive exclusion, the idea of the ecological niche has had a queer history.[20] The expression was apparently first used by Roswell H. Johnson (1877–1967), who had a most curious career, starting with evolutionary zoology, then turning to

20. Roswell H. Johnson's part in the establishment of the concept of the ecological niche was rediscovered accidentally by R. M. Gaffney; see Roots of the Niche Concept, *Amer. Natural.* 109:490, 1973. His role is discussed briefly in *An Introduction to Population Ecology* (p. 155), but it has as yet been impossible to form any idea as to his influence or lack of influence in the period from 1910 to 1914. My friend David Cox tells me that there may be a body of Johnson papers in existence, though he has as yet been unable to consult them.

petroleum geology, and finally becoming director of counseling in the American Institute of Family Relations in Los Angeles. In 1910, he introduced the term *niche* in an essentially modern sense, but did so only to point out the general invalidity of the concept.

There is no evidence that Grinnell knew of this discussion, though it appeared in a publication of the Carnegie Institute of Washington on evolution in ladybug beetles. Johnson clearly disliked competition and the "strong Malthusian leanings of Darwin." He evidently only became happy in his career when he felt he was an intentional promoter of harmony. He retired from that profession in 1960 in his eighty-third year.

Elton developed the idea of the niche rather differently in his *Animal Ecology*, with no thought of competitive exclusion. To him, it meant the role that an animal played in a community. It is curious that he certainly knew of at least one book in which Grinnell had used the word, without noticing that latter worker's meaning.

A deep suspicion of theoretical formulations was probably most marked among the biologists of the middle western states, where plant ecology was rapidly growing. It came very strikingly to my attention later in my career, when I was attempting to get Raymond Lindeman's famous paper "The Trophic-Dynamic Aspect of Ecology" published.[21] This paper was the first one to indicate how

21. Through the kindness of Frank Ruddle, the present chairman of the department of biology at Yale, I have been able to see the letters written when I was being considered for promotion to associate professor, which are still in the files of the department. Two of these, from Paul S. Welch and A. C. Redfield, were quite favorable, though probably not favorable enough to satisfy the standards of today. One was from Chancey Juday, who wrote, "Professor Hutchinson has some very good ideas and, if his mathematical treatises were based on

biological communities could be expressed as networks or channels through which energy is flowing and being dissipated, just as would be the case with electricity flowing through a network of conductors. Though the concept is now regarded as both basic and obvious, like the principle of competitive exclusion, it roused extraordinary opposition. The resistance to publication was the more poignant in that the young author was dying

---

much larger amounts of observational data, his contributions to limnology would be much more valuable in our opinion." This is in the same spirit as the criticism from the same source that delayed the publication of Lindeman's trophic-dynamic paper (see n. 13).

It is ironical that the most important conclusion in those of my contributions submitted, in part in manuscript, to Juday, was largely based on a table giving the mean temperatures at each meter depth in Lake Mendota throughout the summer, based on a very large number of individual determinations over many years. The table had been most kindly sent me by professors Birge and Juday, to whom it had not revealed its secrets. The mechanisms of heating that it suggested were also apparent in Connecticut lakes and are probably general in small lakes in temperate regions.

The fourth letter, from an unidentified correspondent called "Bill," possibly Dr. William Balamuth, writing to George A. Baitsell from Evanston, Illinois, indicated that two distinguished ecologists had never heard of me, that a third had no very high opinion, though one or two of my reprints "contained significant contributions," while a fourth had remarked that I had confined my work to limnology and "did not stand out in that." The last communication was clearly from someone who was not a regular reader of the *International Journal of Psychoanalysis*. The writer of the letter himself, after quoting these opinions, felt that Baitsell had on his "hands a problem in which the only accusations that can be levelled are a general tepidity." I think that this letter, even though accompanied by three fairly good ones, would today be enough to damn any candidate before some committee or other engaged in evaluating promotions. I therefore hope that everyone who does get promoted this year will have a proportionately more brilliant career than I have had. My own promotion clearly must have depended fundamentally on Harrison's judgment.

of an obscure hepatitis as the paper was finally accepted and went to press. The whole history has been recently recounted by Robert Cook. Thinking about the matter, and about a similar difficulty that befell my first graduate student, Gordon Riley, when he submitted a paper on plankton productivity, containing a good deal of statistical theory, to *Ecological Monographs*, I began to wonder whether he and Ray and I had not been suffering from a sort of commonsense backlash generated at the Reformation by the ultra-intellectual and antiempirical aspects of medieval scholasticism, which backlash had flourished in America wherever a Puritan attitude was still strong. I then remembered how when Professor E. A. Birge and Professor Chancey Juday were kind enough to let me spend a week at the Trout Lake Laboratory in Vilas County, in northeastern Wisconsin, I had learned a fabulous amount about limnological technique but had come away with two feelings of dissatisfaction. One was that it would be nice to know how to put all their mass of data into some sort of informative scheme of general significance; the other was that it would be nice to have either tea or coffee, without seeming decadent and abnormal, for breakfast. I now suspect a connection.

My unsuitable assignment to teach embryology lasted until 1936; after that I took over from Petrunkevitch an undergraduate course on the natural history of animals. I tried to make it into an ecology course organized entirely in terms of interaction between individuals and species, as it seemed that at an elementary level it was paradoxically easier to understand what happened when two fantastically elaborate systems met than what happened when one such system encountered its much simpler physiochemical environment. This is a sort of inversion of a theme by that wonderfully philosophical zoologist Carl F. A. Pantin, who said that a physicist was a person who only tackled the easy questions on the examination paper set by nature.[22] My graduate course on ecological principles began in 1939 and was followed by biogeochemistry in 1946. The latter course, which toward the end of my career I happily shared with Catherine Skinner, was, I imagine, the first one taught on the subject outside Russia. All these activities, as well as the informal ecology seminar which reached its apogee in 1957 and the underground seminar in science, philosophy, and art when I had retired, developed long after the date intended for the formal end of this book. A few further thoughts, however, clamor to find expression before that date is reached.

The period of which I have written saw a transformation of the zoology department, which finally fused with botany to form a biology department. Each side felt threatened by the other, but the threats were illusionary. All that happened was a recognition of the end of the usefulness of the nineteenth-century descriptive paradigm. What could have been a threat was not the realization that plants and animals have much in common, which is true, but the belief that only *Escherichia coli* and the T_4 bacteriophage are illuminating objects of study for biologists. Yale escaped being totally inundated by the culture media of such minute beings, partly I suspect because the administration could not persuade their most distinguished proponents to leave their lush fields; our home-grown molecular biologists have subsequently done remarkably well.

In spite of the hopes that all universities have of

22. I had hoped to find this remark in Carl Pantin's admirable posthumous *The Relation Between the Sciences* (Cambridge: Cambridge University Press, 1968), but I can discover it nowhere in the book, nor in his other general writings, though the thought is continually expressed in other ways. It is so characteristic that I am sure he made it; it is probably somewhere in print.

cultivating Nobel Prize winners rather than learning, biology at Yale has come to be more diverse than ever before. In this the overall field is far closer to that in which I grew up than was the case in America in the 1930s. Basically, I think the reason for this has been that as the harder questions on nature's examination paper came to be tackled, the number of interpenetrating aspects of organisms that needed to be known increased. This, as I have noted, was very true in the resurgence of systematics, when deep and difficult genetical and ecological questions arose which depended on taxonomic distinctions. I suspect, moreover, from what my more sensitive friends in the humanities and social sciences tell me, that the whole of learning is evolving in this way.

The need for variety in knowledge increases if we are to continue learning about ourselves and the world in which we live, but a new problem is also arising. Most new basic knowledge is produced in institutions that were founded ostensibly for teaching. This is particularly true of really new ideas, which are unlikely to be produced in any sort of institution set up purely for investigation and thought, for all such institutions, except perhaps All Souls College, Oxford, have their activities defined by certain limits. In universities the concept of academic freedom has arisen as a sort of by-product of teaching activity. Good advanced teaching requires good scholars, who can only be induced to come to teach if they have time for other learned activities, to which intellectual limits are not supposed to be set. As populations stabilize, the number of such positions is declining, and is likely to reach an equilibrium value well below the number of people who by ability, education, and temperament can fill them at a very high level. Meanwhile, general unemployment seems chronic and, in attempting to reduce it, more and more people are likely to be forced into retirement while they are still highly active human beings. It would seem to me that what we need is the return of the really able amateur, because that is what, in the true sense of the word, we should all be. Perhaps ultimately all scholarship that does not involve expensive physical installations should become the province of the amateur virtuoso. The standard of publication could remain the same; many amateurs would, of course, still be teachers. With a slightly reduced working week everyone would be expected to take part in various sorts of volunteer activity, of which scholarship would, for the very gifted, be a particularly attractive one. There are obvious difficulties which have to be expressed so that they can be overcome. The idea at first would probably be academically very unpopular, as the professional status of learning has often been held to be far more important than its beauty and interest. Not long ago the *Yale Alumni Magazine* asked a number of the faculty to write briefly their thoughts on the meaning of education. Two of us quite independently included a plea for the amateur in our replies. Many letters were later published about the series, but no one commented on this matter. I suspect that last year it was unworthy of notice; perhaps it will do better on a second presentation.

I like to think that as a fellow of the Linnaean Society of London, I am a member of one of the few local natural history societies whose province is the whole world.

In education, as in the design of all sorts of social action, I believe that those in charge aim at far too low a standard of achievement. It is obviously desirable to learn how to earn one's living. Sickness, hunger, and cold prevent many people from living satisfying lives and must be alleviated. If it is not realized that this is only a beginning, we are liable to get ant-like societies where painless persistence is the highest value. Everywhere in education we should aim at seeing life as a sacred dance or as a game in which the champions are those who give most beauty, truth, and love to the other players.

Since Sir Thomas Browne accidentally reversed the rotation of the earth when the Quincunx of Heaven ran low and it was time to close the five ports of knowledge,[23] perhaps I may end by looking to the rising sun. In 1931, Hellmut de Terra, a German geologist of great geomorphological insight and imaginative power, persuaded Yale to let him organize an expedition to the western end of the Tibetan Plateau. I was asked to be its biologist. I have already given a detailed account of this extraordinary journey in a book called *The Clear Mirror*.[24] In it, I tried to write of travel solely in terms of the impressions made on the traveler, who is otherwise unidentified. Only what he sees or hears exists, not himself. Looking back on this journey, an incident that cannot be reported in this way, without living human beings, insistently comes into my memory.

We had started from Kashmir and crossed a snow-covered pass called the Zoji-la before dawn. In doing so, we had passed into the great Himalayan rain shadow; the forest of Kashmir was giving way to the semidesert of Central Asia. We traveled through small towns or villages, Kargil and Dras, where the inhabitants were Mohammedan. Then we reached, at Lamayuru, the beginning of Tibetan Buddhist country, though politically we were

23. This is in the last chapter of *The Garden of Cyrus*. As I pointed out in Tuba Mirum Spargens Sonum, Per Sepulchrum Regionum, *Amer. Scient.* 39:145–50, the problems raised by Browne in chap. 5 about the existence of five-rayed echinoderms and flowers still have no real solution in developmental terms.

24. G. E. Hutchinson, *The Clear Mirror: a Pattern of Life in Goa and in Indian Tibet* (Cambridge: Cambridge University Press, 1937; reprint ed., New Haven: Leete's Island Books, 1978).

still in Kashmir. After establishing our camp, we started
walking about, to find our way to a *gon-pa*, or monastery,
on a hill overlooking the village. A small boy of about
six took my hand. Led by this little child, who seemed
fully to understand that we could not know each other's
languages, I was taken into one of the few parts of the
world which for better and for worse still remained in the
high Middle Ages. He stayed with me, still holding my
hand, till dusk, when he returned home and we went to
the tents to dine. It was the most moving human relationship that I experienced on the journey until the
voyage home.

INDEX

italicized numerals refer to pages with illustrations